Mud & Pies & SilverSpoons
A Cookbook

Illustrated by Mike Peters, Pulitzer Prize-winning cartoonist
Foreword by Erma Bombeck

Published by
Dayton Philharmonic Women's Association
Dayton, Ohio

First Edition

First Printing	April, 1985	10,000 copies
Second Printing	July 1985	15,000 copies
Third Printing	March 1988	10,000 copies

International Standard Book Number: 0-9614169-0-4

Library of Congress Catalog Card Number: 84-72752

ii

ABOUT THE BOOK

MUD PIES & SILVER SPOONS is designed for convenient use by busy cooks in the kitchen. Recipes are printed in easy-to-read 11 point Clearface type on 70 pound Mead Moistrite Matte paper. In addition to a multi-referenced index, categories of recipes can quickly be identified by the brown corner tabs at the tops of the pages. The attractive binding is Smythe-sewn, which permits the spine to be "broken" backwards without damage to the book; pages will lie flat while the book is in use.

The companies whose products and creative talents combined to produce MUD PIES & SILVER SPOONS are:

Kramer Graphics   Page Design and Typography

Patterson Graphics   Cover Design

Mead Corporation   Paper and Cover Stock

Additional copies of MUD PIES & SILVER SPOONS may be obtained by using forms in back of book or writing to:

Dayton Philharmonic Women's Association
P.O. Box 632
Dayton, Ohio 45401
Telephone: (513) 222-PIES

Proceeds from the sale of MUD PIES & SILVER SPOONS benefit the Dayton Philharmonic Orchestra.

Printed by Parthenon Press, Nashville, Tennessee

FIRST EDITION
COOKBOOK STEERING COMMITTEE

CHAIRMAN
Eleanor (Chris) Saunders

CO-CHAIRMAN
Susan Sauer

RECIPE TESTING & SELECTION
Lou Mason
Ada Lee Correll

EDITOR
Lorraine Quinlivan

MARKETING
Mary Karr

DISTRIBUTION
Karen Worner

PUBLIC RELATIONS
Judy McCormick
Deborah Corpus

ADVISOR
Sally Thompson

SECRETARY
Helen Marinoff

TREASURER
Esther Chestnut

DPWA PRESIDENT
Jan Rudd

The Cookbook Committee wishes to thank all those who submitted recipes. We regret that some recipes could not be printed due to similarity to other recipes or lack of space. All recipes were tested and some modifications made by the committee. Recipes were edited to conform to style.

The Dayton Philharmonic Women's Association is a non-profit organization founded in 1952 to aid and support the Dayton Philharmonic Orchestra and to promote interest in classical music. For this purpose the DPWA sponsors several educational programs in the schools and community, and provides scholarships to young music students. The proceeds of its many projects, including the Designers' Show House and the Cookbook, benefit the Dayton Philharmonic Orchestra.

FIRST EDITION COOKBOOK COMMITTEES

RECIPE TESTING & SELECTION

Chairmen: Lou Mason
Ada Lee Correll

Mary Davis
Ann Finlay
Gay Hoffman

Joan O'Meara
Susan Seyfarth
Karen Worner

Consultants:

Virginia Grice
Fern Perrett
Maridel Sherk

EDITORIAL

Editor: Lorraine Quinlivan
Graphics Editor: Wanda Carmichael
Index: Evelyn Beason
Special Features: Joan Siebenthaler

Nancy Barber
Laura Fanning
Marilyn Frame
Penny Haddick

Betty Jones
Mary Ellen Martin
Susan Siebenthaler

Proofreaders:

Jane Corbly
Barbara Dierkers
Carolyn Helwig

Helen Marinoff
Rosemarie Sholl

DISTRIBUTION

Chairman: Karen Worner
Jerri Campbell
Sally Murchland

MARKETING

Chairman: Mary Karr
Judy Beriss
Kathleen Compton
Barbara Marshall

PUBLIC RELATIONS & PROMOTION

Chairmen: Judy McCormick
Deborah Corpus

Marilyn Bohlander
Susan Coffin
Sarah Ekkens
Marilyn Erickson

Ann Finlay
Marilyn Hagans
Glenda Shrader
Joan Siebenthaler

Creative Consultant:

Molly Cammerer

COMPUTER OPERATIONS

Chairman: Susan Sauer
Laurie Leach
Judy Scheidt

ACKNOWLEDGMENTS

The Dayton Philharmonic Women's Association wishes to thank the following for their generous contributions of materials, professional services, and talent to the production of this book:

Erma Bombeck
Andrew K. Cherney
Gem Savers' Club
Georgia Johnson
Kramer Graphics
Mead Corporation
NCR Corporation
Patterson Graphics
Mike Peters
Printing Service Company
J. Gordon Rudd

PREFACE

The Dayton Philharmonic Women's Association is proud to present a collection of 470 recipes selected from almost 1000 submitted by members and friends. Each selection has been kitchen-tested at least twice, often three times, and taste-tested by a minimum of twelve people.

The aim has been to select recipes that reflect the new American lifestyle, recipes that stress fresh ingredients and yet are relatively fast and easy to prepare. Included are dishes suitable for busy-day family meals, and also glorious creations to grace your table at elegant dinner parties. All are both delicious and attractive.

Remembering those summer days long ago when we made mud pies in the backyard with Mother's best silver spoon, we selected the title **Mud Pies & Silver Spoons** and challenged Mike Peters, Pulitzer Prize-winning cartoonist, to illustrate the book.

Clutching her magic silver spoon, a zany and befuddled Fairy Godmother attends to her kitchen, finding herself crushed within a huge sandwich, exhausted after stuffing a whole pig, and flying away on a giant carrot after suddenly meeting an equally surprised turkey eyeball to eyeball. Through it all, she will surprise and delight you.

Surely we must be the first cookbook published to include a recipe for garbage, but would you really expect a serious recipe from former Daytonian, Erma Bombeck, who wrote our Foreword?

Explore the special features in this cookbook. Learn from the "Sterling Ideas" on the back of each divider. Let us take you on a cook's tour of "Entertaining with Polish" and suggest sample menus in "Four-Star Events." Your friends will think you a wizard as you turn turnips into tulips and radishes into roses after consulting "The Added Touch."

Most of all, have fun with this cookbook!

Eleanor (Chris) Saunders
Chairman

ABOUT MIKE PETERS

Mike Peters is a mud pie person. Even the initials of his name, M. P., give him away.

Thus it is that when Mike Peters agreed to illustrate MUD PIES & SILVER SPOONS, it was an appropriate and happy marriage of talent and personality with the book's intent. Who better to convey the idea of cooking for enjoyment—the fun of cooking—than a celebrated cartoonist with his own highly developed sense of fun?

Mike Peters has a facility for seeing things and people in a fresh way—a phenomenon of childhood that Mike fortunately has never lost. Few of us "old folks" could be as comfortable making mud pies in the backyard as we are making real chocolate pies in the kitchen; none of us doubt that Mike could be happy doing either.

Because of this special kinship to childhood, Mike has been called the Peter Pan of cartoonists, but he is much more the Superman type.

As a child, Mike was weaned on Superman comic books and learned how to draw from them. So great was his admiration that he asked his mother to make him a Superman costume for Halloween—a set of blue long johns with a big "S" emblazoned across the chest. Long after Halloween, he often wore it to school under his ordinary clothes to the surprise of his school chums and the consternation of the nuns at the parochial school he attended in St. Louis.

Mike Peters, "grown up," has not lost his fascination with Superman. It surfaced again last spring (1984) when he advised graduates at Wright State University's commencement exercises "to find a job they enjoy, even being Superman," and surprised his audience when he threw open his black gown to reveal a Superman suit under it all!

Mike Peters' accomplishments are many. In 1981 he won the Pulitzer Prize for his cartoons, which are nationally syndicated in over 300 newspapers and have appeared as well in such publications as *Time, Newsweek,* and *The New Republic.* Several books of his cartoons are now in print.

In addition to editorial cartoons, he has produced an animated cartoon series, "Peters Postscripts," for NBC's "Nightly News" and, most recently, a popular comic strip, "Mother Goose and Grimm." He has been a regular guest, the cartoonist-in-residence, on NBC's "Today" show and now has his own television series, "The World of Cartooning with Mike Peters."

Mike Peters, who joined the staff of the *Dayton Daily News* in 1969, has now joined the list of nationally-known celebrities from Dayton—a list that includes Erma Bombeck, who has written the Foreword for MUD PIES & SILVER SPOONS.

For those of us who remember fondly those days when we made mud pies, we say, "Thank you, Mike Peters." We hope he has had as much fun creating these delightful illustrations as the readers are sure to have as they turn these pages.

Lorraine Quinlivan
Editor

FOREWORD

When I received a letter from The Dayton Philharmonic Women's Association telling me about the creation of MUD PIES & SILVER SPOONS, there was no doubt in my mind what they wanted.

A Bombeck recipe.

After all, when you want shoes, you go to Gucci. When you want a bauble, you go to Tiffany's. When you want a Designer recipe...who else?

Actually, I was born to cook. My grandmother lived on Bainbridge Street in Dayton and became a legend at feeding vagrants near the railroad. My mother was one of those dedicated disciples of the kitchen who washed out her measuring cup every time she measured water.

When I was raising my kids in Centerville and Bellbrook, I was cheered by the fact that they ate anything—soap, candles, rocks, blacktop driveways, guppies, crayons and rectal thermometers. It was a joy to watch them fight over the baking soda I had put in the refrigerator to remove odors.

You cannot imagine my disappointment when I was informed that 470 recipes had already been tested and selected for this cookbook by a cowardly Board of anonymous volunteers who believe sweetbreads come from a bakery and aspic is a skiing lodge in Colorado.

All the committee wanted from me was a foreword.

Well, tough biscuits!

Here is Recipe No. 471!

MADE FROM SCRATCH GARBAGE

Garbage, if it's made right, takes a full week. Most people think you just take a leftover straight from the table, scrape it right from the plate and dump it into the can. That is not the way Bombeck garbage is made.

The ingredients can vary, but basically you're looking at:

2 tbsp. leftover peas

leftover pot roast the size of a coaster

1 peach pit

DAY I: Transfer leftovers from table to a smaller dish while chanting, "Don't touch this. I'm saving it for vegetable soup."

DAY II: Leftovers enjoy place of prominence and are seen every time door opens. Familiar words are chanted over it, "Don't touch it. I'm saving it for vegetable soup."

DAY III: Leftover is moved to less prominent shelf.

DAY IV: Traumatic time in the life of future garbage. It is either prematurely tossed out or shoved to rear of refrigerator.

DAY V: Leftover is opened, exposed to air and passed around to see if anyone can identify it. If it is recognizable, it is shoved to dark corner and allowed to "ripen" for another day.

DAY VI: Crucial day in which peas and beef curdle, turn green and harden. Pit grows fuzz.

DAY VII: Excited cries resound as children dance around refrigerator shouting, "Is it garbage yet?"

Mother removes leftover, folds back foil and pronounces it dead. She prepares it for burial by wrapping it in newspaper, then placing it in a brown bag, then a plastic one, and finally puts it to rest in garbage can.

Bury no garbage before its time. Bon appetit!

Erma Bombeck

TABLE OF CONTENTS

(continued)

I | Mud Pies &
Similar Delights

Mud Pies

Grown-Ups are the queerest folks; they never seem to know
That mud-pies always must be made just exactly so.
You have to have a nice back yard, a sunny, pleasant day,
And then you ask some boys and girls to come around and play.

You mix some mud up in a pail, and stir it with a stick;
It mustn't be a bit too thin, and not a bit too thick.
And then you make it into pies, and pat 'em with your hand,
And bake 'em on a nice flat board, and my! but they are grand!

Carolyn Wells

MISSISSIPPI MUD PIE

Lois Ross   *Yield: 8-9 servings*

1   package (about 2 dozen)
     chocolate sandwich
     cookies, crumbled
¼   cup butter, melted
     Coffee ice cream

TOPPING
4   teaspoons water
2   tablespoons light corn
     syrup
2   tablespoons butter
1   square (1 oz.) unsweetened
     chocolate
2   squares (1 oz. each) semi-
     sweet chocolate

Combine cookie crumbs with melted butter and press into 10-inch greased pan. Freeze. Fill crust with ice cream and refreeze. Pour topping over frozen pie and return to freezer until ready to serve.

In saucepan, stir water, syrup, and butter until mixture boils; add chocolate and stir until melted. Remove from heat and cool thoroughly.

MOCHA MUD PIE

Gwendolyn McCausland   *Yield: 8-10 servings*

½   cup butter
2   squares (1 oz. each)
     unsweetened chocolate
¾   cup sugar
2   tablespoons Kahlua
2   eggs
½   pint whipping cream,
     whipped and sweetened
     with sugar or 2 cups
     frozen whipped topping,
     thawed
     Prepared chocolate pie
     crust (9-inch)
     Chopped nuts for garnish

Melt butter and chocolate on low heat; cool. In large mixing bowl, combine butter-chocolate mixture with sugar and Kahlua; beat with electric mixer at medium speed for 2 minutes. Add eggs, 1 at a time, beating well after each addition. Fold in whipped cream and pour into chocolate crust. Chill until set (at least 4 hours). Garnish with chopped nuts or additional whipped cream, if desired.

3

MUD-FUDGE PIE

Doris Ponitz *Yield: 8 servings*

NUT CRUST
1½ cups finely chopped walnuts
1 tablespoon all-purpose flour
¼ cup margarine, softened
¼ cup sugar

MUD-FUDGE FILLING
½ cup margarine, softened
1 cup sugar
3 eggs
2 squares (1 oz. each) unsweetened chocolate, melted and cooled
⅓ cup all-purpose flour (unsifted)
1½ teaspoons vanilla
½ teaspoon baking powder
⅛ teaspoon salt

Chop nuts in food processor or by hand. Add flour, margarine, and sugar. Mix well and press over bottom and sides (but not rim) of 9-inch pie pan.

Mix all ingredients until smooth and pour into nut crust. Bake at 325 degrees for 35-45 minutes. (Filling will appear slightly moist when done.)

Delicious served warm or cool with whipped cream or vanilla ice cream.

MEADOWBROOK MUD PIE

Sandi Ingberg *Yield: 8 servings*

1 pint chocolate ice cream
¾ cup peppermint stick ice cream
½ cup chopped pecans
Graham cracker crust (9-inch)
½ cup heavy chocolate icing

Soften ice creams; mix ice creams and pecans thoroughly. Place in crust; freeze. When hard, top with icing. Garnish with whipped cream and additional chopped pecans, if desired.

A favorite dessert at Meadowbrook Country Club in Dayton, Ohio.

MIAMI MUD PIE

Timi Gump   *Yield: 8 servings*

26   chocolate sandwich
     cookies, including filling
1¼   tablespoons instant coffee
6   tablespoons butter or
     margarine, melted
1½-
2   quarts coffee ice cream
1   cup chocolate fudge
     topping
     Whipped cream
     Slivered almonds

Finely crush cookies in food processor. Add coffee and melted butter, processing after each addition. Generously butter 9-inch pie plate. Press cookie crust mixture into pie plate and freeze. Soften ice cream and blend with electric beater until even consistency. Place ice cream in freezer until thick enough to mound. Fill frozen crust with ice cream, mounding high in center to form peak, and freeze for 8-10 hours. Place container of fudge sauce in freezer with pie. Five minutes before serving, remove pie from freezer and allow to stand at room temperature. Remove fudge sauce from freezer and spread on top of ice cream. Cut into 8 portions and serve immediately on chilled dessert plates with chilled forks. Top with whipped cream and almonds.

If desired, coarsely chop 6 squares (1 oz. each) semi-sweet chocolate in food processor and add to softened ice cream before freezing.

TRIPLE-DECKER MUD PIE

Margo Hunter   *Yield: 8 servings*

1   package (13.7 oz.) chocolate fudge frosting mix (divided)
¾   cup flour
½   teaspoon salt (divided)
⅓   cup butter, softened
1   tablespoon water
1   teaspoon vanilla
2   eggs
1¼ cups chopped pecans (divided)
2   packages (3 oz. each) cream cheese, softened
¾   cup sour cream (divided)
    Vanilla ice cream

In small mixing bowl, combine 1 cup frosting mix with flour, ¼ teaspoon salt, butter, water, vanilla, and 1 egg. Beat 2 minutes until smooth. Spread on bottom and sides of 9-inch greased pie pan. Sprinkle with ½ cup nuts. In large mixing bowl, combine cream cheese, ½ cup sour cream, 1 egg, 2 cups frosting mix, and ¼ teaspoon salt. Beat 2 minutes until smooth and creamy. Fold in ½ cup nuts and pour over unbaked crust. Bake at 325 degrees for 35-40 minutes or until filling is set. Cool completely. Mix remaining frosting mix with ¼ cup sour cream. Spread over cooled pie and sprinkle with remaining nuts. Serve with vanilla ice cream.

MUD-PUD PIE

Nancy Abbott   *Yield: 12-16 servings*

1   stick margarine
1   cup flour
1   cup crushed nuts
1   package (8 oz.) cream cheese, softened
1   cup granulated sugar
16   ounces frozen whipped topping, thawed
10   ounces chocolate instant pudding
2½   cups milk
     Baking chocolate, shaved

Mix margarine, flour, and nuts. Spread in 9x13-inch pan and bake at 350 degrees for 15-20 minutes. Cool. Beat together cream cheese, sugar, and half of whipped topping. Spread over crust. Mix pudding with milk. Spread on cheese layer. Spread remaining whipped topping over pudding. Top with baking chocolate. Refrigerate.

May use butterscotch or pistachio pudding.

MARSHMALLOW MUD CAKE

Deborah Corpus (Mrs. Charles)   *Yield: 12 servings*

4	eggs
2	cups sugar
1	cup melted butter
1½	cups flour
⅓	cup unsweetened cocoa
1	cup flaked coconut
½	cup chopped nuts
1	jar (7 oz.) marshmallow creme
1	cup chopped nuts for topping (optional)

Beat eggs until thick; add sugar. Combine butter, flour, cocoa, coconut, and nuts; add to egg-sugar mixture. Stir with wooden spoon. Pour into greased and floured 9x13-inch pan and bake at 350 degrees for 30 minutes or until done. Remove from oven and immediately spread marshmallow creme gently on surface of warm cake. Carefully spread frosting over marshmallow creme, swirling to give marbled effect. If desired, sprinkle nuts over top.

FROSTING

½	cup melted butter
⅓	cup unsweetened cocoa
1	teaspoon vanilla
6	tablespoons milk
4	cups powdered sugar

Combine all ingredients. Beat until smooth.

MUDGE CAKE

Becki Sammons   *Yield: 10-12 servings*

1¾	sticks butter or margarine
4	squares (1 oz. each) unsweetened chocolate
2	cups sugar
1	teaspoon vanilla
4	eggs
1	cup flour
1-2	cups chopped pecans

Grease and line with waxed paper two 8-inch cake pans. Melt butter and chocolate. When cool, add sugar, vanilla, and eggs, beating by hand. Dredge pecans in flour and add last. Place batter in prepared pans and bake at 350 degrees for 40-45 minutes. Cool cake completely before removing from pans.

FROSTING
1	box powdered sugar
2	tablespoons cocoa
¼	cup butter or margarine
	Evaporated milk
1	teaspoon vanilla
1	cup chopped pecans

Mix powdered sugar and cocoa. Add butter and blend until creamy. Beat in evaporated milk until mixture is of spreading consistency. Add vanilla and nuts.

Place pan of water in oven to make cake more moist. Cake may be made ahead and layers frozen. A few hours before serving, defrost cake layers and spread with frosting.

RUDD PIE

Jan Rudd   *Yield: 8 servings*

2	squares (1 oz. each) semi-sweet chocolate
1	stick butter
1	cup sugar
2	eggs, slightly beaten
¼	cup flour
⅛	teaspoon salt
1	teaspoon vanilla
½	cup chopped nuts
	Ice cream, any flavor

Melt chocolate and butter over low heat. Stir in sugar. Remove from heat and add eggs, flour, salt, vanilla, and nuts. Pour into greased 8-inch pie pan. Bake at 350 degrees for 30 minutes. Cut into wedges and serve with ice cream. (Coffee, vanilla, or peppermint flavors are suggested.)

MUD SQUARES

Leona Kincade   *Yield: 12 servings*

1   cup oatmeal (not instant)
1   stick margarine
1¾ cups boiling water
1   cup sugar
1   cup lightly packed brown sugar
2   large eggs or 3 medium-sized
1¾ cups all-purpose flour
1   teaspoon baking soda
½   teaspoon salt
2-4 tablespoons cocoa (according to taste)
1   package (12 oz.) semi-sweet chocolate chips
¾   cup coarsely chopped walnuts or pecans

In large bowl, pour boiling water over oats and margarine. Let stand 10 minutes. Stir in sugars and add eggs (slightly beaten). Combine dry ingredients and add to oats mixture. Stir in half of chocolate chips. Pour batter into greased and floured 9x13-inch pan. Sprinkle remaining chocolate chips and nuts over cake. Bake at 350 degrees for 40 minutes or until toothpick inserted into cake comes out clean. Cool.

CHOCOLATE TORTE

Susan S. Seyfarth   *Yield: 8-10 servings*

8   ounces butter, softened
8   ounces superfine sugar
8   ounces semi-sweet chocolate, melted
8   eggs, separated
1   teaspoon vanilla or brandy
    Grated semi-sweet chocolate

Beat butter, sugar, and chocolate at slow speed; gradually add egg yolks, 1 at a time. Add vanilla (or brandy). Beat 10-15 minutes at medium speed. Beat egg whites until stiff and fold into chocolate mixture. Put ¾ of mixture in lightly greased (bottom only) 10-inch springform pan. Bake at 325 degrees for 30-35 minutes or until straw comes out clean. Let stand until completely cold. Cake will sink in the middle and crack. Spread remaining batter on top and decorate with grated chocolate. Cover and refrigerate.

CHOCOLATE BRANDY CHEESECAKE

Mark Kaplan   *Yield: 15-20 servings*

5	ounces chocolate wafers
6	tablespoons butter, melted
5	squares (1 oz. each) unsweetened chocolate
3	packages (8 oz. each) cream cheese (room temperature)
1	cup sugar
3	eggs (room temperature)
1	cup sour cream (room temperature)
⅓	cup brandy or cognac
2	squares (1 oz. each) semi-sweet chocolate
	Powdered sugar

Process wafers in blender or processor until reduced to powder. Toss with butter and press in bottom of 10-inch springform pan. Melt unsweetened chocolate in double boiler. Beat cheese and sugar with electric mixer until light and fluffy, 5-10 minutes, scraping bottom of bowl occasionally. On low speed, add eggs, 1 at a time. Beat in sour cream, then melted chocolate. Add brandy and beat 5 minutes on medium speed. Pour over crust and place in cold oven. Turn oven to 300 degrees and bake until puffed up, at least 1¼ hours. Turn oven off and allow to cool slowly in oven. With vegetable peeler, make shavings of semi-sweet chocolate and use to fill any cracks and completely cover top of cheesecake. Dust with powdered sugar. Store in refrigerator or freezer. Serve at room temperature.

This recipe was submitted by violinist and dessert-lover Mark Kaplan when he appeared with the Dayton Philharmonic Orchestra the week this book was going to the typesetter. In this case, definitely better late than never!

STERLING IDEAS

Appetizers

Remember that appetizers are meant to whet the appetite, not dull it. Quick cheese, fruit, and cracker appetizers include:

        Bel Paese + grapefruit or melon + garlic rounds
        Brie + pears or apples + party rye
        Edam + apples, oranges, or pineapple + party rye
        Gouda + raspberries or apples + toast points
        Gruyère + apples or pears + sesame crackers
        Provolone + bananas or pears + warm Italian bread
        Ricotta + apples or pineapple + garlic rounds
        Roquefort + grapes or pears + toasted bagels

Blanching cauliflower or broccoli before adding to a crudités platter gives better flavor and color. Also, try adding to the crudités peeled turnip sticks, peeled, sliced broccoli stems, peeled and cut parsnips, or almost any of the winter squashes.

Barely cooked carrots, asparagus spears, or Brussels sprouts, marinated overnight in a vinaigrette sauce, make tasty appetizers.

A platter holding one or two kinds of canapés or hors d'oeuvres is more sumptuous-looking than a tray with a large variety of appetizers. Also, passing a platter with too many choices stops conversation cold while the guests make up their minds.

Beverages

Try freezing cherries, berries, mint leaves, stuffed olives, and lemon twists in ice cube trays to glamorize drinks; freeze leftover coffee or tea to use in iced coffee or tea.

Iced tea requires only half as much sugar if sweetened hot rather than cold.

Ground coffee and coffee beans keep their flavor much better if stored in the refrigerator or freezer.

For instant European-style coffees, add either cocoa, orange rind, or cinnamon to dry milk and instant coffee. To serve, measure the mixes into cups and add boiling water.

For an easy iced tea go-together, have handy a small pitcher of thawed lemonade concentrate.

Mimosas (champagne and orange juice) are a nice touch for a brunch.

AN AMERICAN VERSION OF SUSHI

Mike and Marian Peters   *Yield: 14-16 servings*

Rice
Sushi powder *
Nori sheets *
Vegetables, sliced julienne
(use any of the following):
    asparagus
    carrots
    green onions
    avocado
    cucumber
Crab sticks
Pickled ginger *
Toasted sesame seeds
Wasabi (hot green horseradish) *

*****Sold at Japanese markets**

Wash 1 cup of rice in cold water 3 or 4 times or until water is clear. Add 1 cup of cold water and bring quickly to a boil. When the water has evaporated, immediately reduce heat to lowest setting, cover with tight-fitting lid, and simmer for 20 minutes. (It may be necessary to add a little more water.) While rice is hot, add sushi powder, following directions on container. Meanwhile, toast nori sheets in 325 degree oven. (Roasted nori may be purchased, eliminating toasting step.) When sheets turn green, spread each with thin layer of rice to within 1-inch of edges. Place vegetables and shredded crab down center of rice-covered nori sheets. Add pickled ginger and sprinkle with toasted sesame seeds. Roll up jelly roll fashion, sealing by moistening edges of nori with small amount of water. Slice with sharp knife into 1-inch slices. May roll like ice cream cones and serve unsliced. Serve with small amount of hot green horseradish.

"Sushi is not all raw fish. Well, actually, sushi is raw fish and we don't really make sushi. We make sashimi and maki-seaweed rolls."
Mike Peters

13

SHRIMP IN MUSTARD SAUCE

Mrs. William D. Sawyer   *Yield: 8 servings*

1½ **pounds shrimp, shelled and deveined**
¼ **cup finely chopped parsley**
¼ **cup finely chopped green onions**
¼ **cup tarragon vinegar**
¼ **cup wine vinegar**
½ **cup olive oil**
2-4 **tablespoons Dijon mustard**
2 **teaspoons crushed red peppers (or to taste)**
2 **teaspoons salt**
Freshly ground black pepper

Add cleaned shrimp to boiling salted water. Stir and cook just until water returns to boil. Drain and place in large bowl. Mix remaining ingredients and pour over warm shrimp. Mix well to coat each shrimp. Cover and refrigerate. (Best prepared 2-3 days before serving. Stir several times a day.) Serve shrimp in the marinade with toothpicks.

Also nice served with French bread to enjoy the sauce.

STUFFED SHRIMP

Alexandra Feeman Stevens   *Yield: 10 servings*

20 **jumbo shrimp, cooked, peeled, and deveined**
3 **ounces cream cheese**
1 **ounce Roquefort or Danish bleu cheese**
¼ **teaspoon prepared mustard**
2 **teaspoons finely chopped scallions**
1 **cup finely chopped parsley**
10 **lemon wedges**
10 **sprigs of parsley**

Split shrimp halfway down the spine; chill. Blend cream cheese, Roquefort, mustard, and scallions. Stuff shrimp, smoothing mixture evenly. Dip shrimp backs in parsley. Chill. Serve with lemon wedges and parsley sprigs as garnish.

SHRIMP APPETIZER QUICHES

JoAnn Saunders Maness   *Yield: 2 dozen*

1	package (8 oz.) refrigerated butterflake dinner rolls
¾	cup (4 oz.) small, cooked shrimp
½	cup whipping cream or half-and-half
2	tablespoons minced green onion
½	teaspoon salt
¼	teaspoon dried dill weed
⅛	teaspoon cayenne
½	cup (2 oz.) Swiss cheese, shredded

Generously grease 2 dozen 1¾-inch muffin cups. Separate rolls into 12 equal pieces and cut each in half; press each half over bottom and sides of muffin cup. Divide shrimp among cups. Blend cream, onion, salt, dill, and cayenne and put about 2 teaspoons in each cup. Sprinkle cheese on top. Bake at 375 degrees for 20 minutes, until edges are brown and custard is set. Cool 5 minutes before serving.

May be frozen after baking. To reheat, place frozen quiches on baking sheet; bake at 375 degrees for 15 minutes or until heated through.

SALMON CANAPÉS

JoAnn Saunders Maness   *Yield: 3 dozen*

1	can (7¾ oz.) salmon
1	cup grated Swiss cheese
3	tablespoons mayonnaise
2	tablespoons sliced green onion
1	tablespoon chopped parsley
¼	teaspoon garlic powder
1	package refrigerated butterflake dinner rolls

Flake salmon and combine with cheese and other ingredients. Separate rolls into 3 or 4 natural sections and place rounds on cookie sheet. (If there is great variation of thickness, place thinner sections on 1 cookie sheet and thicker on another for more even baking.) Top with salmon mixture and bake at 375 degrees about 10 minutes.

May be frozen and reheated.

SHRIMP PROSCIUTTO APPETIZER

Susan Mills *Yield: 8 servings*

	Juice of 1 lemon
24	large or jumbo shrimp, peeled, deveined (leave tails on)
12	thin slices prosciutto
½	stick unsalted butter, sliced
1	tablespoon vegetable oil
2	medium cloves garlic, sliced
½	cup tomato purée
¼	cup dry white wine
¼	cup chicken broth
3	tablespoons whipping cream
1	tablespoon coarsely chopped fresh basil or parsley
1	tablespoon capers

Bring large pot of water and lemon juice to rapid boil. Add shrimp and boil 1 minute. Transfer to strainer and cool. Wrap each shrimp with ½ piece of prosciutto and put in shallow flameproof dish. Arrange butter slices between shrimp. Refrigerate until ready to bake. Heat oil and sauté garlic until lightly browned. Stir in tomato purée, wine, broth, and cream. Reduce heat and simmer until flavors are blended, about 10-15 minutes. Stir in basil and capers. Bake shrimp at 500 degrees until butter melts, about 3 minutes. Pour sauce over shrimp. Broil until shrimp tails are reddish. Arrange on serving plates (about 3 each) and top with sauce.

This is great with a Fumé Blanc.

GRAPE-GLAZED SAUSAGE BALLS

Suzanne Pratt *Yield: 8 servings*

1	pound mild sausage
1	small onion, chopped
1	cup grape jelly
1	egg
½	cup dry bread crumbs
¼	teaspoon sage
¼	teaspoon pepper
1	tablespoon prepared mustard
2	teaspoons horseradish

Combine sausage, onion, ¼ cup jelly, egg, crumbs, sage, and pepper. Mix well. Shape into balls and fry until browned evenly. Remove sausage balls; discard half of fat. Stir in remaining grape jelly, mustard, and horseradish. Blend. Add sausage balls and heat 10 minutes, stirring occasionally.

SAUSAGE TARTLETS

Ada Lee Correll   *Yield: 5 dozen*

Favorite pie crust (enough for 2-crust pie)
1   pound mild sausage
3   tablespoons butter
¾   pound mushrooms, chopped
1   onion, chopped
1   egg
¾   cup milk
1½   cups shredded sharp Cheddar cheese
¾   teaspoon salt
¼   teaspoon pepper

Prepare crust. Press into small greased muffin tins; bake at 400 degrees for 5 minutes. Cool. Cook sausage; drain and set aside. Sauté mushrooms and onions in butter. Beat egg slightly; add milk, cheese, salt, and pepper. Stir in sausage, mushrooms, and onion. Fill tartlet shells with mixture. Bake at 375 degrees for 15 minutes. Serve warm.

May be frozen and reheated before serving.

SAUSAGE HORS D'OEUVRES

Doris J. Conway   *Yield: 12 servings*

1   pound bulk sausage
1   package (8 oz.) American cheese, melted
     Party rye bread

Fry sausage and drain; mix with melted cheese. Spread on small rye bread slices. Heat at 450 degrees for 10 minutes.

May be assembled and frozen before baking. Do not defrost; place in oven and bake 15 minutes.

CHICKEN CONSOMMÉ CANAPÉS

Susan T. Sauer   *Yield: 24 servings*

1	can (10¾ oz.) consommé
1	envelope unflavored gelatin
¼	cup water
¼	cup sherry
3	ounces chicken, corned beef, or ham, chopped fine
½	cup mayonnaise
	Curry powder
	Round cocktail crackers

Heat consommé. Dissolve gelatin in water; add to consommé. Add sherry. Lightly oil small muffin tins. Place approximately 1 tablespoon meat in each tin and fill tins with consommé mixture. Chill several hours until set. Mix mayonnaise with curry powder to taste. Spread mayonnaise on crackers. Place 1 consommé circle on each cracker.

BACON TWISTS

Mrs. Ronald Price   *Yield: 18*

6	slices firm sandwich bread
1	package (3 oz.) cream cheese
1	tablespoon mayonnaise
¼	teaspoon onion juice
½	teaspoon seasoned salt
9	slices bacon, halved and partially cooked

Cut crusts from bread and flatten slices with rolling pin. Blend cheese, mayonnaise, onion juice, and salt; spread on bread slices. Place in refrigerator for 15 minutes. Roll each slice in jelly roll fashion and cut in thirds. Wrap bacon around each piece and secure with toothpick. Bake at 375 degrees until bacon is crisp (10-12 minutes).

May be prepared ahead and refrigerated. Bake just before serving.

CORNED BEEF CRUNCHIES

Helen Marinoff   *Yield: 5 dozen*

4   ounces cream cheese
1   teaspoon instant minced
    onion
1   cup chopped, well-drained
    sauerkraut
1   cup flour
½   cup evaporated milk (add
    more if needed)
1   cup corn flake crumbs
5   packages (2½ oz. each)
    dried corned beef, chop-
    ped fine
    Flour

Combine softened cream cheese and instant onion. Add chopped corned beef and sauerkraut. Mix well and chill thoroughly. Shape into 1-inch balls. Roll in flour, dip in milk, and then into crumbs. Fry in batches in deep fat heated to 365 degrees for 1 minute or until golden brown and heated through. Drain and serve.

These freeze well. May be heated from frozen state in single layer on cookie sheet at 400 degrees for about 20 minutes.

CHINESE MEATBALLS

Jane Alter   *Yield: 50*

2   cups fresh, soft bread
    crumbs
½   cup milk
½   pound ground sirloin
    steak (no substitution)
½   pound bulk sausage
½   teaspoon garlic salt
½   teaspoon onion powder
1   tablespoon soy sauce
½   teaspoon Tabasco
½   teaspoon monosodium
    glutamate
½   can (8 oz.) water chest-
    nuts, finely chopped

Mix bread crumbs with milk. Combine all ingredients and mix well. Roll into 1-inch meatballs. Place on baking pan and bake at 300 degrees for 20 minutes. Serve hot with cocktail picks.

These may be made ahead and frozen. Serve with a mustard sauce for dipping.

SAVORY MUSHROOM TARTS

Sue Falter *Yield: 36*

1 egg
1 tablespoon instant minced onion or ¼ cup finely chopped onion
1 can (10¾ oz.) cream of mushroom soup
½ cup shredded Monterey Jack or Swiss cheese
2 tablespoons minced parsley
¼ cup sherry, wine, or milk
5 slices bacon
¼ pound fresh mushrooms, sliced
Pastry for 2-crust pie

Mix egg, onion, soup, cheese, parsley, sherry (or wine or milk) in small bowl. Cook bacon until crisp. Drain and crumble. Reserve 2 tablespoons bacon drippings. Add mushrooms to drippings and cook until limp. Stir bacon and mushrooms into soup mixture. On lightly floured surface, roll pastry to ¹⁄₁₆-inch. With 2½-inch cutter, make 36 rounds from dough. Press pastry into small muffin pans to fit. Spoon 1½ tablespoons mushroom mixture into each shell. Bake at 400 degrees for 20 minutes, until pastry is brown.

May be made ahead and frozen.

STUFFED MUSHROOMS

Patricia Hickernell Donese *Yield: 40*

2 tablespoons butter (no substitutes)
40 large fresh mushroom caps (stems removed), washed and drained
2¼ cups lean ground ham
¼ cup cream cheese
¼ cup mayonnaise
½ teaspoon salt
4 whole green onions, chopped
2 teaspoons chopped green pepper

Melt butter in skillet over medium heat. Sauté mushroom caps in butter, remove from pan, and stuff with mixture of remaining ingredients. (Pile high in caps.) Place filled caps on ungreased cookie sheet and bake at 350 degrees for 8-10 minutes. Serve hot.

May be assembled the night before and refrigerated. Bake for 12-15 minutes.

BACON CRISPS

Jane Sterritt   *Yield: as desired*

Waverly or Club crackers
Sliced bacon
Grated Parmesan cheese

Separate crackers into sections. Wrap each section with ⅓ slice bacon and place on baking pan, seam of bacon under cracker. Sprinkle liberally with cheese. Bake at 200 degrees for 2 hours. Remove from pan and cool on rack.

CHINESE CHICKEN WINGS

Mrs. Richard D. Smith   *Yield: 60*

⅔	**cup soy sauce**
½	**cup honey**
2	**tablespoons vegetable oil**
2	**cloves garlic, minced**
2	**teaspoons allspice**
30	**chicken wings (discard tips and cut in 2 segments)**

Combine ingredients. Marinate chicken at least 1 hour, turning often. Place on broiler pan lined with heavy-duty foil (no seams make cleanup easy). Bake at 375 degrees for 30 minutes, basting often. Turn and bake an additional 30 minutes.

ITALIAN STUFFED MUSHROOMS

Ana M. Schafer   *Yield: 25*

25   large mushrooms
¼   cup chopped onion
½   cup butter
       Salt, pepper, oregano to
       taste
       Dash of Tabasco
1½   cups Italian bread crumbs
       White wine or beer to
       moisten
⅓   cup grated Swiss cheese

C hop and sauté mushroom stems and onion in 2 tablespoons butter. Add salt, pepper, oregano, and Tabasco to taste; add bread crumbs and stir. Moisten with wine or beer; add Swiss cheese. Stuff mushroom caps with filling and drizzle remaining butter over mushrooms. Bake at 400 degrees for 10 minutes. Broil 1 minute and serve hot.

May be made ahead and reheated to serve.

MARINATED MUSHROOMS

Betty Schear (Mrs. Burt E.)   *Yield: 6-8 servings*

2   pounds fresh mushrooms

W ash and clean mushrooms. Cut off lower part of stems. Cut large mushrooms in half lengthwise. Leave small mushrooms whole. Steam mushrooms 1 minute. Add mushrooms to marinade. Refrigerate 12-24 hours, turning once or twice. Remove seasoning bag, drain mushrooms, and serve with cocktail picks.

MARINADE
1   teaspoon Italian seasoning
½   cup vegetable oil
¼   cup white vinegar
¼   cup wine vinegar
½   cup sugar
2   teaspoons dry mustard
1   teaspoon salt

Tie Italian seasoning in cheesecloth. Combine all marinade ingredients in large jar or bowl and mix well.

May be served as a salad on Bibb lettuce.

LEBANESE ARTICHOKE POCKETS

Joan D. Mullen   *Yield: 12-15 servings*

1   clove garlic, crushed
     Juice of 2 lemons
4   tablespoons oil
     Salt and pepper to taste
4   tablespoons minced fresh
     parsley
1   small onion, sliced
     Dash of allspice
1   can (16 oz.) artichoke
     hearts, washed, drained,
     and halved
     Pita bread

Combine garlic and lemon juice and set aside. In another bowl, combine oil, salt, pepper, parsley, onion, and allspice; add garlic and lemon juice. Add artichoke hearts to mixture. Refrigerate overnight. Cut pita bread in half, then cut in half again, and place artichokes into pockets. Serve cold.

Two cans (8 oz. each) mushroom stems and pieces, drained, may be substituted for the artichokes.

ARTICHOKE SQUARES

Alicia M. Kitzman   *Yield: 8-10 servings*

1   bunch scallions, finely
     chopped (use all white
     and ½ green)
1-2 tablespoons butter
2   jars (6 oz. each) marinated
     artichoke hearts, drained
     and chopped
½   pound sharp Cheddar
     cheese, grated
6   single saltines, crushed
     Salt and pepper
     Dash of Tabasco
     Dash of Worcestershire
     sauce
¼-
½   teaspoon dry mustard
4   eggs

Sauté scallions in butter. In mixing bowl, combine remaining ingredients, except eggs. Add scallions. Pour mixture into 8x10-inch greased pan and top with eggs which have been beaten until frothy. Bake at 350 degrees for 35 minutes. Cut into small squares.

Recipe may be doubled and baked in 9x13-inch pan for 45 minutes. May be frozen and reheated.

AVOCADO WITH CRAB

Peg Stuckey   *Yield: 4 servings*

2	egg yolks, slightly beaten
2	tablespoons lemon juice
½	cup cold butter
	Salt to taste
⅛	teaspoon pepper
6½	ounces frozen or canned crabmeat, drained
1	large ripe avocado
	Paprika

In heavy saucepan, using wooden spoon, stir together all ingredients except crabmeat and avocado. Cook over medium heat, stirring constantly, until sauce thickens. Remove from heat immediately. Flake crabmeat with fork and gently stir into sauce. Peel avocado and cut into 8 slices. Top with crab and sauce mixture. Sprinkle with paprika for color.

SPINACH APPETIZERS

Helen Marinoff   *Yield: 6 dozen*

2	packages (10 oz. each) frozen chopped spinach, cooked and drained (press out water)
8	ounces herb-seasoned stuffing (crumb style)
2	small onions, chopped
2	eggs, beaten
¾	cup melted margarine
½	cup grated Parmesan cheese
1	teaspoon garlic salt
½	teaspoon Tabasco
½	teaspoon black pepper

Mix all ingredients well. Form into 1-inch balls. Place on cookie sheet and freeze. When completely frozen, place in freezer bag or container. Bake frozen on ungreased cookie sheet at 350 degrees for 10-12 minutes.

STUFFED COCKTAIL TOMATOES

Flora Sealy *Yield: 15-20*

1   pint cherry tomatoes
½   pound sharp Cheddar cheese, finely grated
¼   cup sour cream
2   tablespoons sherry

Wash tomatoes. Cut off tops and gently squeeze out seeds. Place on paper towels top side down to dry. Mix cheese with sour cream and sherry in blender. With teaspoon, fill tomatoes with mixture. Chill.

ALL-AMERICAN POTATO SKINS

Valerie J. Doll *Yield: 1 dozen*

3   medium baking potatoes
    Vegetable oil
    Seasoned salt
1   cup shredded Cheddar cheese
6   slices bacon, cooked and crumbled (optional)
    Sour cream

Scrub potatoes well and coat skins with oil; bake at 400 degrees for 1 hour or until done. Cool and cut in half lengthwise; carefully scoop out pulp, leaving a ⅛ to ¼-inch shell. (Pulp may be used for mashed potatoes or reserved for another recipe.) Cut shells in half crosswise and deep fat fry in hot oil (375 degrees) 2 minutes or until lightly browned. Drain on paper towels. Place skins on baking sheet; sprinkle with salt, cheese, and bacon. Place under broiler until cheese melts. Serve with sour cream.

25

VEGGIE PIZZA

Beth Swartz   *Yield: 24 servings*

2   packages (8 oz. each) refrigerated crescent rolls
2   packages (8 oz. each) cream cheese, softened
⅔   cup mayonnaise
1½ teaspoons dill weed
    Garlic salt
    Fresh vegetables (choose at least 4 of the following): broccoli tops; cauliflowerets, thinly sliced; carrots, thinly sliced; tomatoes, chopped or cherry tomatoes, halved; celery, chopped; green pepper, chopped; green onions, chopped; black or green olives, sliced; mushrooms, sliced

Unroll crescent rolls on cookie sheet, jelly roll pan, or 2 round pizza pans. Press to edges of pan and press "seams" together. Bake as directed on package; cool. Mix cream cheese and mayonnaise and spread over baked roll layer. Sprinkle with dill weed and garlic salt. Arrange vegetables on pizza. Cut and serve as snack or appetizer.

Broccoli, carrots, green onions, and tomatoes are an attractive combination.

CHEAPIES

Anna-May Jacobsen   *Yield: 16-20 servings*

1   medium onion
½   cup mayonnaise
4-5 slices thin bread
    Parmesan cheese

Mince onion and mix with mayonnaise, or chop and mix in food processor. Remove crusts from bread. Spread mixture evenly on bread. Sprinkle with cheese and cut into triangles or squares. Bake on buttered cookie sheet at 400 degrees for 5-7 minutes or until lightly browned. Serve immediately.

May be made ahead, but cannot be frozen.

LAYERED CHEESE TRIANGLES

Doris J. Conway   *Yield: 50-60*

1   **loaf white bread, sliced thin**
1   **stick butter or margarine**
1   **stick (10 oz.) Coon cheese or extra sharp Cheddar**
3   **egg whites, beaten until stiff**

Remove bread crusts; cut slices into quarters. Place butter or margarine and cheese (in small pieces) in double boiler and melt over hot water. When mixture is completely melted, fold in stiffly beaten egg whites. Dip each bread square into mixture and stack square on square 3 high on cookie sheet. Freeze 2 or 3 hours. Remove from freezer and cut squares diagonally into triangles. Wrap well and return to freezer. Before baking, remove desired number from freezer, place on lightly greased cookie sheet, and let stand at room temperature about 10 minutes. Bake at 350 degrees for 10-15 minutes or until lightly browned. Serve hot.

CHEESE SHORTIES

Josephine F. Bishop   *Yield: 4-5 dozen*

1   **pound sharp Cheddar cheese, grated**
½   **pound butter or margarine**
2   **cups sifted flour**
     Dash of cayenne pepper or paprika

Cream cheese and shortening until well blended. Add flour and mix well. Shape into long rolls 1 inch in diameter. Wrap each roll in waxed paper and then in foil. Refrigerate or freeze until ready to use. To serve, defrost if frozen and cut into ¼-inch slices. Place on cookie sheet 1 inch apart. Sprinkle with cayenne or paprika. Bake at 400 degrees for 10 minutes or until golden brown. Serve hot.

SWEET AND SOUR PINEAPPLE

June H. Decker (Mrs. E. H.)   *Yield: 6-8 servings*

1	can (20 oz.) pineapple chunks
⅔	cup sugar
⅓	cup vinegar
1	teaspoon whole cloves
½	teaspoon allspice
2	cinnamon sticks
	Sour cream

Drain juice from pineapple into saucepan. Put pineapple in large jar with cover. Add remaining ingredients to juice and cook until mixture comes to full boil. Reduce heat and simmer for 10 minutes. Pour over pineapple in jar; cover and cool to room temperature. Refrigerate. Serve with sour cream for dipping.

Must be made at least 24 hours ahead. Also good with meat.

SPICY PECANS

Lou Mason   *Yield: 4 cups*

½	cup butter
½	teaspoon Tabasco
1	teaspoon Worcestershire sauce
1	tablespoon onion salt
1	pound pecan halves

Melt butter in 3-quart saucepan; add seasonings and stir until well mixed. Add pecans and toss to coat. Pour into 10x15-inch jelly roll pan and spread in single layer. Bake at 325 degrees for 20 minutes, stirring once or twice. Remove to paper towels to cool. Store in airtight container.

MILLIE'S SUGARED NUTS

Constance Klarer   *Yield: 2 cups*

1	cup sugar
¼	cup water
1	tablespoon cinnamon
2	cups nuts

In large frying pan, bring sugar and water to soft ball stage. Remove pan from heat and immediately add cinnamon and nuts. Toss until all liquid is absorbed. Spread on waxed paper, working quickly to prevent nuts from sticking together. Cool completely and store in airtight container.

BRANDY-ENGLISH WALNUT PÂTÉ

Barbara (Babs) C. Knapp   *Yield: 10 servings*

½	cup finely chopped English walnuts
1	can (4½ oz.) deviled ham
1	can (4¾ oz.) roast beef spread
2	tablespoons soft butter or margarine
2	tablespoons brandy
¼	teaspoon salt
	Snipped parsley

Combine walnuts, ham, roast beef, butter or margarine, brandy, and salt. Mix well and chill. Top with parsley and serve with rye bread rounds.

MAPLE-GLAZED NUTS

Barbara (Babs) C. Knapp   *Yield: 1½ cups*

1½ cups English walnuts,
     pecans, and almonds
1   cup water
½   cup maple syrup
1   tablespoon honey
⅛   teaspoon salt
4   tablespoons sugar
1½   cups vegetable oil

Combine nuts, water, syrup, honey, and salt in heavy saucepan. Bring to boil and boil 5 minutes over medium-high heat. Drain quickly and discard liquid. Return nuts to empty pan, place over medium heat, and immediately sprinkle with sugar. Immediately remove from heat and toss to coat completely with sugar. Arrange in single layer and dry for 15 minutes on waxed paper. Wash and dry pan; add oil and heat over medium heat until a nut added to the hot oil bubbles almost immediately. Deep fry nuts, stirring until nuts deepen in color and sugar begins to caramelize. (Lower heat if nut color is deepening too quickly.) This whole process should take 2 minutes per batch. Remove nuts to absorbent linen kitchen towel (do not use paper towels); drain in single layer. After nuts have drained and cooled, they will be very crisp. Pull nuts from the towel (nuts will stick a little) and place in airtight jar.

Nuts will keep 3 or 4 days, but are best served the same day they are made.

LIVER SAUSAGE PÂTÉ

Karen B. Tober   *Yield: 12-14 servings*

1¼   **pounds liver sausage**
1   **pound cream cheese, softened**
3   **tablespoons chopped onion**
3   **tablespoons Worcestershire sauce**
3   **tablespoons lemon juice**
   Parsley, chopped

Cut sausage into chunks and mix all ingredients except parsley in mixer. Form mixture into ball; roll ball in parsley. Refrigerate overnight. Serve with crackers or party rye bread.

FROSTED HAM ROLL

Doris J. Conway   *Yield: 20 servings*

1   **pound cooked ham, ground**
½   **cup dark seedless raisins**
1   **medium onion, grated**
¾   **cup mayonnaise**
½   **teaspoon curry powder**
2   **packages (3 oz. each) cream cheese, room temperature**
2   **tablespoons milk**
   Snipped parsley

Combine ham, raisins, onion, mayonnaise, and curry powder and blend well. Mold mixture into ball on serving plate; chill. Blend cream cheese and milk. Frost ham mixture with cream cheese mixture and garnish with parsley. Serve with crackers and rye bread.

May also be used as sandwich spread by mixing all ingredients together.

STEAK TARTARE

Susan S. Seyfarth   *Yield: 15 servings*

1	jar (2½ oz.) chopped mushrooms, drained
	Italian dressing
½	pound fresh ground sirloin
4	tablespoons finely chopped onion
1	egg yolk, beaten
1	tablespoon grated Parmesan cheese
½	teaspoon garlic salt
¼	teaspoon oregano
1	loaf cocktail rye

Place mushrooms in bowl; add Italian dressing to cover. Cover and marinate several hours in refrigerator. Combine sirloin, 2 tablespoons chopped onion, egg yolk, Parmesan cheese, garlic salt, and oregano. Cover and chill. To serve, mound meat mixture in center of serving plate, edge with marinated mushrooms and remaining chopped onion. Surround with sliced cocktail rye.

SPICY CHILI DIP

Shirley Denka   *Yield: 12-15 servings*

1	pound ground chuck
1	can (8 oz.) tomato sauce
1	can (15¾ oz.) hot chili beans
4	teaspoons chili powder
1	cup grated Cheddar cheese
1	red onion, finely chopped

Brown and crumble ground chuck. Place tomato sauce, chili beans, and chili powder in blender; blend until smooth. Add to ground beef and heat thoroughly. Place in chafing dish and cover generously with cheese and onion. Serve hot with king-size corn chips for dipping.

CHICKEN CASHEW BALL

Theda Roup   *Yield: 15-20 servings*

½	cup cubed cooked chicken breast
½	cup chopped mild onion
½	cup shredded Cheddar cheese
	Salt and pepper to taste
2	tablespoons dry sherry
1	package (3 oz.) cream cheese
1	cup chopped cashews

Mix all ingredients, reserving ½ cup nuts. Form into ball and roll in reserved nuts. Serve with rice crackers or any plain crackers.

AVOCADO CAVIAR PIE

Bettie Howdieshell   *Yield: 6-8 servings*

2	avocados
3	green onions, finely chopped
6	hard-cooked eggs
3	tablespoons mayonnaise
	Salt and pepper to taste
½	pint sour cream
1	jar (2 oz.) black caviar

Mash avocados and spread in bottom of glass pie plate. Top with chopped onion. Grate eggs; add mayonnaise, salt, and pepper and spread on onions. Spread with layer of sour cream. Just before serving, spread caviar on top of sour cream. Serve with rye crackers or party rye bread.

EASY ELEGANT CAVIAR

Mrs. Thomas H. Towler   *Yield: 12-18 servings*

8   **ounces cream cheese**
3½   **ounces black lumpfish caviar**
1   **hard-cooked egg, finely chopped**
½   **onion, finely chopped**
       Crackers or melba rounds

Arrange cream cheese on platter; cover with caviar. Put chopped egg and chopped onion in small separate dishes (with demitasse spoons). Serve on crackers and garnish each serving with egg and onion.

"Always have in your cupboard a 3½-ounce jar of black lumpfish caviar. I like Romanoff; it costs about $2.79, but your guests will think it cost $27.90 and that you are very extravagant! This makes the easiest and the most elegant of hors d'oeuvres. There is never any left!"

Sue Towler

SMOKED OYSTER ROLL

Jo Brakebill   *Yield: 8 servings*

1   **package (8 oz.) cream cheese, softened**
1   **can (3½ oz.) smoked oysters, drained and chopped**
       Pecan bits

Press cream cheese flat. Place oysters on top and roll jelly roll fashion, starting from long side. Roll in pecan bits to cover. Chill and serve with crackers.

CLAM DIP

Sonia Goldfarb   *Yield: 16-20 servings*

2	cans (6 oz. each) minced clams
2	packages (8 oz. each) cream cheese, softened
2	tablespoons mayonnaise
1½	teaspoons prepared mustard
1	teaspoon Worcestershire sauce
¼	cup minced green onion Clam juice as necessary

Drain and rinse clams, reserving juice. Mix cream cheese, mayonnaise, mustard, and Worcestershire sauce and beat until smooth. Add green onions and clams; mix well. Add enough clam juice to make desired consistency.

Good served with raw vegetables or crackers.

CHAFING DISH SHRIMP

Sara Rendall   *Yield: 20 servings*

1	stick butter or margarine, softened
3	cartons (8 oz. each) whipped cream cheese with chives
2	tablespoons dry onion soup mix
1	tablespoon sherry
2	cans (7 oz. each) medium shrimp

Mix butter and cream cheese. Add onion soup mix and sherry and mix well. Stir in shrimp. Place in chafing dish over low heat. Do not boil. Serve with favorite chips or crackers.

35

SHRIMP DIP

Sara Rendall   *Yield: 12-15 servings*

1   **package (8 oz.) cream cheese, softened**
1   **teaspoon grated onion**
2   **tablespoons ketchup**
2   **tablespoons crumbled Roquefort**
⅓   **cup mayonnaise**
¼   **teaspoon celery seed**
1   **tablespoon Worcester-shire sauce**
1   **can (6 oz.) shrimp, drained or 1 bag (6 oz.) frozen salad shrimp, thawed**

Beat all ingredients, except shrimp, until blended. Add shrimp to mixture and stir just until well mixed but pieces of shrimp are still visible. Serve with crackers.

CRAB SPREAD

Ruth A. Coleman   *Yield: 8-10 servings*

1   **package (8 oz.) cream cheese**
2   **tablespoons mayonnaise**
½-1   **teaspoon minced garlic**
½   **teaspoon salt**
    Dash of Worcestershire sauce
    Dash of Tabasco
1   **tablespoon lemon juice**
1   **can (6½ oz.) crabmeat, drained**

Mix all ingredients together. Place in small casserole and bake at 350 degrees for 30 minutes. Serve with crackers.

May be made ahead and frozen or refrigerated until needed. Leftovers may be treated the same way.

SWISS EGG SPREAD

Gay Hoffman   *Yield: 2 cups*

¾   **pound Swiss cheese**
2   **hard-cooked eggs**
1   **large slice of onion**
     Mayonnaise
     Salt to taste

Grate cheese. Chop eggs and onion very fine and add to cheese. Blend in enough mayonnaise to make spreadable. Add salt. Serve with crackers or melba toast.

TACO DIP

Elizabeth Donovan   *Yield: 12 servings*

1   **can (10½ oz.) bean dip**
2   **very ripe avocados, mashed with 1 teaspoon lemon juice**
1   **cup sour cream***
½   **cup mayonnaise**
1   **package (1½ oz.) taco seasoning**
½-
¾   **pound Cheddar cheese, shredded**
½   **large onion, diced**
1   **can (2¼ oz.) black olives, sliced**
2   **medium tomatoes, diced and drained**

*****May substitute cottage cheese, blended with lemon juice in blender until creamy.**

Spread bean dip in 10-inch pie plate. Top with avocado mixture. Mix sour cream, mayonnaise, and taco seasoning; spread on avocado layer. Top with layer of cheese, then onion, then olives. May be assembled to this point early in day, covered, and refrigerated. Just before serving, add tomatoes and serve with tortilla chips.

Wonderful as an appetizer with cocktails or as a patio meal for 4 on a hot summer evening.

BRIE EN CROÛTE

Sonnie Kasch (Mrs. William)   *Yield: 6 servings*

2   **frozen patty shells, thawed**
1   **round (4½ oz. pkg.) Brie cheese**
1   **egg yolk, slightly beaten**
    Apple slices
    Pear slices

Form patty shells into a ball and roll out to ⅛-inch thickness. Cut circle of dough size of Brie and place on top of cheese. With remaining dough, cut another circle large enough to cover bottom and sides of cheese. Place Brie in center of this circle. Wrap dough up sides and seal well with dough on top so that cheese is completely encased. Use any remaining dough to decorate top. Brush with egg yolk. (May be frozen at this point; thaw in refrigerator before baking.) Place on ungreased baking sheet and bake at 450 degrees for 10 minutes. Reduce heat to 400 degrees and bake 20-25 minutes until golden brown. Serve with fruit slices.

CHEESE-CHUTNEY SPREAD

Mary Riegel   *Yield: 12 servings*

1   **package (8 oz.) cream cheese, softened**
8   **ounces sharp Cheddar cheese, grated**
2   **tablespoons mayonnaise**
1   **teaspoon curry powder (optional)**
    Chutney
    Green onions, chopped

Put cream cheese, Cheddar cheese, and mayonnaise in food processor or mixer and mix well. Add curry powder if desired. Place on plate and cover with thick layer of drained chutney. Sprinkle with green onion. Serve with crackers.

HOT SWISS CHEESE SPREAD

Sally J. Thompson   *Yield: 4-6 servings*

½   cup chopped onion
½   cup mayonnaise
½   cup chopped Swiss cheese
      Dijon mustard to taste

Mix all ingredients. Place in small casserole and heat at 350 degrees until cheese melts. Serve with crackers.

BAKED EGG AND CRAB SPREAD

Jo Granzow   *Yield: 8 servings*

1   cup crabmeat, flaked
1½   cups soft bread crumbs
1½   cups shredded longhorn
        cheese
1   cup sour cream
1½   cups mayonnaise
6   hard-cooked eggs, diced
1   tablespoon minced parsley
1   teaspoon minced onion
1   teaspoon pepper
        Tabasco and Worcester-
        shire sauce to taste
1   tablespoon butter, melted

Combine all ingredients, except ½ cup crumbs, ½ cup cheese, and butter. Place in greased individual serving shells or 1½-quart casserole. Sprinkle with remaining cheese and top with remaining crumbs mixed with butter. Bake at 350 degrees for 10-20 minutes, until browned. Serve in shells as first course or with crackers as hot spread.

MEXICAN DIP

Jo McCrabb   *Yield: 8 servings*

1   jar (7½ oz.) Jalapeño relish*
8   ounces Monterey Jack cheese, shredded

*Also called Jalapeño sauce or Salsa Jalapeño

Pour relish into oven-proof baking dish. Sprinkle cheese on top. Bake at 350 degrees for about 10 minutes or until cheese is melted and bubbly. Serve with corn chips or nachos.

Very HOT!

WINNIE'S VIDALIA ONIONS

Sue T. Strother   *Yield: 12 servings*

6   large Vidalia onions
2   cups water
1   cup sugar
½   cup vinegar
1   cup mayonnaise
¾-1   teaspoon celery seed
    Salt
    Pepper

Slice onions and put in container. Boil water, sugar, and vinegar; cool and pour over sliced onions. Refrigerate for 24 hours, stirring several times. Drain well; squeeze out liquid. Add mayonnaise, celery seed, salt, and pepper. Serve on crackers.

May substitute Walla Walla or Maui onions.

ARTICHOKE DIP

Sonnie Kasch (Mrs. William) — *Yield: 1½ cups*

1 can (14 oz.) artichoke hearts, chopped
7 strips bacon, crisply fried and crumbled
½ can (8 oz.) water chestnuts, chopped
2 green onions, finely chopped
1 tablespoon fresh lemon juice
¼ cup mayonnaise
½ cup sour cream
Salt and pepper to taste
1 teaspoon Worcestershire sauce

Mix all ingredients and refrigerate overnight. Serve with vegetables or crackers.

SPINACH DIP WITH GREEN CHILIES

Judith Vandenberg Boudreau — *Yield: 8-10 servings*

1 package (10 oz.) frozen chopped spinach
2 teaspoons parsley flakes
½ cup chopped onion
½ teaspoon basil
½ teaspoon salt
¾ cup mayonnaise
½ can (4 oz.) chopped green chilies (mild or hot)

Cook spinach and drain thoroughly. Mix with remaining ingredients. Serve with crackers or raw vegetables.

41

ZUCCHINI SPREAD

JoAnn Saunders Maness   *Yield: 3 cups*

1   cup grated sharp Cheddar
     cheese
1   cup grated zucchini,
     drained
¾   cup mayonnaise
½   cup walnuts, chopped
1   teaspoon fresh lemon juice

Combine all ingredients and refrigerate 1 hour or overnight. Serve with assorted crackers or crudités.

ORIENTAL DIP

Susan S. Seyfarth   *Yield: 2½ cups*

1   cup mayonnaise
1   cup sour cream
¼   cup finely chopped onion
¼   cup minced fresh parsley
¼   cup chopped water
       chestnuts
1-2   tablespoons chopped
       candied ginger
2   cloves garlic, minced
1   teaspoon soy sauce

Mix all ingredients and chill for several hours to blend flavors. Serve with potato chips or crackers.

VEGETABLE DIP

Mrs. John Finlay (Ann)   *Yield: 1½ cups*

1	cup mayonnaise
½	teaspoon lemon juice
¼	teaspoon salt
¼	teaspoon paprika
1	teaspoon dried salad herbs
1	tablespoon grated onion
1	tablespoon chopped chives or parsley
⅛	teaspoon curry powder
½	teaspoon Worcestershire sauce
½	cup sour cream

Combine all ingredients and serve with raw vegetables. Flavor improves if refrigerated overnight.

ANCHOVY DIP

Mary Earl Rogers   *Yield: 2 cups*

2	packages (8 oz. each) cream cheese
2	tablespoons anchovy paste
½	teaspoon dried dill weed
1	tablespoon Worcestershire sauce
½	cup mayonnaise
¼	cup milk
	Paprika

Mix all ingredients, except paprika, in mixer until light and creamy. Place in serving bowl and sprinkle with paprika. Serve with raw vegetables, crackers, or chips. Will keep 1-2 weeks in refrigerator.

WASSAIL BOWL—AMERICAN STYLE

Catherine W. Staley   *Yield: 40 punch cups*

1	pound sugar
1	quart water
12	whole cloves
4	sticks cinnamon
2	tablespoons chopped ginger
4	allspice berries
3	cups orange juice
2	cups lemon juice
2	quarts cider
	Apple slices (optional)
1	quart bourbon or rum (optional)
	Lemon slices (optional)

Make a syrup by boiling sugar and water ten minutes. Add cloves, cinnamon, ginger, and allspice. Let syrup stand, covered, in a warm place for 1 hour or more; strain. Add orange and lemon juices and cider. Bring quickly to a boil and serve at once. Prepare a few slices of apple to float on top. Should a liquor be added, float slices of lemon on top.

In ancient England at the holiday season, the lord of the manor assembled his household around a bowl of hot spiced ale or cider from which he drank to their health, then passed it to the others that they might drink too. As they drank, they said the old Saxon phrase, "wass hael," meaning, "to your health." Hence, this came to be recognized as the wassail or wassel bowl.

ROBERT'S PUNCH FOR GOV. GORE

Catherine E. Baer   *Yield: 30-40 servings*

1	pint fruit brandy
2	pints vodka
	Juice of 3 lemons
¼	cup sugar
4	quarts ginger ale
1	lemon, cut into slices

Mix brandy, vodka, lemon juice, and sugar together in a large punch bowl. Just before serving, add ginger ale. Garnish with lemon slices.

This is the potent punch served by the butler to an early New England governor.

VODKA PUNCH

Constance Klarer   *Yield: 26 (4 oz.) servings*

1   **fifth vodka**
3   **cans (6 oz. each) frozen
      limeade concentrate**
1   **can (6 oz.) frozen
      lemonade concentrate**
8   **cans water**
      **Grenadine to color (about
      ¼ cup)**
      Maraschino cherries
      Lemon slices
      Lime slices

Mix vodka, limeade, lemonade, water, and grenadine together. Serve in punch bowl with ice ring. Garnish with cherries, lemon, and lime slices.

If green punch is preferred, omit grenadine.

WHISKEY SLUSH

Roy Henry   *Yield: 90-100 servings*

1   **can (12 oz.) frozen
       orange juice concentrate**
1   **can (12 oz.) frozen
       lemonade concentrate**
1½   **cups sugar**
5   **cups water**
3   **cups whiskey (may
       substitute brandy)**
       7-Up

Mix together all ingredients, except 7-Up; freeze. To make 1 drink, put 2-3 tablespoonfuls of mix in highball glass with an ice cube and fill glass with 7-Up. Mix well. A maraschino cherry may be added for color.

STRAWBERRY WINE SLUSH

Becki Sammons   *Yield: 10 (4 oz.) servings*

1   can (6 oz.) frozen limeade
     concentrate
1   pint strawberries,
     unsweetened (fresh or
     frozen)
16   ice cubes
1½   cups Sauterne

Place limeade, strawberries, and ice cubes in blender and mix on high speed until smooth. Blend in Sauterne and serve immediately.

PAIN KILLER

Doris J. Conway   *Yield: 4-6 servings*

1   cup bourbon
1   cup strong coffee, cooled
1   quart vanilla ice cream

Process all ingredients in blender until smooth. Serve immediately in champagne glasses as an after-dinner drink.

POLYNESIAN PUNCH

Gwendolyn McCausland   *Yield: 24 servings*

2	cans (20 oz. each) unsweetened crushed pineapple
4	bananas
1	can (12 oz.) frozen lemonade concentrate (undiluted)
½-1	cup sugar
1	can (46 oz.) pineapple juice
3	cups piña colada mix
4	quarts ginger ale
1	quart pineapple sherbet

Blend crushed pineapple and bananas in blender; add lemonade and blend. Continue to blend as sugar is added. Pour into freezer container and freeze. Two hours before serving, remove frozen mixture and thaw. Put mixture in punch bowl; add pineapple juice, piña colada mix, and ginger ale. Stir well. Top with scoops of pineapple sherbet.

CRICKET

Susan T. Sauer   *Yield: 4 servings*

1	pint chocolate chip ice cream
8	ice cubes, crushed
¼	cup crème de cacao
2	tablespoons brandy

Mix all ingredients in blender. Spoon into champagne glasses or punch cups. May be served as dessert in sherbet dishes.

HOLIDAY PERCOLATOR PUNCH

Barbara (Babs) C. Knapp   *Yield: 26 servings*

2   **quarts cranberry juice cocktail**
2   **quarts sweetened pineapple juice**
1   **quart grapefruit juice**
⅔   **cup sugar**
1   **tablespoon whole cloves**
6   **sticks cinnamon**
2   **lemons, sliced and quartered**
1   **lime, sliced and quartered**
     Sliced limes and whole fresh cranberries for garnish

Pour liquids into 30-cup electric percolator. Put all other ingredients, except garnish, in basket. Perk until percolator indicates it is ready. Serve with lime slice and cranberry garnish.

This may also be heated in a large pan. If desired, a shot of rum may be placed in each cup at serving time.

HOT SPICED CRANBERRY PUNCH

Susan T. Sauer   *Yield: 14-16 servings*

1   **pound cranberries**
     Juice of 3 oranges
     Juice of 3 lemons
1½   **cups sugar**
1   **stick cinnamon**
1   **teaspoon whole cloves**

Boil cranberries in 3 quarts water for 5 minutes or until cranberries pop. Strain into large pot and discard berries. Add juice of oranges and lemons, sugar, and spices. Bring back to boil and serve.

HOT BUTTERED RUM PUNCH

Marilyn Erickson   *Yield: 20-30 servings*

1	gallon apple cider
1	fifth rum
1	cup dark brown sugar
½	teaspoon vanilla
½	teaspoon cinnamon
½	teaspoon nutmeg
4	tablespoons butter
1-2	lemons, sliced

Combine cider and rum; simmer. Add sugar, vanilla, spices, and butter. Stirring constantly, bring just to boiling (but do not boil). Add lemon slices and serve.

If using glass punch bowl, temper bowl before adding hot liquid.

TENNESSEE TEA

Pat Reed   *Yield: 1 gallon*

6	tea bags
1	quart boiling water
1-1½	cups sugar
1	can (6 oz.) frozen lemonade concentrate
1	can (6 oz.) frozen limeade concentrate
	Cold water
	Lemon or lime slices for garnish

Place tea bags in 1-gallon container. Add boiling water and steep 5 minutes. Remove tea bags. Add sugar, lemonade, and limeade and stir to dissolve. Add cold water to make 1 gallon. Mix well. Serve over ice with lemon or lime slices for garnish.

GLOP

Steve Mason   *Yield: 12 servings*

1	can (12 oz.) frozen lemonade concentrate
1	can (12 oz.) frozen grape juice concentrate
4	cans (12 oz. each) water
48	ounces 7-Up

Mix first 3 ingredients well and refrigerate. When ready to serve, pour large ice-filled glasses ⅔ full of fruit juice mixture. Fill with 7-Up and stir.

"This was invented when our children were little. They named it, and as adults they still love it."

Steve Mason

WHITE WINE SANGRÍA

Jan Rudd   *Yield: 6 servings*

1	bottle (⅘ quart) dry white wine
⅔	cup Triple Sec liqueur
16	ounces club soda
1	lemon, sliced
1	lime, sliced
1	orange, sliced

Chill wine and club soda. When ready to serve, combine wine and Triple Sec in glass pitcher. Stir in club soda and fruit, add ice cubes, and serve.

Other fruits may be added, i.e., blueberries, strawberries, raspberries.

STERLING IDEAS

Soups

Bite-sized cereals toasted in a bit of butter are an interesting change from croutons.

Try adding these garnishes to soup next time:
> Sliced olive rings on jellied consommé
> Salami slices on tomato, pea, or celery soup
> Grated cheese on all chowders or onion soups
> Browned frankfurter slices on pea, tomato, bean, or asparagus soups
> Toasted walnuts, almonds, or pecans on almost any cream soup

Combine these canned soups for zestier flavor:

Clam chowder and tomato	Consommé and tomato
Chicken with rice and tomato	Mushroom and pea
Chicken noodle and mushroom	Split pea and cream of chicken
Tomato and corn chowder	Tomato and celery
Tomato and pea	Vegetable and bean

Breads

For easier slicing of fresh bread, use a hot knife.

For lighter muffins, heat greased pans in the oven for a few moments before pouring in batter.

Heat a ceramic tile in the oven while baking muffins or rolls. Place hot tile in bottom of bread basket to keep rolls warm at table.

For a soft-crusted bread, place a small dish of water in the oven while bread is baking. For a more crusty loaf, brush top and sides of loaf with an egg white diluted with one tablespoon of water five minutes before end of baking time.

To help yeast dough rise quickly in a cool room, place in covered bowl on a heating pad at medium temperature.

CHICKEN TOFU SOUP

Joan Weinberg   *Yield: 8-10 servings*

1	quart chicken broth
¾	cup white wine
1	teaspoon onion powder
¼	teaspoon sour salt (or 2-3 tablespoons fresh lemon juice)
1	teaspoon dry mustard
½	teaspoon curry powder
	Pinch of garlic powder
	Salt and pepper to taste
½-¾	block tofu
2	cups shredded lettuce

Remove all fat from broth by floating a few ice cubes on surface. Remove cubes when fat adheres; add wine, spices, salt, and pepper. Simmer about 5 minutes to blend. Rinse tofu block and cut in small julienne pieces (size will double). Add tofu and simmer ½ hour. (Tofu will turn a nice saffron color from curry.) If liquid has boiled down, add about ½ cup of water. Cool and refrigerate overnight. Remove fat from surface after refrigerating. Place ¼ cup lettuce in each bowl before adding soup. May be served cold or hot.

FRENCH ONION SOUP

Susan Mills   *Yield: 8-10 servings*

2	tablespoons butter
5	medium onions, cut in half and sliced very thin
8	ounces Chablis
2	quarts beef consommé
	Pepper
	French rolls, sliced ¾-inch thick and toasted
2	cups grated Gruyère cheese

Put butter and onions in large pot, cover, and cook for 10 minutes over medium heat, stirring occasionally. Raise heat and brown onions, stirring to prevent burning. Add wine and cook until liquid is reduced to a little less than ⅓. Add beef consommé. Bring to boil, reduce heat to simmer, and cook for about 10 minutes. Season with freshly ground pepper. Skim off fat. Pour soup into oven-proof bowls. Top each with toasted bread and sprinkle generously with cheese. Bake uncovered at 325 degrees for 45-60 minutes.

BROCCOLI SOUP

Shirley W. Dewire   *Yield: 6-8 servings*

⅓   cup salad oil
1   medium onion, diced
1-2 potatoes, diced
1   cup diced celery
1   clove garlic, minced
½   teaspoon pepper
3   cups chopped fresh broc-
    coli or 1 package (10 oz.)
    frozen chopped broccoli
5   cans (10¾ oz. each)
    chicken broth
1   tablespoon dried basil
    leaves
1   teaspoon lemon juice
2   cups half-and-half
¼   cup Parmesan cheese

Sauté onion in oil until tender. Add potatoes, celery, garlic, and pepper. Cook 10-15 minutes. Stir in broccoli, 1 can chicken broth, basil, and lemon juice. Cover and simmer 20 minutes. Cool enough to blend in blender. Add remaining chicken broth and cream for consistency desired. Add Parmesan cheese and heat, but do not boil.

This is also good served cold.

DILLED CREAM OF GREEN

Sandy Wall   *Yield: 6-8 servings*

4   cups homemade turkey
    or chicken broth
1   pound fresh green beans
2   small potatoes, peeled
    and quartered
1   small onion, quartered
4   tablespoons butter or
    margarine
1   teaspoon dill seed
1   large garlic clove
⅔   cup sour cream
    Salt and freshly ground
    pepper

Combine broth, beans, potatoes, onion, butter, dill, and garlic in large saucepan and bring to boil. Reduce heat; cover and simmer until vegetables are tender, about 20 minutes. Transfer soup to blender in batches and purée until smooth. Strain if desired. Put sour cream in large saucepan. Stir soup into sour cream. Add salt and pepper. Heat gently. Do not boil.

May be made ahead and reheated.

EASY POTATO SOUP

Susan M. Falter   *Yield: 6-8 servings*

¼   cup chopped onion
2   tablespoons butter or margarine
4-5   large potatoes, chopped
¼   cup chopped fresh parsley
2   cans (10¾ oz. each) celery soup
2   soup cans milk
½   pint sour cream

Sauté onion in melted butter until soft. Add potatoes and barely cover with water. Cook potatoes until tender. Mash undrained potatoes. (May substitute 3 cups leftover mashed potatoes.) Add parsley, soup, and milk. Heat almost to boiling. Add sour cream.

CREAM OF ZUCCHINI SOUP

Laurie H. Leach   *Yield: 12 servings*

3   pounds zucchini
1½   cups beef stock or broth
2   cups water
1½   teaspoons salt
3   sprigs parsley
½   teaspoon curry powder
¼   teaspoon thyme
1   small onion, quartered
1   clove garlic, chopped
  Milk or half-and-half
  Parmesan cheese
  Bacon bits
  Crème fraîche

To make soup base, wash and quarter zucchini; combine with next 8 ingredients and cook until tender. Purée in blender in 3 equal parts. Return mixture to pan and bring to simmer, stirring constantly. Freeze in 4 pint jars. To prepare 3 servings, thaw 1 pint soup base. Add 1 cup milk or half-and-half and heat. Garnish with grated Parmesan cheese, bacon bits, and/or crème fraîche and serve.

CARROT SOUP

Mrs. C. Miles Schmidt, Jr.　　　　　　　　　*Yield: 6 servings*

6	medium carrots
1	small onion
3	cups chicken stock
1	small bay leaf
3	tablespoons butter
2	tablespoons flour
1	cup half-and-half
	Salt and pepper

Peel and slice carrots and onion. Place in pan with stock and bay leaf. Cover and simmer 45 minutes. Discard bay leaf and purée mixture in blender. Melt butter in large pan. Remove pan from heat and stir in flour. Return to heat and cook a few minutes. Remove from heat and stir in carrot purée. Bring to boil, stirring constantly. Boil 3 minutes. Add half-and-half and heat, but do not boil again or soup may curdle. Season to taste.

SIMPLE LENTIL SOUP

Sue Falter　　　　　　　　　　　*Yield: 6-8 servings*

2	large onions, chopped
1	carrot, coarsely grated
½	teaspoon marjoram
½	teaspoon thyme
¼	cup vegetable oil
1	can (16 oz.) tomatoes, coarsely chopped
5	cups water
3	beef bouillon cubes
1	cup dry lentils, rinsed (lentils may be soaked overnight for more tender result)
1	teaspoon salt
¼	teaspoon pepper
¼	cup parsley
4	ounces Cheddar cheese, shredded

Sauté onions, carrot, marjoram, and thyme in oil in kettle. Cook about 5 minutes, stirring often. Add tomatoes, water, bouillon cubes, lentils, salt, and pepper, stirring to dissolve cubes. Bring to boil. Lower heat, cover, and simmer 1 hour or until lentils are tender. Sprinkle with parsley and cheese before serving.

MUSHROOM SOUP

Geraldine Waanders   *Yield: 4 servings*

2   cups mushroom stems
1   tablespoon chives or mild
     white onion
3   tablespoons butter
2   chicken bouillon cubes
1   cup hot water
2   tablespoons flour
½   teaspoon salt
½   teaspoon white pepper
¼   teaspoon thyme
2   cups milk or half-and-half

Finely dice mushroom stems and chives; sauté in 2 tablespoons butter. Add bouillon cubes and water; simmer 10 minutes. In another pan, melt 1 tablespoon butter. Add flour, salt, pepper, and thyme; simmer briefly. Add milk and mushroom mixture; heat, but do not boil.

CANADIAN CHEDDAR SOUP

Maureen Brolick   *Yield: 6-8 servings*

5   tablespoons butter or
     margarine
¾   cup shredded carrot
½   cup diced celery
½   cup chopped onion
1   cup sliced fresh mush-
     rooms
¼   cup flour
3   cans (10¾ oz. each) beef
     broth
3   cups shredded extra sharp
     Cheddar cheese
2   cups half-and-half

Melt 3 tablespoons butter in large pot or Dutch oven over low heat. Add vegetables. Cover and simmer 10 minutes. Mix remaining butter with flour; stir into vegetables. Gradually stir in beef broth. Raise heat to medium. Cook, stirring constantly, until smooth, about 5-8 minutes. Add cheese and stir until melted. Gradually add half-and-half. Heat thoroughly, but do not boil. Stir and serve.

A rich, hearty soup and a meal in itself when served with French bread or homemade rolls.

STRAWBERRY SOUP

Janet Bogin   *Yield: 6 servings*

4	cups strawberries
4	cups of water
1	cup sugar
1	cup sour cream
1	cup rosé wine
	Strawberries for garnish

Blend first 5 ingredients in blender or food processor. (Use about half of each at a time to blend well.) Serve cold in bowl or cup with oyster crackers. Garnish with whole strawberry.

CHILLED RASPBERRY BISQUE

Lou Mason   *Yield: 6 servings*

1	tablespoon cornstarch
1	cup cold water
1½	cups rosé wine
¾	cup sugar
1	bag (12 oz.) frozen unsweetened raspberries or 2 cups fresh
	Sour cream

In saucepan, mix well all ingredients, except raspberries and sour cream, and simmer until thickened. Add berries and stir until thawed. Place mixture in blender or processor and blend well. Strain liquid and chill. Serve with dollop of sour cream as first course or dessert.

DOOR COUNTY FISH CHOWDER

Rosemary Malzahn   *Yield: 8-10 servings*

6	medium potatoes
3	medium onions
2	large stalks celery
1	teaspoon salt
	Pepper
2-3	pounds fish, skinned and boned
1	can (16 oz.) cream-style corn
1	can (13 oz.) evaporated milk
¼	pound butter or corn oil margarine
1	teaspoon chili powder

Cut potatoes into ¾-inch cubes. Dice onions and celery. Put into pot with enough water to cook. Add salt and pepper and cook until soft. Cut fish into 1-inch cubes. Rinse and set aside. When vegetables are almost done, place fish on vegetables. Do not stir. Cover and cook until fish is done (about 12 minutes). Do not drain. Add corn and milk. Stir gently and heat, but do not boil. Add butter and chili powder, and stir slowly. Let chowder stand a few minutes before serving.

SHERRIED CRAB SOUP

Betty Vallo   *Yield: 4-6 servings*

1	mild onion, minced
2	tablespoons margarine
1	tablespoon cornstarch or flour
1	can (10¾ oz.) tomato soup
1	quart half-and-half
2	cans (6 oz. each) crabmeat, drained
	Salt and pepper to taste
¼	cup sherry or wine

Sauté onion in margarine; stir in cornstarch or flour. Add soup and gradually stir in half-and-half. Cook 10 minutes. Add crabmeat and season to taste. Heat through, but do not boil. Add sherry or wine and serve at once.

COLD AVOCADO SOUP

Georg Bluhm   *Yield: 4 servings*

1	ripe avocado, peeled and pitted
2	cups condensed chicken broth
1	cup heavy or light cream
2	tablespoons rum (white is preferable)
½	teaspoon curry powder
½	teaspoon salt
	Pepper
1	tablespoon lemon juice
	Lemon slices

Place all ingredients except lemon slices in blender. Blend until smooth. Serve in chilled cups or bowls. Float lemon slice on top of each serving. May be made a few hours ahead and refrigerated to blend flavors.

QUICK BORSCHT

Ellen Jane Porter   *Yield: 4-6 servings*

1	medium onion, coarsely chopped
1	stalk celery (with leaves), cut up
½	cup water
2	bouillon cubes, chicken or beef
1	can (16 oz.) beets, undrained
	Sour cream
	Chives, coarsely chopped

Cook onion and celery in water until soft. Add bouillon cubes and stir until dissolved. Put mixture into blender or processor with beets and their liquid. Blend until smooth. Store in glass jar in refrigerator until thoroughly chilled. Serve in small bowls (looks nice in glass); top with dollop of sour cream and sprinkling of chives.

CHILLED CUCUMBER SOUP

Susan H. Hipps   *Yield: 4-5 servings*

1   can (10¾ oz.) cream of chicken soup
½   cup milk
1   large cucumber, peeled, sliced, and seeded (leaving some skin for color)
1   cup sour cream
     Dash of curry powder
     Dash of minced onion

Combine all ingredients in a blender and blend well. Chill until ready to serve. Serve in chilled cups. Garnish with thinly sliced cucumber.

SUMMER GAZPACHO

Sherri Kohnle   *Yield: 6 servings*

1   cup finely chopped, peeled tomatoes
½   cup each finely chopped green pepper, celery, and cucumber
¼   cup chopped onion
2   teaspoons snipped parsley
1   teaspoon chopped scallions
2   cloves garlic, minced
2-3 tablespoons wine vinegar
2   tablespoons olive oil
1   teaspoon salt
½   teaspoon freshly ground black pepper
½   teaspoon Worcestershire sauce
2-3 cups Beefamato juice
     Sour cream
     Dill weed

Combine all ingredients, except sour cream and dill weed, in stainless or glass bowl. Cover and chill at least 4-6 hours. Serve in chilled bowls. Top with dollop of sour cream and sprinkling of dill weed.

ALL SEASONS GAZPACHO

Lou Mason   *Yield: 2 quarts*

2	cans (28 oz. each) tomatoes
1	medium green pepper, seeded
1	medium onion
1	medium cucumber, peeled
½	teaspoon ground cumin
1	teaspoon salt
¼	teaspoon freshly ground black pepper
¼	cup red wine vinegar
¼	cup olive oil
	Cucumber slices, unpeeled

Drain juice from tomatoes into large bowl. Cut pepper, onion, and cucumber into large chunks. Put half of vegetables, including tomatoes, into food processor or blender and process until even consistency (will not be smooth). Add to juice in bowl. Repeat with remaining vegetables. Add cumin, salt, and pepper; stir well, cover, and refrigerate. When ready to serve, add vinegar and oil and stir well. Garnish each serving with cucumber slice. Keeps several days in refrigerator.

May serve the Spanish way with small bowls of chopped cucumber, green pepper, tomato, and croutons so guests may choose their own garnish.

CAPE COD CLAM CHOWDER

Blanche Palmeter   *Yield: 4-6 servings*

3	large potatoes, diced
1	quart half-and-half
¼	pound salt pork, diced (bacon may be substituted)
2	medium onions, diced
2	cans (6½ oz. each) minced clams with juice
	Salt to taste
	Pepper, coarsely ground, to taste

Boil potatoes in small amount of water until just tender; warm half-and-half and add to undrained potatoes. Fry diced salt pork until brown; remove and set aside. Brown onions in salt pork drippings. Add salt pork and onions to mixture of potatoes and half-and-half. Simmer. Add minced clams and juice. Heat slowly, but do not boil. Add seasonings. Serve with favorite oyster crackers.

TEN-MINUTE CORN CHOWDER

Elsie Mason   *Yield: 8 servings*

1   can (10¾ oz.) cream of
     potato soup
2   cans (16 oz. each) cream-
     style corn
1   can (13 oz.) evaporated
     milk
2   cups milk
¼   cup chopped green pepper
1   medium onion, chopped
     or 1 tablespoon instant
     onion
1   teaspoon salt
¼   teaspoon pepper

Heat first 4 ingredients in large pot. While heating, sauté green peppers and onion; add to corn mixture. Add seasonings and serve hot.

BRAWNY BREAD

Amber Killen   *Yield: 3 loaves*

4½ cups whole wheat flour
     (or graham flour)
2½ cups unbleached flour
½   cup wheat germ
½   cup raw bran
2½ cups hot water (100-
     115 degrees)
½   cup butter
½   cup dry milk
¼   cup molasses
¼   cup sugar
2   teaspoons salt
2   packages yeast
     Extra flour for kneading

Combine flours, wheat germ, and bran and put in slow oven or microwave to warm. Combine other ingredients in 1-quart measure and stir thoroughly. Put half of flour mixture and all of liquid mixture in large mixer bowl and beat for 2 minutes. Add remaining flour mixture a little at a time, kneading by hand. Place on floured surface, adding more flour when dough is sticky. Continue to knead about 8-10 minutes. Form dough into a ball and place in oiled bowl to rise in an area with 80-100 degree temperature. When dough has doubled in bulk, punch down. Form into 3 equal loaves and place in greased loaf pans. (Heavy dark pans make the best crust.) Let rise again for 20 minutes. Bake at 375 degrees in center of oven for 20-25 minutes until browned on top and loaf sounds hollow when tapped. Remove from pans and cool. Alternate method: This bread may be made in heavy-duty mixer with dough hook. Put all ingredients in large mixer bowl and turn to slow speed. Allow dough hook to knead mixture for 7-10 minutes, adding more flour if dough is still sticky. When it is done, dough will gather together and clean the bowl.

Serve this bread warm from the oven to guests. The rest of the menu can be very simple, and every one will feel pampered.

CINNAMON RAISIN BREAD

William Sawyer   *Yield: 2 loaves*

2	packages dry yeast
¾	cup warm water
⅓	cup sugar
1¼	cups butter or margarine, softened
1	tablespoon salt
1¼	cups warm milk
2	tablespoons ground cinnamon (or to taste)
5-6	cups all-purpose flour (slightly more if bread flour)
1	cup raisins, plumped in 1 cup hot water for 10 minutes and thoroughly drained
1	egg, beaten

Stir yeast, warm water, and sugar in large bowl and let stand for 5-10 minutes. Stir butter and salt into warm milk and blend with yeast mixture. Stir in cinnamon. Add 5 cups of flour, 1 at a time. Beat well between additions. Knead on floured board about 10 minutes until smooth. Knead in remaining flour as required to avoid sticking. Spread dough and add half of raisins. Knead to mix, adding flour as needed. Add remaining raisins. Place dough in lightly greased bowl; turn to grease all sides. Cover and let rise in warm place to at least double its size, about ½ hour. Knead briefly. Divide dough and shape to fill half of 2 greased bread pans (5x9-inch). Cover. Let rise until doubled, 1-2 hours. Brush tops with beaten egg. Bake at 425 degrees for 10 minutes. Reduce temperature to 350 degrees and continue baking for 20 minutes. To prevent excessive darkening of bread tops, cover loaves with foil after top has browned, about 10 minutes. When done, loaves will sound hollow when tapped. Remove from pans and cool. Slice and serve or store unsliced loaves in plastic bags in freezer.

Especially good toasted.

PARMESAN HERB BREAD

Lou Mason   *Yield: 15 servings*

½   **cup butter or margarine, softened**
1   **teaspoon dried parsley flakes**
¼   **teaspoon dried oregano, crumbled**
¼   **teaspoon dried dill weed**
¼-
⅓   **cup grated Parmesan cheese**
1   **large loaf Italian bread, sliced in 1-inch slices**

Mix first 5 ingredients well. Spread mixture on 1 side of each slice of bread, reassemble loaf, and wrap in foil. Heat at 400 degrees 10-15 minutes. May be assembled ahead and refrigerated. Heat longer if cold. May be frozen. Variation: Slice loaf in half lengthwise and spread with butter mixture. Bake on cookie sheet at 400 degrees for 10-15 minutes until bubbly and lightly browned. Cut in serving-sized pieces.

HERB BREAD

Glenda Shrader   *Yield: 10-12 servings*

1   **stick butter, softened**
1   **small Spanish onion, chopped**
½   **teaspoon celery seed**
½   **teaspoon dill weed**
    Sprinkle of garlic powder
    Dash of seasoned salt
1   **large loaf French bread, sliced**

Thoroughly combine first 6 ingredients and spread on slices of French bread. Reassemble loaf and spread some of mixture over top. Wrap loaf in foil and warm at 350 degrees for 20 minutes.

66

CINNAMON PECAN ROLL-UPS

Barbara S. Smith   *Yield: 3 dozen*

½   pint sour cream
½   pound butter or margarine,
     melted
1   package yeast, dissolved
     in 4 tablespoons warm
     water
4   cups sifted flour
2   tablespoons sugar
4   egg yolks
1   teaspoon salt
1   egg, beaten
     Powdered sugar

Mix sour cream, butter, yeast, flour, sugar, egg yolks, and salt. (Dough will be very soft.) Form into ball, wrap in foil, and chill overnight. Divide ball into 6 pieces. Roll each piece very thin on floured board to make 6x12-inch rectangles. Sprinkle ⅙ of filling on each rectangle. Roll rectangles up, beginning at long side. Put rolls, seam side down, on cookie sheets (3 to a sheet). Brush each roll with beaten egg. Bake at 375 degrees for 15-25 minutes or until brown. Sprinkle with powdered sugar. Cut each roll into six 2-inch segments. Serve warm.

FILLING
2½   cups chopped pecans
1⅔   cups sugar
3   tablespoons cinnamon

Combine ingredients and mix well.

Perfect with morning coffee or afternoon tea.

BUFFET BREAD

Connie Scofield   *Yield: 10-12 servings*

1   loaf French bread
1   stick margarine, softened
¼   teaspoon thyme
½   package dried Italian
     salad dressing mix
1½   cups shredded Swiss
     cheese

Remove crust from bread. Slice diagonally, not quite all the way through, in 1-inch slices. Combine margarine, thyme, and salad dressing mix. Spread mixture between slices and over top and sides of loaf. Sprinkle cheese over top. Wrap loosely in foil and bake at 350 degrees for 20 minutes or until cheese melts. Serve warm.

SPICED FRUIT BREAD

Matina Thomas   *Yield: 2 loaves*

2	cups warm milk
2	tablespoons sugar
1	tablespoon dry yeast
2	bananas, mashed (1 cup)
1	cup raisins
¼	cup butter, melted
1	tablespoon wheat germ
	Grated peel of 2 oranges
2½	tablespoons cinnamon
1	tablespoon salt
5-7	cups bread flour

Pour ½ cup warm milk into large bowl. Add sugar and yeast; stir until dissolved. Let stand 5-10 minutes. Blend in remaining 1½ cups milk, bananas, raisins, melted butter, wheat germ, orange peel, cinnamon, and salt. Using wooden spoon, stir in flour 1 cup at a time until dough can be kneaded. Turn dough onto floured surface and knead until smooth and elastic (about 10 minutes), adding remaining flour as needed. Place dough in greased bowl, turning to grease all surfaces. Cover with plastic wrap and place in warm area until doubled in size, about 1½ hours. Grease two 5x9-inch loaf pans. Punch dough down and knead lightly. Divide in half and shape each into loaf; transfer to prepared pans. Cover with towel and let rise in warm, draft-free area until doubled, about 40 minutes to 1 hour.

GLAZE

1	egg, beaten
1	tablespoon milk

Blend glaze ingredients and brush tops of loaves with mixture. Bake at 375 degrees (350 degrees for glass pans) until loaves sound hollow when tapped, about 35-50 minutes. Turn out onto racks to cool completely before slicing.

Delicious toasted.

ORANGE DATE BREAD

Chris Saunders   *Yield: 2 small loaves*

1	cup sour cream
2	eggs
½	cup butter, softened
1½	cups sugar
	Peel of 1 orange, grated
1	cup chopped walnuts
½	cup chopped dates
2	cups flour
½	teaspoon baking powder
½	teaspoon salt
1	teaspoon baking soda

GLAZE

¼	cup orange juice
½	cup sugar

Grease 2 loaf pans (3¾x7¾-inch) and line with waxed paper. Mix sour cream, eggs, butter, and sugar. Add orange peel, nuts, and dates. Sift flour, baking powder, salt, and soda together. Add to blended mixture. Pour batter into prepared pans. Bake at 350 degrees. After 1 hour check to see if it is done, but do not bake over 1 hour 15 minutes.

Mix orange juice and sugar. Brush or pour on hot bread and let it soak in.

CAROLINA TEA BREAD

Joyce Privette Carr   *Yield: 2 large loaves or 5 small loaves*

3	cups flour
3	cups sugar
1	tablespoon baking powder
1	tablespoon cinnamon
3	eggs
1½	cups milk
1½	teaspoons salt
1½	sticks margarine (do not use butter)

SPICE BUTTER

1	stick butter or margarine
	Grated rind of 1 orange
¼	teaspoon cinnamon
	Pinch of mace
¼	teaspoon vanilla

Mix well all ingredients, except margarine. Melt margarine, cool, and add to other ingredients. Grease pans with butter and dust with flour. Pour mixture into pans and bake at 375 degrees for 45 minutes (or until center is done; test with straw). Cool 10 minutes; turn out on brown paper. Loaves freeze well.

Beat butter with rind, spices, and vanilla. Serve with tea bread.

Bread may be sliced and toasted for breakfast or tea.

CHOCOLATE PUMPKIN NUT BREAD

Beth Wharff   *Yield: 1 loaf*

1½   cups sugar
¼   teaspoon baking powder
1   teaspoon baking soda
¾   teaspoon salt
½   teaspoon each ground
     cloves, cinnamon, ginger,
     nutmeg, allspice (or 2 tea-
     spoons pumpkin pie spice)
1⅔   cups flour
⅓   cup water
2   eggs
½   cup salad oil
1   cup pumpkin
1   cup chocolate chips
½   cup chopped nuts

Combine sugar, baking powder, soda, salt, spices, and flour. Add water, eggs, salad oil, and pumpkin. Beat until thoroughly combined and smooth. Add chocolate chips and nuts. Oil loaf pan (5x9-inch) and line with foil. Oil the foil. Pour in pumpkin mixture and bake at 350 degrees for 1 hour 15 minutes. Cool in pan; remove and chill.

EASY ROLLS

Jane Hilty   *Yield: 2-3 dozen*

½   cup shortening
1   cup milk, scalded
2   eggs, beaten
¼   cup sugar
1   teaspoon salt
2   packages yeast
¼   cup warm water
4   cups flour

Combine shortening and milk; stir to melt shortening; cool. Add eggs, sugar, and salt. Soften yeast in warm water 5 minutes; add to milk mixture. Add flour, 1 cup at a time, beating well with wooden spoon after each addition. Refrigerate, covered, for 4 hours or overnight. Shape into rolls. Let rise 1 hour. Bake at 350 degrees for 10-20 minutes, depending on size of rolls.

May be shaped several hours in advance and then refrigerated. Remove from refrigerator 1 hour before baking.

ALMOND CRESCENT ROLLS

Kathy Cavers   *Yield: 16 rolls*

¼	cup butter
1¼	cups sifted powdered sugar
1	tablespoon flour
1	egg yolk
¼	cup finely ground almonds
2	cans (8 oz. each) refrigerated crescent rolls

Cream butter, sugar, and flour. Beat in egg yolk; add almonds. Spread each triangle of dough with almond mixture. Roll up and bake according to package directions for crescent rolls.

One can (8 oz.) of almond paste may be used in place of the homemade mixture.

DILLED CHEESE BREAD

Jan Rudd   *Yield: 12-14 servings*

3	cups biscuit mix
1½	cups grated sharp Cheddar cheese
1	tablespoon sugar
1¼	cups milk
1	egg, slightly beaten
1	tablespoon vegetable oil
1	teaspoon dill weed
½	teaspoon dry mustard

Combine biscuit mix, cheese, and sugar in large bowl. Mix remaining ingredients well in another bowl and stir into dry mixture, blending thoroughly. Beat lightly to remove lumps. Turn into greased 5x9-inch loaf pan and bake at 350 degrees for 45-50 minutes or until golden. Cool slightly and turn out onto wire rack.

Excellent toasted.

PECAN ROLLS

Caryl Weckstein   *Yield: 30 rolls*

2	packages yeast
½	cup warm water
½	cup lukewarm milk (scalded and cooled)
½	cup sugar
½	teaspoon salt
2	eggs
5	cups flour
1½	cups margarine, softened
1	cup brown sugar
1	cup pecan halves
4	tablespoons butter or margarine, melted
½	cup sugar
4	teaspoons cinnamon
½	cup raisins

Dissolve yeast in warm water. Stir in milk, sugar, salt, eggs, 2½ cups flour, and ½ cup margarine. Beat until smooth. Add remaining flour and mix until easy to handle. Knead well. Place in greased bowl, turn greased side up, cover, and let rise until double in size. Punch down dough. In each of two 9x13-inch baking pans, melt ½ cup margarine and sprinkle with ½ cup brown sugar and ½ cup pecan halves. Set pans aside. Divide dough into 2 equal portions. Roll each portion of dough into 9x15-inch rectangle. Spread each with 2 tablespoons of melted butter; sprinkle with half of combined sugar and cinnamon and half of raisins. Roll up, beginning at wide side; seal edges. Cut each roll into 15 slices; place cut side down over pecans in prepared pans. Let dough rise in pans until double in size. Bake at 375 degrees for 20-25 minutes. Remove from oven and immediately turn pans upside down on large platters.

To freeze rolls, bake as directed and immediately turn pan over on large piece of foil. Wrap well and put in freezer while still warm. When ready to use, take directly from freezer to 375 degree oven and bake at least 15 minutes.

CINNAMON STICKS

Lou Mason   *Yield: about 36 sticks*

1	**cup butter, melted**
1½	**cups sugar**
2	**tablespoons cinnamon**
1	**loaf unsliced white bread**

Melt butter in large shallow skillet. Mix sugar and cinnamon in shallow bowl. Remove crusts from bread and cut into approximately 1x1x2-inch sticks. Roll bread sticks quickly in butter (to just coat surface), then in cinnamon sugar. Place on cookie sheet. Bake at 425 degrees for 12 minutes. Cool on rack. Wrap in foil to store. May be frozen. To serve, warm in foil.

QUICK CREAM CHEESE PASTRIES

Mrs. John Grunkemeyer   *Yield: 16-20 servings*

2	**packages (8 oz. each) cream cheese, softened**
1	**egg, separated**
1	**tablespoon lemon juice**
1	**tablespoon vanilla**
¾	**cup sugar**
2	**packages (8 oz. each) refrigerated crescent rolls**

Using electric mixer, combine cream cheese, egg yolk, lemon juice, vanilla, and sugar. Unroll 1 package of rolls on cookie sheet and pat to close perforations. Spread cheese mixture on roll layer. Unroll second package of rolls, pat to close perforations, and lay on cheese layer. Brush with slightly beaten egg white. Bake at 325 degrees for 20 minutes. Cover loosely with foil and bake an additional 10 minutes. Cool before cutting in strips or squares.

For variation, spread with cherry pie filling or strawberry glaze. Serve as breakfast cake or dessert.

BREADS

CHEESE DINNER MUFFINS

Beverly Strodtz   *Yield: 1 dozen*

1½ cups flour
½   cup yellow cornmeal
¼   cup sugar
1   tablespoon baking powder
¾   teaspoon salt
⅔   cup shredded extra sharp
    Cheddar cheese
1   egg, beaten
1   cup milk
½   cup cream-style cottage
    cheese
¼   cup vegetable oil

Combine flour, cornmeal, sugar, baking powder, and salt and stir well. Mix in shredded cheese. Combine egg, milk, cottage cheese, and oil. Pour into dry ingredients and stir until just moistened. Spoon batter into well-greased muffin tins. (Do not use paper liners.) Bake at 400 degrees for 20-25 minutes.

BLEU CHEESE MUFFINS

Virginia Kober   *Yield: 10 muffins*

1   can refrigerated biscuits
6   tablespoons butter
1   package (4 oz.) bleu
    cheese (may use Cheddar
    or Swiss)

Grease muffin tins. Cut each biscuit into 3 pieces and place 3 pieces in each muffin cup. Melt butter and bleu cheese. Pour mixture equally over biscuits. Bake at 350 degrees for 10-12 minutes. Invert pan on rack for 3-5 minutes and serve hot.

To serve as hors d'oeuvre, place biscuit pieces in single layer in 9x9-inch pan. Drizzle cheese mixture over pieces and bake as directed above.

74

TO YOUR HEALTH MUFFINS

Ruth Layman   *Yield: 12 large or 36 miniature muffins*

¼   cup dark molasses
2   tablespoons oil or melted
      margarine
1   egg, well beaten
1   cup milk
1   cup All-Bran cereal
¼   cup wheat germ
¼   cup whole wheat flour
¾   cup all-purpose flour
1   tablespoon baking powder
½   teaspoon salt (optional)
¾   cup raisins
½   cup chopped nuts

HONEY BUTTER
½   cup butter or margarine
½   cup honey

Blend molasses, oil, egg, and milk. Stir in All-Bran and wheat germ. Let soak about 10 minutes. Sift flours with baking powder and salt; add to liquid mixture. Stir only until ingredients are combined. Add raisins and nuts. Fill muffin tins half full. Bake at 400 degrees for 30 minutes. Serve with honey butter.

Whip butter in mixer until fluffy. Slowly add honey and continue beating until all honey is absorbed.

This recipe is rich in vitamin B, iron, and fiber, and is low in cholesterol.

BRAN MUFFINS

Mollie McCoy   *Yield: 24-36 muffins*

1   cup boiling water
1   cup 100% wheat bran
1½ cups brown sugar
½   cup shortening
2   eggs
2   cups buttermilk
2   cups whole wheat flour
½   cup white flour
2½ teaspoons baking soda
2   cups All-Bran cereal
½-1 cup raisins or dates
      Chopped nuts (optional)

Pour boiling water over wheat bran and let stand. Cream sugar and shortening. Add eggs, then remaining ingredients. Mix slightly. Fill greased muffin tins half full. Bake at 400 degrees for 10-20 minutes. Batter can be refrigerated up to 3 weeks.

OATMEAL MUFFINS

Matina Thomas   *Yield: 16 servings*

1	cup oatmeal
1	cup buttermilk
1	cup all-purpose flour
½	teaspoon salt
½	teaspoon baking soda
1½	teaspoons baking powder
½	cup salad oil
1	egg, room temperature and beaten
1½	tablespoons sesame seeds, toasted
½	cup firmly packed brown sugar
1	tablespoon wheat germ (optional)

In large bowl, soak oatmeal in buttermilk about 30 minutes. Sift together flour, salt, baking soda, and baking powder. Stir oil and egg into oatmeal mixture. Blend in dry ingredients and mix only long enough to moisten. Sprinkle sesame seeds, brown sugar, and wheat germ onto batter and stir gently. Sugar should remain suspended in pea-sized chunks. Spoon batter into greased muffin tins. Bake at 350 degrees for 25-30 minutes. Turn muffins from tins while still hot.

BROWN SUGAR COFFEE CAKE

Mrs. William D. Long (Julie)   *Yield: 12 servings*

2	cups brown sugar
½	cup margarine, softened
2	cups flour
2	teaspoons cinnamon
1	cup buttermilk
1	teaspoon baking soda
1	egg
1	teaspoon vanilla
½	teaspoon salt
½	cup raisins or nuts (optional)

Mix sugar, margarine, flour, and cinnamon with wooden spoon until crumbly; reserve 1 scant cup for topping. Mix buttermilk and baking soda and add to the sugar and margarine mixture. Add remaining ingredients. Pour batter into greased, floured 9x13-inch pan or two 8-inch round pans. Sprinkle with reserved topping. Bake at 350 degrees for ½ hour.

Freezes well.

BREADS

OLD-FASHIONED PANCAKES

Mrs. Fred B. Davis   *Yield: 3-4 servings*

1	cup unbleached flour
1	teaspoon baking soda
½	teaspoon salt
2	eggs, well beaten
1	cup buttermilk
2	tablespoons butter, melted

Sift dry ingredients together and add to eggs alternately with buttermilk. Add butter. Stir until blended. Cook pancakes on griddle.

MAPLE-NUT COFFEE CAKE

Betty Sue Wydman   *Yield: 16-20 servings*

1	package (16 oz.) hot roll mix
1	cup warm water
1	egg
2	tablespoons sugar
1	teaspoon maple flavoring
6	tablespoons butter, melted

FILLING

½	cup sugar
½	teaspoon cinnamon
½	teaspoon maple flavoring
½	cup chopped nuts

GLAZE

1½	cups sifted powdered sugar
½	teaspoon maple flavoring
2-3	tablespoons milk

Dissolve yeast in roll mix package in warm water. Stir in egg, sugar, and maple flavoring; add roll mix and blend. Knead until glossy, 2-3 minutes. Place in greased bowl and turn once to oil top. Cover and let rise until double in size, about 1 hour. Mix filling ingredients. Divide dough into 3 balls. On lightly floured surface, roll out first ball to 12-inch circle. Fit into bottom of pizza pan. Brush with 2 tablespoons melted butter and sprinkle with ⅓ of filling. Repeat with other 2 portions of dough, forming 3 layers, and ending with filling. Use glass to mark 2-inch circle in center of dough. Cut from outside edge just to circle, forming 16 pie-shaped wedges. Twist each wedge 5 times. Let rise until double. Bake at 375 degrees for 20-25 minutes. Mix glaze ingredients. Drizzle on warm cake.

Makes an excellent gift. Great for Christmas breakfast.

77

PEANUT BUTTER COFFEE CAKE

Donna Hawkins   *Yield: 8 servings*

¼	cup butter
¾	cup sugar
1	egg
1½	cups flour
1½	teaspoons baking powder
¼	teaspoon salt
½	cup milk
1	teaspoon vanilla

TOPPING

½	cup brown sugar
2	tablespoons flour
1	tablespoon cinnamon
3	tablespoons melted butter
¼	cup peanuts or 6 teaspoons peanut butter

GLAZE

½	cup powdered sugar
1	tablespoon milk

Cream butter and sugar. Add egg. Mix together flour, baking powder, and salt. Add to butter and sugar mixture alternately with milk; add vanilla. Spread half of batter in greased 9-inch square pan. Mix first 4 topping ingredients and crumble half over batter. Repeat layers. Sprinkle with peanuts or drop twelve ½ teaspoons peanut butter on cake. Bake at 350 degrees for 30 minutes. Mix glaze and drizzle on cooled cake.

APPLE NUT COFFEE CAKE

Diane W. Colaizzi   *Yield: 10 servings*

3	cups flour
2	cups sugar
1	teaspoon baking soda
1	teaspoon salt
1½	teaspoons cinnamon
3	eggs, beaten
1	cup oil
4	cups chopped peeled apples
1	cup chopped nuts

Mix all ingredients with wooden spoon. Bake in greased and floured 9x13-inch pan or two 9-inch pie pans at 350 degrees for 50 minutes.

This is great for brunch. May be made in foil pans and used for gifts.

SOUR CREAM RIPPLE COFFEE CAKE

Nancy F. Horlacher (Mrs. Jeffrey)   *Yield: 12 servings*

1	cup margarine
2	cups sugar
2	eggs
1	cup sour cream
½	teaspoon vanilla
2	cups cake flour or 2 cups minus 4 tablespoons all-purpose flour
1	teaspoon baking powder
¼	teaspoon salt

TOPPING

½	cup chopped pecans
2	teaspoons cinnamon
¼	cup brown sugar

In mixer, cream margarine, sugar, and eggs. At low speed, add sour cream, vanilla, flour, baking powder, and salt. Spoon half of batter into 10-inch tube or bundt pan (greased and floured). Mix topping ingredients. Sprinkle half of topping over batter in pan. Spoon remaining batter into pan. Sprinkle on remaining topping. Bake at 350 degrees for 1 hour.

FROZEN BREAD COFFEE CAKE

Marilla Eschbach   *Yield: 10 servings*

2	cups white sugar
1	cup brown sugar
1	tablespoon cinnamon
2	loaves frozen bread, thawed
½	cup chopped almonds, walnuts, or pecans
¼	pound butter, melted

Mix together sugars and cinnamon. Cut each bread loaf into quarters and each quarter into 10 pieces. Shape each piece into a ball. Place nuts on bottom of greased angel food cake pan. (Use cake pan that does not come apart.) Coat balls in melted butter, then in sugar and cinnamon mixture. Place balls in pan in uncrowded layers. Let rise until triple in bulk, 2- 2½ hours. Bake at 325 degrees for ½ hour; reduce temperature to 300 degrees and bake for 15 minutes more.

79

GERMAN COFFEE CAKE

Jenny Donaldson   *Yield: 12 servings*

1	package active dry yeast
½	cup warm water
½	cup lukewarm milk
⅓	cup sugar
⅓	cup butter or margarine, softened
1	teaspoon salt
1	egg
3½-4	cups all-purpose flour, sifted

TOPPING

⅓	cup sugar
1	teaspoon cinnamon
½	pint cream (whipping cream is best, but light cream or half-and-half may be used)

Dissolve yeast in warm water in large bowl. Stir in milk, sugar, butter, salt, and egg. Add 2 cups flour. Beat until smooth. Mix in enough of remaining flour, about 1 cup, to make dough easy to handle. Turn dough onto lightly floured surface; knead until smooth and elastic, about 5 minutes. Place in greased bowl; turn greased side up. Cover with damp cloth; let rise in warm place until double, about 1½ hours. (Dough is ready when indentation remains.) Punch down dough. Roll into rectangle and place in greased 9x13-inch pan. Let rise until double in size, about 40 minutes. With finger, punch holes in dough (the more holes the better). Sprinkle with sugar and cinnamon mixture until dough is covered. Pour cream over dough. Bake at 350 degrees for 25-30 minutes.

Place sheet of foil under pan as cream may bubble over.

CHEESE STREUSEL COFFEE CAKE

Marcia Nicholson   *Yield: 12-15 servings*

1	package (18 oz.) yellow cake mix
1	package active dry yeast
1	cup flour
2	eggs
⅔	cup warm water

Mix 1½ cups cake mix and remaining batter ingredients for 2 minutes at medium speed with electric mixer. Pour batter into greased 9x13-inch pan.

CHEESE FILLING

2	packages (8 oz. each) cream cheese, softened
2	eggs
¼	cup sugar
1	tablespoon flour
1	tablespoon lemon juice

Blend filling ingredients. Drop by spoonfuls onto batter; spread.

TOPPING

6	tablespoons butter
	Remaining cake mix

Mix topping ingredients until crumbly. Sprinkle topping over cheese filling. Bake at 350 degrees for 40-45 minutes.

GLAZE

1	cup powdered sugar, sifted
1	tablespoon corn syrup
1	tablespoon water

Mix glaze ingredients and drizzle on baked coffee cake.

OVERNIGHT COFFEE CAKE

Mrs. Fred B. Davis   *Yield: 12 servings*

2	cups sifted flour
1	teaspoon baking powder
1	teaspoon baking soda
1	teaspoon cinnamon
¼	teaspoon salt
⅔	cup margarine
1	cup white sugar
½	cup brown sugar
2	eggs
1	cup buttermilk

TOPPING
½	cup brown sugar, packed
¾	cup chopped pecans
½	teaspoon cinnamon
¼	teaspoon nutmeg

Sift flour, baking powder, baking soda, cinnamon, and salt. Cream margarine and sugars until light and fluffy. Add eggs, 1 at a time, beating well after each addition. Add dry ingredients alternately with milk. Spread in 9x13-inch greased pan. Combine topping ingredients and sprinkle over batter. Refrigerate 8 hours or overnight. Bake at 350 degrees for 30-35 minutes.

SOUTHERN SPOON BREAD

Suzanne Scutt   *Yield: 8 servings*

1	cup boiling water
1	cup white cornmeal
1	teaspoon salt
1	tablespoon sugar
1	egg
2	tablespoons bacon drippings
1	cup buttermilk
1	teaspoon baking soda

Pour boiling water over cornmeal. Cover and let stand 10 minutes. Mix salt, sugar, and egg with cornmeal. Stir in bacon drippings; add buttermilk and soda. Place in greased 1-quart casserole. Bake at 400 degrees for 20-30 minutes. Serve warm.

Makes a good base for cornbread stuffing for turkey.

FRUITED BREAD DRESSING

Virginia Grice   *Yield: 8-10 servings*

1½   cups chopped celery
1   medium onion, chopped
¼   cup butter or margarine
2   medium apples, unpeeled,
     chopped
½   cup dark seedless raisins
1   package (8 oz.) herb-
     seasoned stuffing
1   can whole cranberry sauce
¼   cup brown sugar
1   teaspoon salt
     Grated peel of 1 orange
¼   cup orange juice (optional)

Sauté celery and onion in butter or margarine until transparent but not browned. In large bowl, toss with apples, raisins, and stuffing. Heat remaining ingredients; add to stuffing and toss lightly. Place in well-buttered 2-quart casserole with lid. Bake at 350 degrees for about 50 minutes. Uncover for last few minutes. If a very moist dressing is desired, add orange juice when mixing.

Excellent with poultry, ham, and pork.

PAIN (EXTRA)-ORDINAIRE

Becki Sammons   *Yield: 5 loaves*

6   cups flour
2   packages yeast
1   tablespoon salt
1   tablespoon sugar
2¼   cups warm water (100-
     115 degrees)
     Butter

Preheat oven to 200 degrees for 5 minutes, then turn off oven. Mix all ingredients, except butter, and knead well until smooth and elastic. Form dough into ball and place in large oiled bowl; turn dough to oil entire surface. Place bowl in warm oven and let rise 1 hour. Form dough into 5 thin loaves about 12 inches long. Place on greased cookie sheets (2 or 3 to a sheet), cut 3 diagonal slashes in top of each loaf, and place in oven (it will still be warm) for 45 minutes to rise. Remove from oven; heat oven to 325 degrees and bake loaves for 45 minutes, until crusty and golden. While warm, rub loaves with butter.

BUTTER AND BONUS

Barbara (Babs) C. Knapp *Yield: enough for 12-person dinner party*

1 pint whipping cream

VARIATIONS
To make garlic salted butter, add garlic salt; or add table salt and mashed garlic cloves to taste before refrigerating. To make herb salted butter, add favorite herbs and salt to taste before refrigerating.

Place ½ pint whipping cream in any convenient jar and tighten lid. Shake... any direction... as hard and as long as necessary. In approximately 5 minutes cream will thicken past whipped cream stage to English spreading cream stage. It may be salted and used as spread at this point, but it cannot be stored for any significant period of time. To produce true storable butter, continue shaking another few minutes until cream breaks. (You will hear and feel it do this.) You will think it has returned to a liquid stage, but not so; close inspection will reveal that the cream has separated into buttermilk and pure yellow sweet cream butter. Drink or store the buttermilk and put butter aside. Repeat process with second ½ pint. Place butter from both shakings in serving bowl and refrigerate.

"This recipe may be made in a food processor, but that will eliminate the bonus, the terrific arm exercise! Made as directed, it is wonderful for working off tensions and great for occupying young children (who love to help with the shaking). It makes for incredible dinner table conversation and is wonderful for the working woman who hasn't time or inclination to bake, but still wants to show off."
Babs Knapp

STRAWBERRY BUTTER

George Zimmerman   *Yield: 2 cups*

4	**sticks sweet butter, softened**
5	**tablespoons powdered sugar**
1	**egg yolk, beaten**
¾-1	**cup fresh strawberries or 1 package (10 oz.) frozen strawberries**

Blend butter with sugar; add egg yolk, blending until smooth. Add strawberries, mix well, and chill.

Tasty spread for yeast breads, nut breads, Hawaiian bread, etc.

IV | Salads, Dressings & Sauces

STERLING IDEAS

Salads, Dressings & Sauces

Fresh basil leaves can be stored up to three months in a jar of olive oil. Be sure leaves are submerged.

Ginger roots keep indefinitely in wine in the refrigerator.

To keep garlic fresh, section a whole bulb and place in a half-pint jar of olive or safflower oil. Garlic buds may be chopped fine and kept in the same way. Store in the refrigerator indefinitely. Great for salads.

To crush garlic easily, put cloves between two layers of waxed paper and hit with hammer or with flat side of chef's knife. No crusher to clean.

White pepper is stronger than black pepper because it is ground from ripe pepper-corns. Use about half as much as black pepper.

An easy way to wash salad greens for 100 people is to put them in a clothes basket and hose them down; to dry, put them in a pillowcase in the spin cycle of the washing machine.

To keep watercress fresh, place the stems in water, cover with a plastic bag secured with a rubber band, and refrigerate.

To keep parsley fresh, wash, spin dry in salad spinner, and place in tightly covered glass jar in the refrigerator. Will keep for two to three weeks.

Add frozen peas directly from the bag or box to tossed salads. They will chill the salad and are delicious without cooking.

A whole lemon heated in hot water for five minutes or in a microwave about one minute will yield one or two tablespoons more juice than a cold lemon.

To get whole walnut meats, soak the nuts overnight in salt water before you crack them. Warming shelled nuts before chopping brings out the natural nut oils.

For quick seasoning, keep on hand a large shaker containing six parts salt to one part pepper.

To easily remove white membrane from oranges, soak them in boiling water for five minutes before peeling.

Freeze lemon rinds for grating later; frozen rind grates easily.

SHOW HOUSE PASTA PRIMAVERA

Linda Marshall   *Yield: 12 servings*

1   package (16 oz.) pasta shells
1   pint cherry tomatoes, halved
1   yellow squash, halved and sliced
1   zucchini, halved and sliced
1   cup small broccoli flowerets, blanched and chilled
1   pound fresh asparagus or green beans, cut in diagonal 1-inch slices, blanched and chilled
½   pound fresh mushrooms, sliced
1   carrot, sliced paper-thin
3-4   green onions, chopped
      Salt
      Pepper, coarsely ground
1   cup freshly grated Parmesan cheese
2   ounces prosciutto or pepperoni, chopped (optional)
      Lettuce leaves

FRENCH DRESSING
3   cloves garlic
½   tablespoon salt
¾   tablespoon freshly ground pepper
1   tablespoon sugar
½   tablespoon Dijon mustard
1   tablespoon water
½   cup vinegar
2   cups olive oil or vegetable oil
2   tablespoons chopped fresh basil (or 1 teaspoon dried)

C ook pasta al dente and drain. Pour ½ cup dressing over pasta; toss. Set aside to cool to room temperature. Mix remaining ingredients with pasta and toss with more dressing. Serve at room temperature in large bowl lined with lettuce leaves.

Place garlic, salt, pepper, sugar, mustard, water, and vinegar in blender. Blend 1 minute. Add oil and basil. Blend until well mixed.

Delightful main dish served at luncheon for volunteers following the 1983 Designers' Show House in Dayton, Ohio.

MAIN DISH MACARONI SALAD

Helen Potter   *Yield: 6-8 servings*

1   package (8 oz.) elbow
       macaroni
¾   cup mayonnaise (add
       more if needed)
3   tablespoons ketchup (or
       to taste)
½   teaspoon prepared horse-
       radish
¼   teaspoon dry mustard
2   tablespoons sliced scallions
2   cups slivered cooked ham
1   cup sliced or diced celery
       Watercress
       Cherry tomatoes

C ook macaroni as directed; drain in colander. Rinse with cold water and drain again. In bowl, blend mayonnaise, ketchup, horseradish, mustard, and scallions. Add macaroni, ham, and celery and mix until blended. Garnish with watercress and cherry tomatoes.

SUMMER PASTA SALAD

Becki Sammons   *Yield: 4 servings*

1   pound fresh ripe tomatoes
       or cherry tomatoes, halved
½   cup olive oil
       Basil to taste
¼   cup pitted and sliced
       black olives
¼   cup Parmesan cheese
       Salt
       Pepper
8   ounces mozzarella cheese
1   package (8 oz.) pasta shells

P eel and core tomatoes; cut in half and remove seeds. Cut into ¼-inch strips. Toss with oil. Add basil, olives, Parmesan, salt, and pepper. Toss and cover. Marinate in refrigerator for 2 or more hours. Just before serving, cut mozzarella cheese into ½-inch cubes and place in large serving bowl. Cook pasta al dente; drain. Add to mozzarella and toss. Add marinated tomatoes. Toss and serve immediately.

SPIRAL PASTA SALAD

Mrs. Gayle B. Price, Jr.

Yield: 8 servings

1   package (8 oz.) spiral pasta
½   pound broccoli flowerets
½   green pepper, cut in strips
¼   pound pea pods
2   tablespoons olive oil
½   pint cherry tomatoes
¼   cup chopped parsley
1   avocado

DRESSING
½   cup olive oil (or ¼ cup olive
     oil and ¼ cup salad oil)
¼   cup lemon juice
1   teaspoon salt
½   teaspoon coarsely ground
     pepper
2   cloves garlic, crushed
2   tablespoons chopped
     chives
1   tablespoon chopped fresh
     basil or 1½ teaspoons
     dried basil
2   teaspoons chopped fresh
     dill or 1 teaspoon dried
     dill weed

Make dressing and set aside. Cook pasta al dente. Refresh in cold water and drain. Sauté broccoli, pepper strips, and pea pods in olive oil until tender-crisp. Mix with pasta, tomatoes, and parsley. Toss entire salad with dressing. Garnish with sliced avocado.

Combine all ingredients and mix well.

ARTICHOKE RICE SALAD

Isabel A. Bowden   *Yield: 6-8 servings*

2   **jars (6 oz. each) marinated artichoke hearts**
1   **package (6 oz.) chicken-flavored rice mix**
4   **green onions, sliced thin**
½   **green pepper, chopped**
12   **pimento-stuffed olives, sliced**
⅓   **cup mayonnaise**
¾   **teaspoon curry powder**

Drain artichoke hearts, reserving marinade. Cook rice as directed, omitting butter; cool. Add onions, pepper, olives, and artichoke hearts, mixing gently. Combine marinade from artichokes with mayonnaise and curry powder. Mix thoroughly, but gently, with rice mixture. Cool before serving.

BROWN RICE SALAD

Ginny Foley   *Yield: 10-12 servings*

5   **cups cooked brown rice**
1   **cup cooked peas**
⅔   **cup each finely chopped carrots, celery, red onion**
2   **tablespoons minced parsley**
8   **slices cooked bacon, crumbled**
⅓   **cup chopped black olives**
½   **cup chopped walnuts or almonds (optional)**

DRESSING
¼   **cup vinegar**
¼   **cup oil**
2   **cloves garlic, pressed**
½   **teaspoon each salt, brown sugar, Dijon mustard, thyme, dill weed**
¼   **teaspoon pepper**

Toss rice, peas, carrots, celery, onion, parsley, bacon, and olives. (Ingredients may be varied to suit your taste.) Add nuts if desired. Pour dressing over rice mixture, toss well, and chill.

Combine all dressing ingredients. Allow to mellow a few hours before using.

CONFETTI RICE SALAD

Mrs. Gerald T. Meier (Barbara)   *Yield: 8-10 servings*

2	cups cooked rice
½	cup chopped green onions, including tops
½	cup chopped green pepper
½	cup chopped celery
¼	cup chopped pimento (optional)
1	can (8 oz.) baby peas, drained or 1 cup frozen or fresh peas, uncooked (save some for garnish)
1	cup crumbled bacon
4	ounces sharp cheese, grated
½-1	cup mayonnaise
	Salt and pepper (to taste)
	Lettuce leaves

Mix rice with vegetables. Add bacon and cheese. Add enough mayonnaise to moisten. Season with salt and pepper. Serve on lettuce leaves, and garnish with reserved peas.

TABBOULEH

Do Winkler (Mrs. Ralph H.)   *Yield: 6 servings*

1	cup bulgur wheat (fine grind)
1	bunch green onions
2	large bunches parsley (about 1½ cups chopped)
1	cup fresh mint leaves (or ¼ cup dried mint)
4	tomatoes
2-4	lemons (according to tartness desired), juiced
⅓	cup olive oil
	Salt to taste
	Lettuce leaves

Rinse wheat twice, then soak in hot water while chopping onions, parsley, mint leaves, and tomatoes very fine. Squeeze wheat dry with palms of hands. Combine wheat, chopped vegetables, lemon juice, olive oil, and salt. Toss well. Adjust seasonings to taste. Serve in a mound on bed of fresh lettuce leaves.

May also be served with cabbage leaves or wild grape leaves used as scoops.

PASTA, SEAFOOD & BASIL CREAM

Betty Sue Wydman   *Yield: 12-16 servings*

PASTA (prepare 1-3 days ahead)
1   pound Italian fettuccine
      in 2-inch pieces
⅓   cup light olive oil
¼   cup white wine vinegar
      Salt and freshly ground
      pepper

VEGETABLES (prepare 1-2 days ahead)
16   very thin asparagus spears
      in 2-inch pieces
2-3   cups broccoli flowerets
6   green onions
1   pint cherry tomatoes
      Bibb lettuce leaves

SEAFOOD (prepare no more than 1 day ahead)
2   pounds bay or sea scallops
2   pounds uncooked large
      shrimp
⅓   cup olive oil
6   tablespoons wine vinegar
1   clove garlic, minced
2   green onions, minced

BASIL CREAM (prepare 1-2 days ahead)
⅓   cup white wine vinegar
2   tablespoons Dijon mustard
3-4   tablespoons dried basil,
      crumbled
1   clove garlic
⅓   cup vegetable oil
1   cup sour cream
½   cup milk
7   tablespoons minced fresh
      parsley
      Salt and pepper

Cook pasta until tender but still firm. Drain and rinse. Put into large bowl. Add oil and vinegar and toss. Season with salt and pepper. Refrigerate until serving time.

Cook asparagus and broccoli until crisp-tender. Rinse with cold water. Store in plastic bags in refrigerator. Mince green onions and halve tomatoes. Transfer to small bowl and refrigerate. Rinse lettuce leaves, wrap in plastic, and chill.

If using sea scallops, cut in half. Gently poach scallops until barely firm, about 2 minutes. Drain. Poach shrimp in shells until pink and firm but not rubbery. Rinse and shell. Cut shrimp in half lengthwise. Transfer seafood to large bowl; add oil, vinegar, and garlic and refrigerate. Chill green onion separately.

Combine vinegar, mustard, basil, and garlic in food processor. With machine running, drizzle in oil. Add sour cream, milk, and parsley, and purée until smooth. Season to taste. Refrigerate until shortly before serving. Stir before adding to salad.

To assemble: About 30 minutes before serving, arrange lettuce leaves around edge of platter. Gently toss pasta with

PASTA, SEAFOOD & BASIL CREAM *(Continued)*

vegetables and green onion-tomato mixture. Arrange on platter. Make well in center of pasta. Drain seafood, toss with remaining green onion, and season to taste. Mound seafood in center of pasta. Drizzle some basil cream over all. Pass remaining basil cream separately.

Although this recipe has several steps, they are not difficult and may all be done in advance.

HERRING SALAD

Jenny Southwood   *Yield: 4-6 servings*

1	jar (8 oz.) Gaffelbitar herring (or in brine)
1	large apple, peeled and cubed
2	dill pickles, cubed
1-2	tomatoes, cubed
2	small onions, thinly sliced
8	ounces sour cream
2	tablespoons vinegar
1	teaspoon sugar
	Salt
	Pepper
1	egg, hard-cooked

Drain herring; remove skin and any bones. Cut into neat pieces. Combine herring, apple, pickles, tomatoes, and onions. Make dressing with sour cream, vinegar, sugar, and seasonings. Pour dressing over salad and mix thoroughly. Cover and refrigerate for several hours. Garnish with quartered hard-cooked egg.

Nice addition to a salad buffet.

MEDITERRANEAN SHRIMP SALAD

Nicoletta Thompson *Yield: 4-6 servings*

2	cups large shrimp, lightly cooked and peeled
1	tablespoon finely chopped parsley
2	tablespoons finely chopped chives or green onions
2	tablespoons butter
½	teaspoon rosemary, finely crumbled
1	cup walnut halves
6	pitted ripe olives
6	stuffed green olives
½	green pepper, sliced in strips
3	firm ripe tomatoes, cut in wedges
¾	cup crumbled Feta cheese
½	cup small pickled onions (optional)
	Salad greens

MARINADE

1	cup olive oil or corn oil
½	cup lemon juice
1	teaspoon sugar
1	teaspoon seasoned salt
¼	teaspoon pepper
⅛	teaspoon garlic powder
½	teaspoon oregano
½	teaspoon marjoram

Pour marinade over shrimp in bowl; add parsley and chives. Mix lightly and cover. Marinate in refrigerator at least 1 hour. Melt butter with rosemary in heavy skillet. Add walnuts; sauté over low heat, stirring occasionally, for about 5 minutes or until lightly browned. Combine shrimp mixture, walnuts, and remaining ingredients, except greens, in large bowl; toss until well mixed. Arrange on greens in chilled serving dish or individual dishes.

Pour oil into pint jar; add lemon juice, sugar, salt, pepper, garlic powder, oregano, and marjoram. Cover and shake well.

ASPARAGUS SALAD MOLD

Susan S. Seyfarth   *Yield: 8 servings*

1	package (3 oz.) lime gelatin
½	cup boiling water
1	can (10¾ oz.) cream of asparagus soup
½	cup mayonnaise
1	tablespoon vinegar
1	tablespoon chopped onion
½	cup hand-shredded, un-peeled, seeded cucumber, drained well
¼	cup chopped celery
1	tablespoon chopped parsley
½	cup unpeeled, shredded zucchini (optional)

Dissolve gelatin in boiling water. Handbeat soup and mayonnaise into gelatin. Add remaining ingredients and pour into greased 4-cup mold. Refrigerate to set.

May be served with crackers as appetizer spread.

TOMATO ASPIC SALAD

Gwendolyn McCausland   *Yield: 8-10 servings*

3	cups V-8 juice
1	bay leaf
¼	teaspoon celery salt
¼	teaspoon onion salt
2	packages (3 oz. each) lemon gelatin
¾	cup Clamato juice
¼	cup vinegar
1	cup chopped green olives
½	cup finely chopped celery
½	cup finely chopped green pepper
½	cup finely chopped green onion (optional)

Heat 2 cups of V-8 juice, bay leaf, celery salt, and onion salt to boiling. Add gelatin and stir until dissolved. Discard bay leaf. Add remaining V-8, Clamato juice, and vinegar. Chill until partially set. Gently fold in olives, celery, and green pepper. Pour into 6½-cup ring mold or make 10 individual small molds. Chill until firm. Unmold onto serving plate.

ORIENTAL CHICKEN SALAD

Tina Schuman   *Yield: 8-10 servings*

2   **whole chicken breasts, cooked and cut into bite-sized pieces**
1   **small head iceberg lettuce, torn in pieces**
1⅓   **cups broken rice sticks, fried***
1   **bunch green onions, sliced**
½   **cup slivered almonds, toasted**
¼   **cup sesame seeds, toasted**

DRESSING
¼   **cup sugar**
2   **teaspoons salt**
1   **teaspoon monosodium glutamate**
½   **teaspoon pepper**
¼   **cup wine vinegar**
½   **cup salad oil**

*Rice sticks are available at oriental food stores. To fry, break off a small handful and fry in hot (375-400 degree) oil. They will "puff up" immediately. Remove from oil and drain on paper towel.

Combine chicken, lettuce, fried rice sticks, onions, almonds, and sesame seeds in large bowl. Toss with dressing just before serving.

Combine sugar, salt, monosodium glutamate, pepper, vinegar, and oil in blender, or blend with whisk.

CHICKEN LUNCHEON SALAD

Florence Hobbs   *Yield: 4-6 servings*

2-3 whole chicken breasts,
     cooked and cut in bite-
     sized pieces
1   can (8 oz.) water chestnuts
1   pound seedless grapes
¾   cup sliced celery
1   cup slivered almonds,
     toasted
1   cup mayonnaise
1   teaspoon curry powder
2   teaspoons soy sauce
2   teaspoons lemon juice
     Bibb lettuce
     Pineapple chunks
     Mandarin orange sections

S lice water chestnuts and add to chicken with grapes, celery, and half of toasted almonds. Mix mayonnaise, curry powder, soy sauce, and lemon juice. Mix thoroughly with chicken mixture and chill. Serve on bed of lettuce leaves and garnish with remaining almonds, pineapple chunks, and mandarin orange sections.

Turkey may be used in place of chicken.

CANTALOUPE-CHICKEN SALAD

Kay Staehlin   *Yield: 2-3 servings*

2   whole chicken breasts,
     cooked
½   cup diced celery
½   cup diced apple
2   green onions, sliced
2   tablespoons chopped
     walnuts
⅓   cup mayonnaise
3   tablespoons yogurt
1   teaspoon prepared mustard
1   teaspoon chopped fresh
     parsley
1   cantaloupe, cut into
     1½-inch slices, peeled and
     seeded
     Bibb lettuce

T ear chicken into large chunks. Combine with celery, apple, green onions, and walnuts. Stir together mayonnaise, yogurt, mustard, and parsley. Add to chicken mixture. Lay cantaloupe circles on Bibb lettuce leaves. Heap chicken salad in centers.

99

CURRIED CHICKEN SALAD

Marty Ebeling *Yield: 4 servings*

3-4 **whole chicken breasts, poached, cooled, and cut in bite-sized chunks**
½ **cup prepared cole slaw dressing**
1 **teaspoon curry powder**
1 **can (11 oz.) mandarin orange sections, drained**
½-
¾ **cup seedless grapes**
Lettuce
Slivered almonds, toasted
Bacon, cooked and crumbled

Combine chicken, dressing, curry powder, oranges, and grapes. Refrigerate for several hours to blend flavors. Serve on lettuce leaves. Top with almonds and crumbled bacon.

SAUCY SPINACH SALAD

Kathleen E. Compton *Yield: 14-16 servings*

2 **pounds spinach**
½ **pound fresh mushrooms, sliced**
1 **large red onion, sliced**
½ **pound bacon, cooked, drained, and crumbled**
4 **eggs, hard-cooked and sliced**

Combine vegetables, bacon, and eggs in large bowl. Pour dressing over all and toss just before serving.

DRESSING
½ **cup salad oil**
1 **tablespoon soy sauce**
¾ **cup chili sauce**
¾ **cup wine vinegar**
½ **cup sugar**

In jar, mix all ingredients for dressing. Shake well before using.

CHARLYE'S CHICKEN SALAD

Charlye Maloney   *Yield: 10-12 servings*

½   head iceberg lettuce
2   heads Bibb lettuce
1   head romaine lettuce
3-4 whole chicken breasts,
     cooked and cut in bite-
     sized pieces
1   cup sliced celery
3   tomatoes, peeled and cut
     in wedges
1   can (14 oz.) artichoke
     hearts, drained and halved
1   large avocado, peeled and
     sliced
½   cup tiny stuffed olives
6   ounces bleu cheese,
     crumbled
8   slices bacon, cooked,
     drained, and crumbled
1   egg, hard-cooked and
     chopped

DRESSING
½   cup salad oil
½   cup olive oil
½   teaspoon salt
¼   teaspoon dry mustard
3   tablespoons lemon juice
⅛   teaspoon curry powder
½   teaspoon sugar
½   teaspoon onion salt
2   tablespoons cold water

Tear lettuce into bite-sized pieces and put into large salad bowl. Toss with small amount of dressing. To serve, mound chicken in center of lettuce bed; arrange celery, tomatoes, artichokes, avocado, and olives around chicken. Sprinkle cheese, bacon, and egg over all. Add more dressing. Pass remaining dressing.

Combine all ingredients. Whisk or shake until well blended.

Makes a hearty luncheon with Parmesan Herb Bread (see Index).

ENDIVE SALAD

Susan Stayton Schindel　　　　　　　*Yield: 4 servings*

Endive
1 **can (1⅝ oz.) shoestring potatoes**
1 **can (9¾ oz.) beets, sliced julienne**
½ **cup chopped onion**
½ **cup crumbled bacon**
¼ **cup grated Parmesan cheese**
Bottled Italian dressing

Fill large salad bowl with endive. Add remaining ingredients. Pour dressing over salad and toss lightly. Serve immediately.

HAWAIIAN TURKEY SALAD

Carol C. Pohl　　　　　　　*Yield: 10-12 servings*

1½ **pounds turkey, cooked and cubed**
1 **fresh pineapple, cut into small chunks**
1 **can (14 oz.) bean sprouts, drained**
1 **can (8 oz.) water chestnuts, drained and sliced**
2 **cups seedless green grapes**
1 **cup chopped celery**
Lettuce

MAYONNAISE DRESSING
2 **egg whites (room temperature)**
½ **teaspoon dry mustard**
½ **teaspoon sugar**
½ **teaspoon salt**
2 **tablespoons white vinegar**
1 **cup no-cholesterol oil**

Combine turkey, pineapple, bean sprouts, water chestnuts, grapes, and celery. Spoon on dressing and toss lightly. Serve in large bowl lined with lettuce leaves.

Put egg whites, seasonings, vinegar, and ¼ cup oil into blender; cover and blend 15 seconds. Remove lid and pour in remaining oil in slow stream. Process for about 15 seconds after oil has been added. May be made ahead and stored up to 1 week in refrigerator.

A good recipe for low cholesterol diets.

CONTINENTAL POTATO SALAD

Laurie Leach   *Yield: 4-6 servings*

2   pounds potatoes
½   small onion or 1 shallot,
     finely chopped
4   ounces ham, cubed
3-4 ounces Swiss or Emmen-
     thal cheese
6   slices bacon, fried crisp,
     drained, and crumbled
1   tomato, coarsely chopped
     Tomatoes, sliced
3   tablespoons chopped
     parsley

VINAIGRETTE
2   tablespoons white wine
2   tablespoons vinegar
1   teaspoon Dijon mustard
     Salt
     Pepper
½   cup oil (part olive)

Cook potatoes in salted water until just tender; peel and cut into cubes. Place in bowl with chopped onion. Add vinaigrette and toss until well moistened. Add ham and cheese and refrigerate. When ready to serve, add bacon and chopped tomato, and mix gently. Garnish with sliced tomatoes and chopped parsley.

Combine wine, vinegar, mustard, salt, and pepper in bowl and stir with whisk. Add oil slowly. Beat well with whisk until all ingredients blend.

POTATO SALAD WITH CUCUMBERS

Sherri Kohnle   *Yield: 6 servings*

4   cups pared, sliced potatoes
1   cup sour cream
½   cup mayonnaise
¼   cup finely chopped fresh
     dill
1½   teaspoons salt
⅛   teaspoon freshly ground
     pepper
1   cup pared, seeded, chop-
     ped cucumber

Cook potatoes in large pan of boiling water until firm-tender, about 10 minutes. (Do not overcook.) Drain thoroughly. Do not cool. Whisk sour cream, mayonnaise, and dill in medium bowl until smooth. Stir in salt, pepper, and cucumber. Add warm potatoes to sour cream mixture; toss gently. Cover and refrigerate until well chilled.

FROZEN FRUIT SALAD

Marty Ebeling   *Yield: 6-8 servings*

1   **package (3 oz.) cream cheese**
½   **cup mayonnaise**
1   **cup crushed pineappple, drained**
½   **cup chopped maraschino cherries**
½   **cup chopped green pepper**
½   **cup chopped pecans**
1   **cup whipping cream**

Mash cream cheese and blend with mayonnaise until smooth. Add pineapple, cherries, green pepper, and nuts. Whip cream and fold into cheese/fruit mixture. Freeze in freezer tray or 6-inch square freezer-proof container. Before serving, allow to stand at room temperature for approximately 10 minutes to facilitate slicing.

For large parties or buffet, freeze in cupcake papers

FROZEN DAIQUIRI SALAD

Marjorie Sando   *Yield: 6 servings*

⅔   **cup mayonnaise**
1   **can (6 oz.) frozen daiquiri mix, thawed**
1   **package (4½ oz.) custard mix**
1   **package (8 oz.) cream cheese, softened**
1   **can (13¼ oz.) crushed pineapple, drained**
     Fruit for garnish (optional)
     Mint leaves (optional)

Combine mayonnaise, daiquiri mix, and dry custard mix. Add gradually to softened cream cheese; beat to blend well. Fold in pineapple. Pour into 9-inch pie plate. Freeze. Cut into wedges. Garnish with fruit and mint leaves, if desired.

May also be served as a dessert.

HEARTY ANTIPASTO SALAD

Mrs. Donald F. Thompson   *Yield: 8 servings*

2	pounds fresh green beans
1	tablespoon Jane's Krazy Mixed-Up Salt (or mixture of salt, flaked onion, pepper, garlic powder, celery seed, thyme, oregano)
8	ounces fresh mushrooms, halved
16	cherry tomatoes or 3 fresh tomatoes, cut into wedges
1	small onion, sliced thin and separated into rings
1	large green pepper, cut into strips
1	clove garlic, minced
½	pound hard salami, thinly sliced and halved
12	ounces provolone cheese, cubed

Clean green beans. Bring 12 cups of water to boil in open pan. Drop in green beans and return to rolling boil. Boil beans for 6-9 minutes. Beans should be bright green and crisply done. Drain, sprinkle with Krazy Salt, and chill. Combine beans with prepared vegetables, garlic, meat, and cheese. Cover with dressing. Marinate 1-2 hours.

DRESSING

1	cup safflower oil
1	cup lemon juice, frozen or fresh
2	tablespoons granulated artificial sweetener (or sugar to taste)

Put dressing ingredients in glass jar. Shake well to mix thoroughly. Shake again before pouring over salad.

As a side dish, this will serve 20.

PICNIC SALAD WITH HERB DRESSING

Doris Ponitz Yield: 6-8 servings

1 pound fresh asparagus or 1 pound fresh whole green beans
1 small head fresh cauliflower, cut into flowerets, or 1 package (10 oz.) frozen cauliflower
2 jars (4 oz. each) marinated artichoke hearts, drained
   Cherry tomatoes

HERB DRESSING
1 teaspoon salt
¼ teaspoon coarse black pepper
½ teaspoon thyme
½ teaspoon marjoram
¼ cup chopped parsley
¼ cup chopped chives
⅓-
½ cup salad oil (use part of artichoke oil)
¼ cup tarragon vinegar

Cook asparagus (or beans) and cauliflower tender-crisp. Drain artichokes (reserve oil). Pour herb dressing over vegetables. Chill at least 1 hour. Garnish with cherry tomatoes.

Put salt, pepper, thyme, marjoram, parsley, chives, oil, and vinegar into jar and shake well.

BEST-EVER CAULIFLOWER SALAD

Mrs. William Schaff Yield: 8-10 servings

1 head cauliflower, broken into flowerets
½ medium red onion, thinly sliced
¼ cup grated Parmesan cheese
1 pound bacon, fried crisp and crumbled
1 cup mayonnaise
3-4 tablespoons sugar
   Carrot curls

Toss cauliflower, onion, cheese, and bacon to mix. Combine mayonnaise and sugar. Pour over salad. Toss to coat. Cover and refrigerate at least 30 minutes. Garnish with carrot curls.

Variation: One small head of iceberg lettuce, torn, may be added.

VEGETABLE POTPOURRI

Mrs. M. T. Smith   *Yield: 6-8 servings*

1   can (14 oz.) artichoke
    hearts, drained and halved
½   pound mushrooms, sliced
    Salt
    Garlic salt
    Pepper
1   bottle (8 oz.) Italian
    dressing
4   tomatoes, cut into wedges,
    or cherry tomatoes, halved
1   avocado, peeled and sliced

Combine artichokes and mushrooms in salad bowl. Season with salts and pepper to taste. Add dressing and marinate 1 hour. Add tomatoes and avocado. Marinate at least 2 hours more. Drain and serve.

Attractive served in glass bowls.

KAY'S GREEK SALAD

Ginny Schwankl   *Yield: 12-16 servings*

1   head cauliflower
1   bunch broccoli
6   green onions
8   ounces fresh mushrooms
2   packages (9 oz. each)
    frozen artichoke hearts,
    cooked and drained
1   pint cherry tomatoes
1   can (3¼ oz.) ripe olives
1   can (2 oz.) stuffed olives
3-4 carrots (optional)
1   bag radishes (optional)
2-3 celery stalks (optional)
1   zucchini (optional)
1   yellow squash (optional)

Cut vegetables into bite-sized pieces. Pour dressing over vegetables. Marinate 1-8 hours before serving.

DRESSING
1   cup olive oil
½   cup wine vinegar
2   teaspoons sugar
    Garlic salt
    Generous dash of thyme
    and basil

Combine oil, vinegar, sugar, and salt. Add thyme and basil. Mix well.

Feta cheese may be added before serving, if desired.

GENTLEMAN'S CHOICE

Ann C. Karter   *Yield: 6 servings*

2	carrots, pared and sliced
2	tablespoons butter
1	teaspoon garlic powder
2	pounds beef tenderloin, cut into ½-inch cubes
½	pound fresh mushrooms, thickly sliced
2	cans (14 oz. each) artichoke hearts, quartered
2	celery stalks, sliced
1	can (3½ oz.) small pitted black olives
2	tablespoons chopped chives
1	cup Italian dressing
2	medium tomatoes
	Lettuce leaves
1	small avocado, sliced

Cook carrots 5 minutes until tender-crisp; drain and cool. Melt butter with garlic; sauté tenderloin quickly. Drain and transfer meat to large bowl to cool. In remaining butter in pan, sauté mushrooms. Drain and add to meat. Add cooled carrots, artichoke hearts, celery, olives, and chives. Pour dressing over all; toss, cover, and refrigerate overnight. An hour before serving, cut tomatoes into wedges and marinate in some of dressing from salad. At serving time, arrange salad on lettuce and garnish with tomatoes and sliced avocado.

MUSHROOM SALAD

Susan Mills   *Yield: 4-6 servings*

1	jar (5 oz.) Dijon mustard
10	tablespoons vinegar
1	cup olive oil
¼	teaspoon tarragon
¼	teaspoon oregano
½	teaspoon salt
¼	teaspoon freshly ground pepper
¾	pound fresh mushrooms, sliced
	Crisp salad greens
	Beefsteak tomatoes, sliced

Beat mustard slowly with wire whisk. Add vinegar and oil alternately while beating (may do this in blender or food processor). Add seasonings and blend well. Pour dressing over mushrooms and toss to coat. Serve on bed of greens and tomato slices.

CAULIFLOWER VINAIGRETTE

Barbara Burkard   *Yield: 6 servings*

2	cups thinly sliced cauliflower
½	cup chopped stuffed green olives
⅓	cup finely chopped green pepper
3	tablespoons chopped red or green onion

Combine all ingredients; mix with dressing. Marinate in refrigerator for several hours.

DRESSING

1½	tablespoons lemon juice
1½	tablespoons wine vinegar
4½	tablespoons salad oil
1	teaspoon salt
½	teaspoon sugar
	Dash of pepper

Put all ingredients into glass jar and shake well. (Blender may be used.)

For dieters, reduce amount of salad oil and increase vinegar accordingly.

SWISS MUSHROOM SALAD

Lou Mason   *Yield: 12 servings*

12	ounces mushrooms, sliced
6	ounces Swiss cheese, grated
¾	cup chopped green onion
1-1½	cups chopped parsley
½	cup salad oil
¼	cup red wine vinegar
1	tablespoon Greek seasoning*

Combine mushrooms, cheese, onion, and parsley in salad bowl. Mix oil, vinegar, and Greek seasoning. Pour over salad and toss. Refrigerate up to 8 hours.

*A prepared spice available at specialty food shops.

PEA POD SALAD

Sonnie Kasch (Mrs. William)   Yield: 4-6 servings

1	cup fresh pea pods
1	cup sliced fresh yellow squash
1	cup sliced fresh mushrooms
4	green onions, chopped
½	cup salad oil
⅓	cup white wine vinegar
½	teaspoon sugar
¾	teaspoon salt
½	teaspoon dried basil, crushed
	Fresh greens or spinach leaves
	Alfalfa sprouts
	Cherry tomatoes or tomato slices
	Sunflower seeds

Cook pea pods 1-2 minutes; drain and rinse in cold water. Store separately in refrigerator. Combine squash, mushrooms, and onions in bowl. In jar combine oil, vinegar, sugar, salt, and basil. Shake well and add to squash mixture. Marinate several hours or overnight. Just before serving, add pea pods to vegetable mixture; toss gently. Drain marinade from vegetables. To serve, arrange fresh greens on serving platter or individual plates; spoon drained vegetables onto greens. Garnish with sprouts, tomatoes, and sunflower seeds.

Serving suggestion for buffet: Make individual salads in lettuce cups and place on large platter for easy serving.

TUNA MOUSSE

Gracey P. Weisbrod   Yield: 6 servings

2	egg yolks
1	teaspoon salt
1	teaspoon dry mustard
¼	teaspoon paprika
1½	tablespoons butter, melted
¾	cup milk
2½	tablespoons vinegar or lemon juice
1	envelope unflavored gelatin
¼	cup cold water
2	cups flaked tuna (or salmon or crab)
	Celery (optional)

Mix slightly beaten egg yolks with salt, mustard, and paprika; add butter, milk, and vinegar. Cook over boiling water, stirring until thick. Soften gelatin in cold water; add to cooked mixture with tuna and turn into cool mold; chill. Celery may be added with tuna for crunch. If using fish-shaped mold, slice ripe olive for eye of fish.

May also be served on crackers or used as sandwich filling.

110

POLYNESIAN SALAD

Rachel Sperry   *Yield: 12-15 servings*

1   head lettuce
1   package (10 oz.) frozen
     peas, thawed and drained
2   medium green peppers,
     diced
1   medium red onion, sliced
     thin
2   cans (8 oz. each) water
     chestnuts, drained and
     sliced thin
3   medium carrots, grated
2   cans (15½ oz. each)
     crushed pineapple, drained
2   cans (4 oz. each) sliced
     mushrooms, drained

TOPPING
2   cups mayonnaise
1   cup sour cream
5   tablespoons sugar
¾   pound Cheddar cheese,
     grated
¾   pound bacon, cooked
     and crumbled

L ine 9x13-inch pan or glass bowl with shredded lettuce. Layer remaining ingredients, in order listed, on lettuce bed.

Blend mayonnaise, sour cream, and sugar. Spread evenly over salad to cover. Refrigerate overnight. Two hours before serving, sprinkle with cheese and bacon.

TANGY TOMATOES

Florence Hobbs   *Yield: 8-10 servings*

3	large tomatoes, sliced or quartered
5	small green onions, chopped (include green tops)
1	teaspoon dried basil

DRESSING

1	teaspoon salt
1	teaspoon sugar
½	teaspoon paprika
¼	teaspoon dry mustard
⅛	teaspoon pepper
⅓	cup vinegar
⅔	cup salad oil

Arrange tomatoes in shallow dish. Sprinkle onions over tomatoes. Sprinkle basil over all and cover with dressing. Marinate in refrigerator several hours.

Combine salt, sugar, paprika, mustard, and pepper in jar with vinegar. Add oil and shake well. Shake again before using.

DOUBLE HEARTS VINAIGRETTE

Mrs. Paul T. Welch (Mary)   *Yield: 4 servings*

1	can (14 oz.) hearts of palm, drained and cut lengthwise about thickness of pencil
1	can (14 oz.) artichoke hearts, rinsed and drained
1	bottle (16 oz.) Italian dressing
	Bibb lettuce
2	hard-cooked eggs, quartered
1	tomato, quartered
	Black olives

Marinate hearts of palm and artichoke hearts separately in dressing. Refrigerate for several hours or until well chilled. To serve, remove hearts of palm and artichoke hearts from dressing and place on Bibb lettuce. Garnish with eggs, tomato, and olives. Dressing may be saved and reused.

An easy, elegant, and fast last-minute salad made with pantry-shelf items.

TOMATOES WITH ARTICHOKE HEARTS

Jean Collins   *Yield: 5-6 servings*

5-6   **tomatoes**
     Salt
     Pepper
     Dill weed
5-6   **artichoke hearts, well
     drained**

Peel tomatoes and cut out stem end deeply. Rub tomatoes with salt, pepper, and dill. Drain upside down on plate for several hours in refrigerator. Place an artichoke heart inside each tomato. Spoon dressing generously in and over tomatoes. Sprinkle with dill.

DRESSING
1   **cup mayonnaise**
½   **cup sour cream**
1   **teaspoon curry powder**
2   **teaspoons fresh lemon
     juice**
2   **green onions, finely
     chopped**
     Dill weed to taste

Combine mayonnaise, sour cream, curry, lemon juice, onion, and dill a day or more ahead to blend seasonings.

MARINATED TOMATO-PEPPER SALAD

Joyce C. Young   *Yield: 4-6 servings*

¾   **cup olive or salad oil**
3   **tablespoons wine vinegar**
2   **teaspoons ground cumin**
1   **teaspoon salt**
1   **teaspoon pepper**
     Chopped parsley
2   **large green peppers, cut
     into 1-inch squares**
3   **medium tomatoes, peeled
     and chopped**

Combine oil, vinegar, cumin, salt, pepper, and 1 tablespoon parsley. Add green peppers and tomatoes and toss. Refrigerate at least 2 or 3 hours. At serving time, toss again and add more parsley.

SALADS

MOLDED CORNED BEEF SALAD

Ann Simione   *Yield: 12-15 servings*

1   package (3 oz.) lemon
     gelatin
1   cup mayonnaise
1   can (12 oz.) corned beef,
     flaked
1   medium onion, finely
     chopped
1   cup peas, cooked and
     drained
1   cup chopped celery
     Parsley
     Cherry tomatoes

Mix gelatin as package directs and cool. Add mayonnaise to gelatin, stirring constantly. Add beef, onion, peas, and celery to gelatin mixture. Pour into 6-cup ring mold and chill until set. Remove from mold and garnish with parsley and cherry tomatoes.

SHRIMP ASPIC

Donna Harte   *Yield: 6-8 servings*

1   package (3 oz.) lemon
     gelatin
1   cup hot water
1   can (10¾ oz.) tomato soup
12   stuffed green olives, sliced
½   cup diced celery
⅓   cup chopped walnuts
1   cup cooked shrimp
⅛   teaspoon Tabasco
½   teaspoon Worcestershire
     sauce

Dissolve gelatin in water. Add tomato soup. Refrigerate. When partially set, add remaining ingredients. Pour into 5-cup mold. Chill until set.

HEARTY SEAFOOD TOSS

Jocelyn Feeman

SALADS

Yield: 10-12 servings

1 pound raw mushrooms, sliced
1 can (14 oz.) artichoke hearts, drained and chilled
1 jar (2 oz.) pimento, thinly sliced
1 small onion, thinly sliced
1 small cucumber, thinly sliced
6-8 radishes, thinly sliced
6 anchovies, coarsely diced
1 teaspoon capers
¼ cup chopped fresh parsley
12 black Greek olives, cut up, or 1 can (2¼ oz.) sliced black olives
2 cans (6½ oz. each) white meat tuna or 1 pound cold cooked shrimp, halved
½ head crisp romaine lettuce or other favorite lettuce, torn into bite-sized pieces

DRESSING
1 large clove garlic
½ cup olive oil
3 tablespoons wine vinegar
1 tablespoon Dijon mustard
1 teaspoon salt
¼ teaspoon freshly ground pepper

In bowl, combine all salad ingredients, except lettuce, and toss well with dressing. Refrigerate, covered, several hours. Just before serving, add lettuce and toss lightly.

Crush garlic. Let stand overnight in olive oil in refrigerator. Next day, discard garlic. Combine remaining dressing ingredients with olive oil.

115

PIQUANT MOLDED BEET SALAD

Virginia Grice   *Yield: 6 servings*

1   can (16 oz.) beets, drained
     well and shredded (reserve
     juice)
1   package (3 oz.) lemon
     gelatin
3   tablespoons vinegar
½   teaspoon salt
2   tablespoons onion juice
     or finely chopped onion
2   tablespoons horseradish
¾   cup chopped celery
     Salad greens
     Sour cream

Drain liquid from beets; add enough water to make 1½ cups. Bring to boil in saucepan. Stir in gelatin until dissolved. Mix in remaining ingredients, except greens and sour cream. Pour into 1-quart mold and chill until firm. Remove from mold and serve on salad greens with sour cream.

CUCUMBER SALAD

Jean N. Vesper   *Yield: 6-8 servings*

1   package (3 oz.) lemon
     gelatin
½   cup hot water
1   tablespoon vinegar
½   cup mayonnaise
2   small unpeeled cucumbers,
     grated
1   pint small curd cottage
     cheese or sour cream for
     extra richness
1   small onion, grated
½   cup chopped pecans

Dissolve gelatin in hot water; add vinegar. Add to mayonnaise, stirring to prevent lumping. Drain as much liquid from cucumbers as possible. Combine cucumbers, cottage cheese, and onion; add to mayonnaise mixture. Add pecans and pour into 5-cup mold. Chill several hours.

Salad keeps well for several days.

116

LIME VELVET SALAD

Peggy Horner   *Yield: 16 servings*

1	package (3 oz.) lime gelatin
1	package (3 oz.) lemon gelatin
2	cups boiling water
2	packages (3 oz. each) cream cheese, softened
1	can (13 oz.) evaporated milk
1	cup chopped celery
¾	cup chopped pecans
1⅓	cups crushed pineapple, undrained

Dissolve gelatins in boiling water in large bowl; add cream cheese. Beat with electric mixer until smooth. Chill gelatin mixture until consistency of unbeaten egg white. While gelatin mixture is chilling, pour evaporated milk into loaf pan and place in freezer until milk is frozen ¼ inch around edge of pan. Chill beaters and bowl. Pour chilled milk into chilled bowl and beat at high speed until stiff peaks form. Fold celery, nuts, and pineapple into gelatin mixture; fold in whipped milk. Pour into 10-cup mold or 9x13-inch glass pan. Chill until firm.

CITRUS DELIGHT

Mrs. Dennis (Aggie) Schaffer   *Yield: 15-18 servings*

2	packages (3 oz. each) orange gelatin
2	cups boiling water
1	can (6 oz.) frozen orange juice concentrate
2	cans (11 oz. each) mandarin oranges, drained
1	can (8 oz.) crushed pineapple, drained
1	envelope dry whipped topping
1	package (3½ oz.) instant lemon pudding
1	cup cold milk

Combine gelatin and water; stir to dissolve. Add orange juice concentrate, mandarin oranges, and pineapple. Pour into 3-quart rectangular pan or 9x13-inch pan. Refrigerate until set. Make whipped topping according to package directions; set aside. Combine pudding mix with milk and stir until smooth. Fold into whipped topping and spread on gelatin. Keep refrigerated.

FAVORITE SALAD

Jane Speyer   *Yield: 10 servings*

2	packages (6 oz. each) lemon gelatin
2	cups boiling water
1½	cups cold water
1	can (20 oz.) crushed pineapple, drained (reserve juice)
1	cup small marshmallows
2	bananas, sliced

Dissolve gelatin in boiling water; add cold water and let set until syrupy. Add pineapple, marshmallows, and bananas. Place in 2-quart mold and refrigerate until firm.

TOPPING

1	egg
2	tablespoons flour
½	cup sugar
2	tablespoons butter
1	cup pineapple juice
1	cup whipping cream, whipped

Mix together egg, flour, sugar, butter, and juice; cook until thick. Cool. Fold in whipped cream. Spread on jelled salad and chill.

ORANGE FLUFF

Patricia Metcalf   *Yield: 6-8 servings*

1	package (3 oz.) orange gelatin
1	quart small curd cottage cheese
1	can (20 oz.) crushed pineapple, drained
1	can (11 oz.) mandarin oranges, drained
4	ounces shredded coconut
1	cup miniature marshmallows
1	carton (8 oz.) frozen whipped topping, thawed

Mix orange gelatin powder with cottage cheese. Add pineapple, oranges, coconut, and marshmallows. Fold in whipped topping. Refrigerate at least 1 hour or overnight. Whip with fork before serving.

Delicious as salad or dessert.

CRANBERRY SALAD

Bette Huter   *Yield: 12 servings*

1   package (6 oz.) orange
     gelatin
2   cups boiling water
1   cup 7-Up
½   cup sugar
1   cup finely chopped celery
2   McIntosh or Delicious
     apples
1   orange, including peel
1   pound raw cranberries
     Mayonnaise
     Parsley

C ombine gelatin and boiling water. Add 7-Up; add sugar and celery. Quarter apples and orange; remove cores and seeds. Place apples and orange in food processor with cranberries and coarsely chop, or grind in food grinder. Add to gelatin mixture and chill in 2-quart mold or 9x13-inch glass dish until firm. Serve with mayonnaise and garnish with parsley.

CRANBERRIES IN THE SNOW

Rosemarie S. Sholl   *Yield: 12-15 servings*

1   can (14 oz.) sweetened
     condensed milk
¼   cup lemon juice
1   can (16 oz.) whole berry
     cranberry sauce
1   can (20 oz.) crushed
     pineapple, drained
1½   cups chopped pecans
1   carton (12 oz.) frozen
     whipped topping, thawed

C ombine condensed milk and lemon juice in large bowl. Stir in cranberry sauce, pineapple, and 1 cup pecans. Fold in 8 ounces whipped topping. Spread mixture in 9x13-inch baking dish. Freeze until firm. Frost with remaining whipped topping and sprinkle with ½ cup pecans. Return to freezer. Remove from freezer 10 minutes before serving.

May also be served as dessert.

SPRING SALAD

Patti Ballard   *Yield: 6 servings*

1½   pounds small new potatoes
3   teaspoons salt
¼   pound fresh green beans
½   cup chopped pecans
¼   cup minced shallots
¼   cup chopped fresh parsley
      Pepper
      Bibb or Boston lettuce
      leaves

Cook unpeeled potatoes with 1 teaspoon salt in boiling water to cover, about 20 to 25 minutes. Drain and let cool. Trim ends from beans and cut in half. Drop into boiling water with 2 teaspoons salt; cook 8 minutes. Drain and rinse with cold water. In large bowl, combine potatoes (cut into ½-inch slices), beans, pecans, shallots, parsley, and half the dressing. Add pepper to taste. Toss and arrange on lettuce leaves.

DRESSING
4   egg yolks (room
      temperature)
⅓   cup red wine vinegar
1   teaspoon Dijon mustard
½   teaspoon salt
      Freshly ground pepper
½   cup plus 2 tablespoons
      olive oil
½   cup salad oil

In blender or food processor, combine egg yolks, vinegar, mustard, salt, and pepper. Cover and process until well mixed. With motor running, drizzle oil into mixture in thin stream. Process until all oil is added. Makes 1¾ cups.

GOOBER PEAS

Donna Harte   *Yield: 6 servings*

1   package (10 oz.) frozen
      peas (do not cook or thaw)
½   cup salted peanuts
4-6   green onions, thinly sliced
⅓-
½   cup diced celery (optional)
      Mayonnaise

Just before serving, combine all ingredients, adding enough mayonnaise to suit your taste. Serve on lettuce leaves. Variations: Add cooked, diced chicken or cooked shrimp or ham.

This is a great last-minute recipe for guests. It's quick, different, and delicious.

BANANA-NUT SALAD

Mrs. Charles D. Ross   *Yield: 8 servings*

2	eggs
½	cup sugar
2	tablespoons cornstarch
¼	teaspoon salt
1¼	cups milk
1	teaspoon vinegar
5	bananas
½-1	cup finely chopped peanuts

Beat eggs in saucepan. Mix sugar, cornstarch, and salt; stir into beaten eggs with milk. Stir constantly over medium heat until mixture is smooth and thick. Remove from heat and add vinegar. Cool. Place in refrigerator overnight. When ready to serve, slice bananas lengthwise, then cut into quarters. Alternate bananas and dressing in serving dish, preferably round. Top with nuts.

An easy, but different fruit salad!

QUICK FRESH CUCUMBER PICKLES

Doris J. Conway   *Yield: 3-4 pints*

4	cucumbers (7 cups), unpeeled
2	onions, sliced
2	green peppers, cut into strips

DRESSING

1½	teaspoons salt
2	teaspoons celery salt
2	cups sugar
1½	cups white vinegar

Score cucumbers lengthwise with fork and thinly slice. Mix with onions and peppers. Pour dressing over vegetables. Store covered, in a non-metal container, overnight in refrigerator.

Combine all ingredients and mix well.

These pickles do not need to be canned. They will keep several weeks in the refrigerator.

121

BLEU CHEESE DRESSING

Gwendolyn McCausland   *Yield: 1½ quarts*

1	quart mayonnaise
½	cup salad oil
¼	cup white vinegar
3	tablespoons lemon juice
2	tablespoons Worcester-shire sauce
½	teaspoon garlic salt
½	teaspoon ground black pepper
½	teaspoon paprika
1	pound bleu cheese, crumbled

Mix together all ingredients, except bleu cheese. Stir until smooth. Add bleu cheese. Store in refrigerator. Keeps for weeks.

GREEN GODDESS DRESSING

Kathleen Compton   *Yield: 2½ cups*

4	cloves garlic, chopped
6	small green onions, chopped
6	sprigs fresh parsley
2	cups mayonnaise
½	tube anchovy paste
1	teaspoon lemon juice
½	cup sour cream

Put all ingredients in blender or food processor and purée.

May also be used as dip with raw vegetables, corn chips, or potato chips. For dip, omit sour cream.

HEARTY SALAD DRESSING

Maureen Brolick   *Yield: 4-6 servings*

6	tablespoons olive oil
2½	tablespoons lemon juice
1	clove garlic, crushed
½	teaspoon salt
½	teaspoon sugar
⅛	teaspoon pepper
⅛	teaspoon dry mustard
1	egg yolk

Mix dressing ingredients. Pour over salad greens and toss. Serve immediately.

This salad dressing is well suited for the heartier salad greens. Try it on your favorite spinach-mushroom-bacon salad or on a romaine-based salad.

CELERY SEED DRESSING

Ruth C. Mead   *Yield: 2 quarts*

2	medium onions, finely grated
2	cups sugar
4	teaspoons dry mustard
4	teaspoons salt
⅔	cup white vinegar
⅔	cup cider vinegar
4	cups salad oil
4	tablespoons celery seed

Put first six ingredients in large bowl of electric mixer. Turn on lowest speed and slowly add salad oil in thin stream. Keeping mixer on lowest speed, add celery seed. Pour into glass containers and refrigerate. Dressing will keep indefinitely in refrigerator. Shake container well before using.

Makes a nice Christmas gift.

POPPY SEED DRESSING

Ann Macaulay   *Yield: 8-10 servings*

½ **medium onion, coarsely chopped**
⅓ **cup cider vinegar**
½ **cup sugar**
1 **teaspoon salt**
1 **teaspoon dry mustard**
1 **cup salad oil**
1½ **tablespoons poppy seed**

Blend onion and half of vinegar in blender or food processor. Add remaining vinegar, sugar, salt, and mustard; blend well. Slowly add oil, blending constantly until thick. Stir in poppy seed. Serve over Bibb lettuce topped with sliced kiwi, or other salad of your choice.

CREOLE SAUCE

Elsie Mason   *Yield: 6 servings*

2	medium onions, chopped
1	green pepper, cut into strips
¼	cup oil
2	teaspoons flour
1	tablespoon sugar
¼	teaspoon pepper
½	teaspoon salt
1	teaspoon oregano
1	can (16 oz.) tomatoes
1	can (8 oz.) tomato sauce

Sauté onions and pepper in oil until tender. Blend in flour and other ingredients. Cook over low heat 20 minutes.

This sauce is especially tasty. May be used over cheese soufflé, stuffed peppers, hamburgers; or add 1 pound cooked shrimp and serve over rice. May be made ahead and frozen for later use.

MUSTARD SAUCE

Suzie Holloway   *Yield: 2 cups*

⅔	cup sugar
1	tablespoon (heaping) flour
2	tablespoons dry mustard
½	cup white vinegar
2	egg yolks
1	cup milk

Mix sugar, flour, and mustard in top of double boiler. Add vinegar, egg yolks, and milk. Cook, stirring constantly, over simmering water until thickened. Chill.

Delicious served with baked ham.

MOCK HOLLANDAISE

Sara J. Thomason   *Yield: 1 cup*

½   cup sour cream
½   cup mayonnaise
1   teaspoon prepared mustard
2   teaspoons lemon juice

Mix all ingredients in saucepan. Stir over low heat until mixture begins to boil. Remove from heat immediately.

Add a few drops of yellow food coloring for true hollandaise appearance.

GARLIC DILL SAUCE

Pamela Stockmyer   *Yield: 3½ cups*

2½ cups mayonnaise
1   cup sour cream
1   tablespoon vinegar
2   teaspoons lemon juice
2   teaspoons Worcester-
     shire sauce
2   cloves garlic, crushed
3   tablespoons chopped fresh
     dill or 1 teaspoon dried dill

Blend ingredients in food processor or blender; chill. Serve with cold poached salmon. Also delicious as dip for fresh steamed artichokes or asparagus.

PESTO SAUCE

Barbara Neroni   *Yield: Enough for 3-4 pounds pasta*

1   cup olive oil
2   medium cloves garlic
½   cup pine nuts or walnuts
3   cups fresh basil leaves
1   cup fresh Italian parsley
     leaves*
½   cup grated imported cheese
     (Parmesan, Romano, or
     pecorino)
1   teaspoon freshly ground
     pepper
     Salt (only if needed,
     depending on cheese)

*Available in specialty food
stores.

Blend oil and garlic in blender at high speed until smooth. Gradually add nuts until well blended. Add basil leaves a few at a time, following with parsley leaves. Blend until smooth. Add grated cheese and pepper, continuing to blend to smooth consistency. Taste for salt. For immediate use, cook linguine in salted water with a little oil. Drain well and add a little butter to hot linguine. Mix with small amount of pesto sauce and place in warm serving dish. Top with generous amount of pesto. (A little boiling water from pasta may be added to pesto sauce to thin, if desired. Pesto sauce should be at room temperature when served; if heated, cheese may lump.)

This sauce is very rich; a little goes a long way. Keeps in refrigerator for several weeks (cover with layer of olive oil). Freezes well.

QUICK SHRIMP SAUCE

Helen Marinoff   *Yield: ¾ cup*

½   lemon (juice and pulp)
½   cup ketchup
2-3 drops Tabasco
1   tablespoon Worcester-
     shire sauce
1   tablespoon horseradish

Mix all ingredients. Adjust to taste, adding more horseradish or Tabasco if desired. Ready to serve immediately.

Good with seafood or raw cauliflower.

FUNGHETTO SAUCE FOR BEEF

Barbara Neroni   *Yield: 12 servings*

1   stick butter
1   large onion, chopped
3-4 green peppers, cut into
     wedges
1   pint mushrooms, sliced
2   cloves garlic, halved
1-2 tablespoons tomato paste
1   cup or more Marsala wine
     (dry)

Sauté vegetables with garlic in butter; remove garlic. Add tomato paste and wine. Simmer briefly, but do not overcook vegetables. May be prepared early in day. When ready to serve, add additional wine to taste and heat thoroughly. Serve with sliced tenderloin steak or other cooked beef.

GRANDMOTHER'S CHILI SAUCE

Constance Klarer   *Yield: 3 quarts*

18   large ripe tomatoes
6   onions
3   green peppers
⅓   cup salt
1   cup sugar
2½   cups vinegar
1   small hot red pepper
     (optional)

Peel and quarter tomatoes. Finely chop onions and green peppers. Combine all ingredients in open kettle and cook at slow boil for 1 hour. Bottle in sterile jars or store in freezer.

STERLING IDEAS

Vegetables

Add a little lemon juice or vinegar to the water in which cauliflower is cooked to keep it snowy white.

Cut corn over an angel food cake pan using the center tube to support the ear. The cut corn accumulates neatly in the pan.

If parsley is washed with hot water instead of cold, it keeps its flavor and is easier to chop.

Always rub fresh or dried herbs between the fingers to release the flavor oils.

Start new potatoes cooking in boiling water; start old potatoes in cold water. A few drops of lemon juice in the water will whiten potatoes.

To keep fresh-like color, cook green vegetables uncovered, white vegetables covered.

Potatoes soaked in salt water for 20 minutes before baking will bake more rapidly.

A nice addition to cooked broccoli is a sauce made from sliced almonds lightly browned in butter or margarine to which two tablespoons of fresh lemon juice have been added.

Try adding lightly browned sesame seed, butter, and one teaspoon soy sauce to cooked spinach, broccoli, Brussels sprouts, or asparagus.

Don't throw away raw broccoli stems. Peel and slice for a crudités platter, or add to stir-fries, or use in Chinese dishes as a substitute for water chestnuts.

Don't cook spinach in aluminum. The spinach loses its color and picks up a metallic taste.

Try adding mint leaves to peas or green beans for a different taste.

Raw tomatoes sliced vertically will keep their shape better.

Winter squash cut into small chunks adds flavor to soups or stews.

ARTICHOKE & MUSHROOM CASSEROLE

Mrs. John R. Fischrupp — *Yield: 8 servings*

- 1 pound fresh mushrooms, sliced
- 2 tablespoons butter or margarine
- 1 package (¾ oz.) chicken gravy mix
- 1 cup milk
- 6 ounces Swiss cheese, grated
- 2 tablespoons white wine
- 2 cans (14 oz. each) artichoke hearts, drained
  Buttered bread crumbs

Sauté mushrooms in butter. Mix gravy mix with milk as directed on package, substituting milk for the water. Add mushrooms, cheese, and wine to prepared gravy. Add artichoke hearts. Put in casserole with circle of bread crumbs around edge. Bake at 350 degrees for ½ hour.

GREEN BEANS SUPREME

Mary Guenin — *Yield: 6-8 servings*

- 2 packages (10 oz. each) frozen French-cut green beans
- 2 tablespoons butter
- 1 small onion, minced
- 1 tablespoon chopped fresh parsley
- 1 teaspoon salt
- ¼ teaspoon white pepper
- 1 tablespoon flour
- ¼ teaspoon grated lemon rind
- 1 cup sour cream
- 1 tablespoon dry sherry
- 1 cup grated Cheddar cheese
- ½ cup bread crumbs

Cook beans according to package directions; set aside. Place butter, onion, and parsley in saucepan and sauté for 5 minutes. Add salt, pepper, flour, lemon rind, sour cream, and sherry. Cook for 3 minutes (do not boil). Add beans to mixture. Pour into buttered 1½-quart casserole. Sprinkle with cheese and bread crumbs. Bake uncovered at 350 degrees for 30 minutes.

SPICY STIR-FRIED GREEN BEANS

Gertrude C. Derby   *Yield: 4-6 servings*

1	pound fresh green beans
1	tablespoon vegetable oil
1	thin slice fresh ginger, peeled and minced
	Garlic to taste
½	sweet red pepper, cut into thin strips
½	teaspoon beef bouillon granules dissolved in ¼ cup water
1-2	teaspoons cornstarch
1	tablespoon dry sherry
2	tablespoons soy sauce
1	teaspoon chili paste*

*Can be found in Chinese grocery

Wash and trim beans into bias strips. Heat oil in heavy skillet or wok. Stir-fry ginger and garlic a few seconds; add green beans and sweet red pepper. Cook, stirring, for 2-3 minutes. Add bouillon mixture. Cover and steam 4-5 minutes or until beans are tender-crisp. Combine remaining ingredients and stir gently into beans. Heat until thickened and bubbly. If sauce is too thin, add more cornstarch.

EGGPLANT PARMESAN

Betty Sue Wydman   *Yield: 6 servings*

1	large eggplant
3-4	tablespoons oil
1	can (16 oz.) tomatoes
1	can (6 oz.) tomato paste
2	cloves garlic
1	teaspoon salt
	Dash of pepper
1	can (4½ oz.) mushroom crowns
2	cups bread cubes
½	cup grated Parmesan cheese
½	pound mozzarella cheese, sliced

Cut eggplant in half lengthwise; scoop out, leaving ¼-inch rim. Cube eggplant pulp and sauté in oil 5 minutes; set aside. Combine tomatoes, tomato paste, garlic, salt, and pepper in saucepan. Simmer 5-10 minutes. Add mushrooms, bread cubes, Parmesan cheese, and eggplant. Place half of eggplant mixture in shells, dividing evenly. Top with half of mozzarella. Add remainder of eggplant mixture; top with remaining cheese broken into small pieces. Bake at 375 degrees for 15-20 minutes.

QUICK AND SIMPLE LIMA BEANS

Mary Houpis   *Yield: 6-8 servings*

1   package (14 oz.) frozen
      lima beans
3   carrots, sliced
1   large onion, sliced
1   can (8 oz.) tomato sauce
1   tablespoon chopped fresh
      parsley
½   teaspoon salt
¼   teaspoon pepper
¼   cup salad oil

Mix all ingredients in saucepan and simmer approximately 35 minutes or until all vegetables are tender.

Alternate cooking method: Microwave, covered, in 1½-quart glass casserole for 12-15 minutes on high.

SWEET-SOUR BEANS

Rebecca Drake   *Yield: 12 servings*

8   slices bacon
4   small onions, chopped
1   cup brown sugar
1   teaspoon dry mustard
⅔   cup vinegar
1   can (32 oz.) pork and beans
1   can (16 oz.) New England-
      style baked beans
1   can (8 oz.) butter beans
1   can (16 oz.) green lima
      beans
1   can (16 oz.) white lima
      beans
1   can (16 oz.) kidney beans

Fry bacon; set aside. Brown onions in bacon grease and set aside. Combine brown sugar, mustard, and vinegar. Bring to boil; simmer 5 minutes. Drain all beans, except pork and beans and baked beans; mix all beans with onions in 4-quart casserole. Pour brown sugar mixture over beans; crumble bacon on top. Bake, uncovered, at 350 degrees for 1 hour.

HARVARD BEETS AND PINEAPPLE

Florence Robbins   *Yield: 4-6 servings*

3   tablespoons sugar
1   tablespoon cornstarch
¼   teaspoon (scant) salt
¼   cup vinegar
1   can (16 oz.) whole beets, cut into chunks
1   can (8 oz.) pineapple chunks
2   tablespoons butter or margarine

Mix sugar, cornstarch, salt, and vinegar in pan. Drain beets and pineapple, reserving liquid. Add ⅓ cup of combined liquid and butter to cornstarch mixture. Cook, stirring constantly, until thickened. Add beets and pineapple; cover and simmer slowly for 12-15 minutes. Serve hot.

BROCCOLI MOZZARELLA

Bettie Howdieshell   *Yield: 8 servings*

3   packages (10 oz. each) frozen broccoli spears
4   tablespoons butter
2   tablespoons flour
1   teaspoon salt
¼   teaspoon pepper
1   teaspoon sugar
1   small onion, grated
1   cup sour cream
3   ounces sliced blanched almonds, toasted
4   ounces mozzarella cheese, shredded
1   cup corn flake crumbs

Cook broccoli until tender-crisp. Melt 2 tablespoons butter; stir in flour, salt, pepper, and sugar. Add grated onion, sour cream, and almonds. Alternate layers of broccoli and cream mixture in buttered casserole. Cover with cheese and top with corn flake crumbs which have been browned in 2 tablespoons butter. Bake at 400 degrees for 20 minutes.

BROCCOLI SOUFFLÉ

Caryl Weckstein   *Yield: 8 servings*

3	packages (10 oz. each) frozen chopped broccoli
2	tablespoons butter or margarine
2	tablespoons flour
¾	cup milk
¾	cup mayonnaise
1	tablespoon onion juice
4	eggs, well-beaten
	Salt and pepper to taste

Cook and drain broccoli; place in greased 2-quart casserole. Combine butter and flour in saucepan; heat until bubbly. Slowly add milk; cook until thick. Add remaining ingredients, stir well, and pour over broccoli. Bake at 350 degrees for 45 minutes or until firm.

May also be baked in well-greased ring mold set in pan of hot water. Unmold and fill center with cooked carrot slices or sautéed cherry tomatoes.

BROCCOLI AU GRATIN

Marjorie Saunders   *Yield: 6-8 servings*

2	packages (10 oz. each) frozen broccoli spears
1	can (10¾ oz.) cream of shrimp soup
½	cup cream
½	cup tomato juice
¼	cup fresh bread crumbs
3	tablespoons butter or margarine
½	cup grated sharp Cheddar cheese

Cook broccoli until tender-crisp and drain well. In saucepan, combine soup, cream, and juice and heat until hot. Arrange broccoli in shallow 8x8-inch dish. Pour soup mixture over broccoli. Toss crumbs with melted butter and sprinkle over soup. Sprinkle cheese over all. Bake uncovered at 350 degrees for 10 minutes until bubbly hot.

BROCCOLI-ONION DELUXE

Helen Marinoff   *Yield: 6 servings*

1	pound fresh broccoli or 2 packages (10 oz. each) frozen broccoli
3	medium onions, quartered
4	tablespoons butter or margarine
2	tablespoons flour
¼	teaspoon salt
	Dash of pepper
1	cup milk
1	package (3 oz.) cream cheese
½	cup shredded sharp processed American cheese
1	cup soft fresh bread crumbs

Split fresh broccoli spears lengthwise and cut into 1-inch pieces. Cook in boiling salted water until tender; drain. (Cook frozen broccoli according to package directions.) Cook onions in boiling salted water until tender; drain. In saucepan, melt 2 tablespoons butter; blend in flour, salt, and pepper. Add milk; cook until thickened, stirring constantly. Reduce heat; blend in cream cheese until smooth. Place vegetables in 1½-quart casserole. Pour sauce over vegetables and mix lightly. Top with shredded cheese; cover and chill. Bake covered at 350 degrees for 30 minutes. Remove from oven. Melt remaining butter; toss with crumbs. Sprinkle around edge or over top of casserole and bake uncovered for 30 minutes more.

If desired, may be baked without chilling; reduce first baking time by 15 minutes.

QUICK BROCCOLI WITH CHEESE

Virginia L. Hill   *Yield: 8 servings*

3   packages (10 oz. each) broccoli flowerets, thawed and drained
4   ounces shredded Cheddar cheese
1   can (5⅓ oz.) evaporated milk
1   can (10¾ oz.) cream of mushroom soup
1   can (2.8 oz.) onion rings

Arrange broccoli in greased 2-quart casserole. Combine remaining ingredients, except onion rings, and pour over broccoli. Bake at 350 degrees for 25 minutes. Sprinkle onion rings on top and bake 10 minutes more.

GARDEN PATCH CASSEROLE

Chris Saunders   *Yield: 6-8 servings*

2   packages (10 oz. each) frozen chopped broccoli
1   can (17 oz.) whole kernel corn
1½ cups cottage cheese
½   cup sour cream
1   tablespoon flour
3   eggs
2   tablespoons minced onion
1½ teaspoons salt
¼   teaspoon pepper
¼   cup grated Parmesan cheese

Cook chopped broccoli until tender-crisp and drain well. Drain corn. Combine cottage cheese, sour cream, flour, eggs, onion, and seasonings. Fold in vegetables. Pour into buttered 2-quart casserole and top with Parmesan cheese. Bake at 325 degrees for 45 minutes.

CABBAGE CASSEROLE

Jane Corbly   *Yield: 8-10 servings*

1	medium head cabbage, thinly sliced
1	can (10¾ oz.) cream of celery soup
½	cup mayonnaise
½	cup milk
½	teaspoon salt
2¼	cups corn flake crumbs
2½	tablespoons butter or margarine, melted
½-¾	cup shredded sharp Cheddar cheese

Boil cabbage in water for 3-4 minutes; drain. Combine soup, mayonnaise, milk, and salt. Mix well and heat. Combine corn flake crumbs and butter. Put half of crumbs in bottom of 1½-quart casserole; alternate layers of cabbage and sauce. Top with remaining crumbs and cheese. Bake at 375 degrees for 20 minutes or until heated through.

A very hearty vegetable.

BAKED CABBAGE

Becki Sammons   *Yield: 6 servings*

1	medium head cabbage
2	teaspoons salt
2	tablespoons flour
1-2	tablespoons sugar
⅛	teaspoon pepper
3	tablespoons butter or margarine
1	cup hot milk
1	cup grated cheese (Cheddar or Colby)

Cut cabbage into wedges. Boil until tender-crisp, drain, and place in single layer in baking dish. Sprinkle with dry ingredients; dot with butter. Add milk and sprinkle with cheese. Bake at 350 degrees for 35 minutes.

CARROTS IN MUSTARD SAUCE

Catherine E. Baer   *Yield: 6-8 servings*

8-10 carrots, pared and cut
     diagonally into thin slices
     (5 cups)
     Salt to taste
2   tablespoons butter or
     margarine
¼   cup light brown sugar
1   tablespoon light corn syrup
2   tablespoons prepared
     mustard
¼   teaspoon salt

Put carrots in saucepan, salt to taste, and barely cover with water. Cover and cook until tender, about 15 minutes; drain. Put butter and remaining ingredients into small saucepan and heat, stirring constantly, until blended. Pour sauce over drained carrots and toss gently until coated. If sauce is too thick, blend in small amount of water. Serve hot.

LEMON-BUTTERED CARROTS

Maureen Brolick   *Yield: 4 servings*

1   pound carrots
2   tablespoons butter
1   tablespoon lemon juice
1   teaspoon dried basil,
     crushed
½   teaspoon garlic salt
⅛   teaspoon white pepper

Peel and slice carrots into ¼-inch "coins." Cook briefly in small amount of boiling water until tender-crisp. Refresh with cold water in colander. Melt butter in saucepan and add lemon juice, basil, garlic salt, and pepper. Return carrots to pan with lemon-butter mixture and cook until carrots are heated through.

Whole baby carrots are also well suited to this recipe.

VEGETABLES

CARROTS AND CELERY IN VERMOUTH

Lillian M. Kern   *Yield: 5-6 servings*

1   **pound carrots**
1   **pound celery**
1   **can (10¾ oz.) cream of celery soup**
6   **tablespoons white vermouth**
     Black pepper (or white)

Trim vegetables; cut into chunks. Steam or microwave (no water in microwave) until tender-crisp. Dilute soup with vermouth. Add ground pepper. Heat to "piping." Combine vegetables and sauce in hot dish or bowl. May be reheated.

The quantity of sauce can be adjusted according to amount desired. Start with ½ can of soup and 2-4 tablespoons vermouth and gradually increase ingredients.

CORN CUSTARD

Mrs. Dan Elliott   *Yield: 6 servings*

1   **package (10 oz.) frozen corn or 1 can (17 oz.) whole kernel corn**
3   **eggs**
3   **tablespoons sugar**
1   **teaspoon salt**
1   **tablespoon cornstarch**
2   **cups milk**
1   **tablespoon butter**

Place corn in greased 1 to 1½-quart casserole. Beat eggs, sugar, and salt slightly. Make paste of cornstarch and 2 tablespoons milk. Scald remaining milk; add to cornstarch mixture. Add butter. Slowly add egg mixture to milk mixture, blend well, and pour over corn. Set casserole in pan of hot water 1 inch deep. Bake at 350 degrees for 45-50 minutes or until a knife inserted comes out clean.

BLACK-TIE RED BEANS

Wanda P. Carmichael　　　　　　　　　*Yield: 8 servings*

2　cans (15 oz. each) dark red
　　kidney beans, undrained
½　cup red wine
¼　cup soy sauce
1　onion, chopped
1　teaspoon brown sugar
1　clove garlic, chopped
1　teaspoon prepared mustard
　　Sour cream
　　Chopped chives

Mix all ingredients, except sour cream and chives, and place in 1-quart crock or casserole. Bake, covered, at 325 degrees for 1 hour. (If too juicy, uncover and cook ½ hour longer.) Serve with side dishes of sour cream and chives for topping.

Good served with steak sandwiches and carrot and celery sticks.

EGGPLANT SOUFFLÉ

Fern Perrett　　　　　　　　　*Yield: 6 servings*

1　medium eggplant
1　can (10¾ oz.) Cheddar
　　cheese soup
4　ounces Velveeta cheese,
　　cubed
¾　cup soft bread crumbs
2　teaspoons grated onion
2　tablespoons ketchup
2　eggs, separated

Peel eggplant, cut in ½-inch cubes, and cook in boiling water to cover until soft, about 10 minutes. Drain well, pressing out excess water, and mash. Heat soup and cheese until cheese melts. Add mashed eggplant, crumbs, onion, ketchup, and beaten egg yolks. Beat egg whites until stiff and fold into eggplant mixture. Pour into buttered 1½-quart baking dish. Bake at 325 degrees until firm in center, about 1 hour. Serve immediately.

L'OIGNON À LA GRILLADE

Bella Freeman   *Yield: 1 serving*

1	large sweet onion
2	tablespoons sweet butter
1	teaspoon granulated beef bouillon
	Brandy or sherry (optional)

Skin and core onion to half its depth. Place onion on square of heavy-duty foil large enough to cover completely. Mix butter and bouillon together and place in onion core. Add brandy or sherry, if desired. Wrap onion tightly in foil and place in coals of grill for 20 minutes or bake in oven at 350 degrees for 1 hour.

Great picnic fare! Serve in foil or put in soup bowl with fresh croutons and freshly grated cheese.

GREEN PEPPER SAUTÉ

Alice Hebert   *Yield: 6 servings*

1	cup sliced onion
1	tablespoon salad oil
3	green peppers, sliced into ¼-inch rings
2	cans (3 oz. each) sliced mushrooms, drained
1	teaspoon salt
⅛	teaspoon dried red pepper, crushed
⅛	teaspoon dried oregano

In skillet, sauté onion in hot oil, stirring until golden, about 5 minutes. Add remaining ingredients. Cook, covered, over medium heat 5 minutes, stirring occasionally.

Fifty calories per serving!

GRANDMOTHER'S PARSNIPS

Gertrude Derby   *Yield: 4-6 servings*

1   **pound parsnips**
¼   **pound bacon, diced**
     Salt

Pare parsnips; cut into spears. Place in skillet with bacon and add water to barely cover. Cook down slowly until parsnips "candy" and brown. Turn occasionally to brown evenly. Salt as needed.

A delicious way to prepare an old-fashioned vegetable. Parsnips will "candy" naturally without adding sugar.

SNAP PEA STIR-FRY

Chris Saunders   *Yield: 4 servings*

2   **cups sugar snap peas or**
     pea pods
2   **tablespoons soy sauce**
1   **teaspoon cornstarch**
⅓   **cup water**
2   **tablespoons dry sherry**
1   **teaspoon sugar**
1   **tablespoon cooking oil**
½   **cup walnut halves**
½   **cup sliced water chestnuts,**
     drained

Remove strings from peas. In small bowl, blend soy sauce into cornstarch; stir in water, sherry, and sugar. Set aside. In wok or skillet, heat oil. Stir-fry peas until tender-crisp, about 2 minutes. Add walnuts and stir-fry 1 minute (add more oil if necessary). Stir soy mixture and add to wok. Cook and stir until bubbly and thickened. Stir in water chestnuts and cook 1 minute longer.

BAKED POTATO SOUFFLÉS

Bettie Howdieshell   *Yield: 12 servings*

6   **large Idaho potatoes, baked**
4   **eggs, separated**
4   **tablespoons light cream**
¾   **cup butter**
    Salt
    Pepper
    Buttered bread crumbs

Cut potatoes in half lengthwise and scoop out pulp. Reserve shells. Mash pulp slightly and place in mixer. Add egg yolks, cream, and butter; add salt and pepper to taste. Whip until smooth and light. Fold in stiffly beaten egg whites. Pile high in reserved shells. Sprinkle lightly with buttered bread crumbs. Bake potatoes at 350 degrees for 10 minutes to set egg whites, and refrigerate 1-2 days. When ready to serve, bake at 350 degrees for 20 minutes or until hot and browned.

BUFFET POTATOES

Nancy M. Pearson   *Yield: 6 servings*

5   **medium potatoes**
3   **tablespoons butter**
    Salt
½   **cup grated cheese**
½   **cup light cream or evaporated milk**

Pare potatoes and cut as for French fries. Place potatoes in large piece of heavy-duty aluminum foil shaped to fit serving dish. Dot potatoes with butter; sprinkle salt and cheese on top. Cover with cream. Fold foil over and seal edges. Bake at 400 degrees for 40-50 minutes. To serve, remove foil and transfer to attractive serving dish.

May be prepared ahead and refrigerated. Allow additional 15 minutes baking time.

MAKE-AHEAD POTATOES

Sue Falter — *Yield: 10 servings*

9   medium baking potatoes
1   tablespoon grated onion
½   cup butter or margarine
1½ teaspoons salt
¼   teaspoon pepper
⅔   cup warm milk
1½ cups shredded Cheddar cheese
1   cup whipping cream, whipped

Boil potatoes until tender. Peel and mash potatoes; add onion, butter, seasonings, and milk. Place mixture in shallow buttered casserole. Fold cheese into whipped cream and spread over potatoes. Bake at 350 degrees for 25 minutes or until golden brown.

May prepare potatoes ahead and add topping just before baking.

POTATO AND ONION BAKE

Alice Hebert — *Yield: 4 servings*

4   medium baking potatoes
¼   cup butter or margarine, softened
2   medium mild onions, sliced
Salt and pepper to taste
Chopped parsley or Parmesan cheese

Cut each potato into four crosswise slices; spread butter between slices and on top. Reassemble with onion rounds between potato slices. Sprinkle generously with salt and dash of pepper. Wrap each potato tightly in double thickness of foil. Bake on baking sheet at 375 degrees for 60-65 minutes or until done. Open foil, sprinkle with chopped parsley, and serve; or sprinkle with grated Parmesan cheese and return to oven for few minutes before serving.

POTATOES FLORENTINE

Rosemarie S. Sholl   *Yield: 8 servings*

10 potatoes, cooked, drained, salted, and mashed
1   package (10 oz.) frozen chopped spinach, cooked, drained, and cooled
1   stick butter or margarine
1½ cups sour cream
¼   teaspoon dill weed
8   green onions, chopped, including tops
    Pepper
    Grated Cheddar cheese

Combine potatoes, spinach, butter, sour cream, dill weed, onions, and pepper. Place in buttered 3-quart casserole. Sprinkle with cheese. Bake at 350 degrees for 15 minutes.

May be made ahead. Omit cheese topping and refrigerate until ready to bake. Increase baking time to 30 minutes. Add cheese last 15 minutes.

RICH POTATO CASSEROLE

Virginia Grice   *Yield: 10-12 servings*

1   package (1½-2 pounds) frozen hash-brown potatoes
2   cups sour cream
½   cup chopped onion
2   cups shredded Cheddar cheese
1   can (10¾ oz.) cream of mushroom soup
½   teaspoon salt
    Pepper to taste
1   stick butter or margarine, melted
2   cups corn flakes, slightly crushed

Butter 9x13-inch baking pan. Break up frozen hash-brown potatoes in pan. Mix sour cream, onion, cheese, soup, salt, pepper, and half of melted butter. Pour over potatoes. Top with corn flakes and drizzle with remaining melted butter. Bake at 350 degrees for 1 hour.

May be assembled ahead and baked just before serving.

SWEET POTATO SOUFFLÉ

Barbara B. Beegle *Yield: 6-8 servings*

3 cups cooked, mashed sweet
  potatoes
½ teaspoon salt
⅓ stick butter or margarine
1 teaspoon vanilla
½-1 cup sugar
2 eggs
½ cup milk

TOPPING
1 cup brown sugar
1 cup chopped pecans
⅓ cup flour
⅓ stick butter or margarine,
  melted

Mix potatoes, salt, butter, vanilla, sugar, eggs, and milk. Pour into 9x13-inch baking dish. Combine topping ingredients and sprinkle over potato mixture. Bake at 350 degrees for 35 minutes.

JAMAICAN SWEET POTATOES

Anna Carr *Yield: 4 servings*

3 tablespoons flaked coconut
1 pound cooked yams, peeled
  and cut into ½-inch slices
  Salt
2 under-ripe bananas, thinly
  sliced
1¼ teaspoons cornstarch
½ cup orange juice
¼ teaspoon cinnamon
¾ teaspoon nutmeg

Sprinkle coconut on piece of heavy foil and toast lightly in pre-heated 350 degree oven. (Watch closely; 2 minutes may be long enough.) Place yam slices in buttered 1-quart casserole. Sprinkle with salt. Cover with banana slices. Dissolve cornstarch in orange juice; heat until thickened. Add cinnamon and nutmeg and pour over yams and bananas. Top with toasted coconut. Cover and bake at 350 degrees about 30 minutes.

WILD RICE CASSEROLE

Barbara Neroni   *Yield: 10-12 servings*

1   **pound bulk pork sausage**
1   **pound mushrooms, sliced**
1   **cup chopped onion**
2   **cups wild rice, washed**
½   **cup slivered almonds,
     toasted**

SAUCE
½   **cup flour**
½   **cup heavy cream**
2   **cans (10¾ oz. each) con-
     densed chicken broth**
1   **teaspoon monosodium
     glutamate**
     **Pinch of oregano, thyme,
     marjoram**
     Salt to taste
⅛   **teaspoon pepper**

Sauté sausage, breaking into small pieces. Drain on paper towels. Sauté mushrooms and onion in sausage fat. Return sausage to pan; set aside. Meanwhile, cook wild rice in boiling salted water 10-12 minutes; drain and repeat. (This method of boiling wild rice assures thorough cleaning.) Make cream sauce and combine with rice, sausage, mushrooms and onion. Pour into casserole. Bake at 350 degrees for 35-40 minutes or until bubbly and heated thoroughly. Garnish with toasted slivered almonds.

Mix flour with cream in heavy sauce-pan until smooth. Add chicken broth and cook until thickened. Add seasonings.

May be prepared a day ahead and refrigerated. Bring to room temperature before baking. Sometimes rice will absorb more liquid than if baked immediately. If mixture looks dry, stir in a little more chicken stock before baking. This is an elegant accompaniment to beef or pork and goes equally well as stuffing for poultry.

GREEN CHILIES RICE RING

Mrs. Richard Salamone   *Yield: 12 servings*

6	cups cooked rice
½	pound Monterey Jack cheese (plain), shredded
½	pound Monterey Jack cheese with peppers, shredded
1	can (4 oz.) green chilies, drained and chopped
2	teaspoons salt
1	teaspoon pepper
2	cups sour cream
	Celery leaves
	Tomato wedges
	Shredded lettuce
1	pimento, cut into strips

Combine rice, cheese, chili peppers, salt, and pepper in large bowl; toss lightly to mix. Fold in sour cream. Spoon into 8-cup mold, packing mixture lightly with back of spoon. Bake at 350 degrees for 30 minutes. Cool in mold on wire rack 5 minutes. Unmold and fill center with celery leaves and tomato wedges. Frame base with shredded lettuce; top with pimento.

EASY SPINACH BAKE

Sue Seifert Williams   *Yield: 4-5 servings*

1	package (10 oz.) frozen chopped spinach
1	egg, slightly beaten
1	cup grated sharp cheese
1	can (10¾ oz.) cream of chicken soup
1	cup herb-seasoned stuffing or 2 slices bread, cubed
3	tablespoons melted butter
	Dash of garlic salt

Cook spinach; drain thoroughly. Combine spinach, egg, cheese, and soup; put in greased 1½-quart casserole. Toss stuffing in butter and add garlic salt. Sprinkle stuffing on spinach mixture. Bake at 350 degrees for 1 hour.

May be assembled ahead and baked just before serving.

SPINACH LOAF

Sally Forbes   *Yield: 8-10 servings*

2	packages (10 oz. each) frozen chopped spinach, cooked, drained, and cooled
1	container (24 oz.) cottage cheese
¾	cup Parmesan cheese (reserve some for topping)
¾	cup bread crumbs
6	whole eggs, beaten
	Sour cream
	Lemon wedges

Thoroughly blend all ingredients, except sour cream and lemon wedges. Line loaf pan with aluminum foil; generously brush foil with oil. Pour in mixture and sprinkle top with reserved Parmesan cheese. Bake at 350 degrees for 30 minutes. Serve with sour cream and lemon wedges.

A good buffet item served cold. Place overlapping slices on platter and garnish with lemon slices. Serve sour cream in side dish.

SPINACH-ROSEMARY BAKE

Ann Buck   *Yield: 10-12 servings*

2	packages (10 oz. each) frozen chopped spinach, cooked and drained
2	cups cooked rice
2	cups shredded sharp cheese
4	eggs, beaten
¼	cup margarine
⅔	cup milk
¼	cup chopped onion
1	teaspoon Worcestershire sauce
¾	teaspoon salt
½	teaspoon rosemary
	Buttered bread crumbs or corn flakes
	Cheddar cheese for topping

Combine all ingredients, except crumbs and cheese for topping, and pour into greased 8x12-inch casserole. Top with buttered bread crumbs or crushed corn flakes, mixed with Cheddar cheese. Bake at 350 degrees for 30 minutes.

SPINACH ROLL

Mary Houpis   *Yield: 8 servings*

1	onion, chopped
¼	cup vegetable oil
2	packages (10 oz. each) frozen chopped spinach, thawed and drained
2	eggs, beaten well
¼	cup chopped parsley
1	cup cottage cheese
½	cup Feta cheese
	Pepper to taste
½	pound butter or margarine, melted
6	pastry sheets of filo
1	tablespoon cream of wheat

Brown chopped onion in oil. In large bowl, mix spinach with eggs; add onion, parsley, cheeses, and pepper. Mix well. Brush melted butter generously on each filo leaf and place leaves on top of each other. On narrow end of top leaf, sprinkle cream of wheat; spread filo with spinach mixture, leaving 1-inch border all around. Fold in long sides 1 inch and roll. Seal with melted butter. Place seam-side down on ungreased baking sheet. Brush top with melted butter. Bake at 350 degrees for 35 minutes.

Versatile recipe; may be served as an appetizer or as accompaniment to a main course. Spinach roll may be frozen. After preparing, bake for 15 minutes and freeze. When ready to serve, thaw only a few minutes; bake at 350 degrees for 30-40 minutes.

FRUIT-FILLED ACORN SQUASH

Mary Houpis   *Yield: 8 servings*

4	medium acorn squash
3	cups chopped apples
1	medium orange, peeled and diced
½	cup brown sugar
¼	cup butter or margarine
¼	cup raisins (optional)
¼	cup pecans (optional)

Wash squash; cut in half and remove seeds. Bake (cut side down) in about ½ inch of water at 350 degrees for 30 minutes. Combine remaining ingredients and fill squash cavities. Bake 35 minutes longer.

Acorn squash may be cooked in microwave.

ESCALLOPED SPINACH AND TOMATOES

Mrs. D. H. Rickard   *Yield: 9 servings*

2   cans (16 oz. each) tomatoes
     or tomato purée
1   bay leaf
3   teaspoons salt
1   teaspoon sugar
1   whole clove
1   tablespoon minced onion
⅓-
½   green pepper, seeded and
     diced
7   tablespoons butter or
     margarine
3-4 tablespoons flour
3   packages (10 oz. each)
     frozen chopped spinach
⅛   teaspoon pepper
½   cup fresh bread crumbs

In saucepan, combine tomatoes or purée, bay leaf, 2 teaspoons salt, sugar, clove, onion, green pepper, 3 tablespoons butter, and flour. Simmer 30 minutes; remove bay leaf and clove. Cook spinach and drain well. Season with 3 tablespoons butter, 1 teaspoon salt, and pepper. Arrange alternate layers of spinach and tomato mixtures in 2 to 3-quart casserole, ending with tomato layer. Top with bread crumbs mixed with 1 tablespoon butter. Bake at 350 degrees until crumbs brown, about 30 minutes.

May be prepared ahead; add crumbs before baking. Reheats well. A colorful vegetable dish for the holidays.

BROILED TOMATO SLICES

Mrs. Fred B. Davis   *Yield: 4 servings*

1   large tomato, cut into ½-
     inch slices
½   cup mayonnaise
4   tablespoons crumbled,
     cooked bacon
2   teaspoons oregano
¼   cup chopped fresh mush-
     rooms
¼   cup chopped water
     chestnuts
4   ounces Muenster cheese

Place tomato slices in single layer in flat pan. Mix together mayonnaise, bacon, oregano, mushrooms, and water chestnuts. Spread over tomato slices. Cover with sliced Muenster cheese. Broil until golden brown.

HERBED TOMATO BAKE

Gertrude C. Derby   *Yield: 4-6 servings*

6	tablespoons butter or margarine
4-6	tablespoons brown sugar
¼	teaspoon salt
1½	cups croutons
¼	cup finely chopped onion
2	cans (16 oz. each) tomatoes, drained

Melt 4 tablespoons butter and stir in 2 tablespoons brown sugar and salt. Add croutons, toss lightly, and set aside. Cook onion in 2 tablespoons butter until soft, not brown. Coarsely chop tomatoes and combine with onion and 2-4 tablespoons brown sugar in 6x10-inch baking dish. Add crouton mixture and blend with tomatoes. Bake at 375 degrees for 20 minutes or until thoroughly heated. May be baked longer at lower temperature.

STUFFED SUMMER SQUASH

Lou Mason   *Yield: 8 servings*

4	medium summer squash (2 lbs.)
½	cup chopped onion
3	tablespoons butter
1	can (4 oz.) chopped mushrooms, drained
½	cup grated Muenster cheese
1	egg, lightly beaten
½	teaspoon salt
	Pepper, freshly ground
½	cup saltine cracker crumbs
1	cup coarse fresh bread crumbs, buttered

Cook squash in boiling water until able to pierce with fork, 5-10 minutes. Drain and cover with cold water until cool enough to handle. Cut in half lengthwise. Remove and reserve pulp, leaving ¼-inch shell. Place shells in single layer in 9x13-inch glass pan. In skillet, sauté onion in butter; chop and add squash pulp and drained mushrooms. Cook until pulp is soft, 5-10 minutes. Add cheese, egg, salt, pepper, and cracker crumbs. Mix well and fill squash shells. Top with bread crumbs. Bake at 350 degrees for ½ hour.

May be refrigerated after assembling. Bring to room temperature before baking or bake 5-10 minutes longer.

TOMATOES PROVENÇAL

Betty Sue Wydman   *Yield: 6 servings*

2	pounds tomatoes
4	slices bacon, diced
1	clove garlic
1	onion, sliced
¼	pound mushrooms, sliced
2	teaspoons seasoned salt
1	tablespoon flour
6	tablespoons Parmesan cheese
1	tablespoon butter

Cut tomatoes into ½-inch slices. In skillet, sauté bacon until crisp; add minced garlic, onion, and mushrooms and sauté until golden; stir in 1 teaspoon seasoned salt and flour. Spread half of tomato slices in 6x10-inch baking dish. Sprinkle with ½ teaspoon seasoned salt. Top with mushroom mixture. Sprinkle with 3 tablespoons Parmesan cheese; dot with butter. Add layer of remaining tomatoes and sprinkle with remaining seasoned salt and Parmesan cheese. Bake at 350 degrees for 40 minutes or until tomatoes are just tender.

JULIENNE ZUCCHINI

Ellie Shulman   *Yield: 4-6 servings*

3-4	medium (5-inch) zucchini or yellow summer squash
2	tablespoons butter
2	scallions, finely shredded (optional)
	Salt
	Pepper, freshly ground
	Dash of cayenne
	Dash of nutmeg

Wash zucchini. Leave skin for color. Cut in half lengthwise and remove seed core. Cut into julienne pieces (may use food processor). Melt butter in large skillet; add zucchini and scallions and stir quickly to coat. Add seasonings to taste. Remove immediately to serving dish and serve.

Squash should be cooked less than 2 minutes to preserve its crisp appearance and taste.

QUICK ZUCCHINI CASSEROLE

Suzie Holloway — *Yield: 4-6 servings*

- 4 cups thinly sliced zucchini
- ¼ cup water
- 1 cup shredded sharp cheese
- 1 egg
- ½ cup sour cream
- 1 tablespoon flour
- 4 slices bacon, cooked and crumbled
- ¼ cup browned bread crumbs

Microwave zucchini and water in glass casserole, covered, on high for 7 minutes; drain. Mix cheese, egg, sour cream, and flour and stir into zucchini. Microwave on high, covered, for 3 minutes; stir. Combine bacon and bread crumbs; sprinkle over casserole. Microwave on high, covered, for 2 minutes longer.

PARISIAN ZUCCHINI

Chris Saunders — *Yield: 4-6 servings*

- 1 medium onion, thinly sliced
- 1 clove garlic, minced
- 3 tablespoons butter or margarine
- 4 cups thinly sliced zucchini (unpeeled)
- 1 teaspoon salt
- Pepper
- 1 teaspoon Italian seasoning
- 1 medium-sized, ripe tomato
- 3 ounces sharp Cheddar cheese, grated
- 3 tablespoons grated Parmesan cheese

Sauté onion and minced garlic in half of butter until golden, but not brown. Remove from skillet. Add remaining butter and sauté zucchini slices quickly until just tender-crisp, sprinkling with seasonings while cooking. Add more butter if necessary. Add wedges of tomato and heat through. (Do not overcook tomato or zucchini.) Gently toss onion and garlic with zucchini and tomatoes and place on flat oven-to-table dish. Top with cheeses and place under broiler until cheese melts.

"This was a specialty of a fine French cook whom I knew many years ago."
Chris Saunders

155

MEDITERRANEAN CASSEROLE

Mrs. Thomas P. Davis   *Yield: 6-8 servings*

½ cup chopped onion
½ cup sliced mushrooms
1 tablespoon chopped garlic
6 tablespoons butter
3 cups sliced zucchini
3 cups sliced yellow summer squash or additional 3 cups zucchini
½ teaspoon marjoram
½ teaspoon basil
½ teaspoon oregano
1 can (16 oz.) stewed tomatoes
1 can (8 oz.) tomato sauce
3 tablespoons tomato paste
1½ cups bread crumbs
1 cup grated Cheddar cheese
1 cup grated mozzarella cheese

Sauté onion, mushrooms, and garlic in 4 tablespoons butter for 3 minutes; add zucchini and yellow squash. Mix marjoram, basil, and oregano; add 1 teaspoon herb mixture to zucchini mixture. Add tomatoes, tomato sauce, and tomato paste. Cook 3 minutes. Place in 3-quart casserole. Mix bread crumbs, Cheddar and mozzarella cheeses, and remaining herb mixture; spread over vegetables. Dot with 2 tablespoons butter. Cook, uncovered, on high in microwave for 10 minutes or bake at 350 degrees for 30 minutes.

May be assembled ahead. Add cheese mixture, herbs, and butter just before baking.

EASY VEGETABLE CASSEROLE

Susan T. Sauer   *Yield: 5-6 servings*

4 cups vegetables (broccoli, Brussels sprouts, green beans, or cauliflower)
3 tablespoons mayonnaise
1 teaspoon Dijon mustard
1 cup grated cheese (Swiss or Cheddar)

Cook desired vegetable until tender-crisp; drain. Mix with mayonnaise and mustard. Place in shallow baking dish, top with grated cheese, and broil until cheese melts. If vegetable has been allowed to cool, bake at 375 degrees for 10 minutes.

A great way to use leftover vegetables!

VEGETABLES

ZUCCHINI SOUFFLÉ

Helen Marinoff   *Yield: 4-6 servings*

2	pounds zucchini (5-6 medium-sized)
1	cup fresh bread crumbs
2	eggs, beaten
¼	cup oil
1	teaspoon salt
½	teaspoon pepper
1	small onion, grated
½	cup chopped parsley
	Butter
	Grated Romano cheese

Grate zucchini, drain, and blot with paper towel. Add bread crumbs, eggs, oil, salt, pepper, onion, and parsley. Mix well and place in buttered 1½-quart casserole. Dot with butter. Bake uncovered at 325 degrees for 40 minutes. Top with cheese and bake 10 minutes more or until set. Let stand 5 minutes before serving.

ZUCCHINI CUSTARD

Chris Saunders   *Yield: 6-8 servings*

6	slices firm white bread, crusts removed
¼	cup butter or margarine
1	can (17 oz.) whole kernel corn, drained
2	cups thinly sliced zucchini
4	ounces California green chilies, seeded and chopped or ¼ cup chopped onion
½	pound Monterey Jack cheese, shredded
4	eggs, lightly beaten
2	cups milk
	Salt and pepper

Spread bread with butter and arrange buttered side down in 9x13-inch baking dish. Spread corn evenly over bread, and arrange zucchini on top of corn. Spread chilies and cheese over zucchini. Combine eggs, milk, salt, and pepper and pour over all. Refrigerate 4 hours or overnight. Bake, uncovered, at 375 degrees for 30-40 minutes or until lightly browned and puffed. Let stand 10 minutes before serving.

BAKED VEGETABLE MÉLANGE

Gerry Meyer   *Yield: 10-12 servings*

2	packages (10 oz. each) frozen broccoli spears
2	packages (10 oz. each) frozen Brussels sprouts
2	packages (10 oz. each) frozen cauliflower
8	tablespoons butter or margarine
1½	tablespoons flour
1	can (13 oz.) evaporated milk
1	jar (8 oz.) Cheese Whiz
1	teaspoon salt
1	teaspoon garlic salt
4	ounces herb-seasoned stuffing mix

P our boiling water over vegetables to separate; drain. Cut broccoli into bite-sized pieces. Place vegetables in 9x13-inch baking dish. In saucepan, melt 1 tablespoon butter. Add flour, evaporated milk, Cheese Whiz, salt, and garlic salt. Pour sauce over vegetables. Pour stuffing mix over sauce. Melt remainder of butter and pour over stuffing mix. Bake, uncovered, at 350 degrees for 1 hour.

VEGETABLE FETTUCINI

Susan S. Seyfarth   *Yield: 6 servings*

1	package (10 oz.) fettucini
1½	cups fresh broccoli flowerets, sliced
1	cup sliced fresh mushrooms
½	cup fresh (or frozen) peas or fresh snow peas
2	tablespoons sliced pimento
2	tablespoons sliced green onions
3	tablespoons oil
1	cup grated Parmesan cheese
¼	cup butter, melted
⅓	cup whipping cream

C ook fettucini according to package directions. Meanwhile, stir-fry vegetables in oil until tender-crisp. Add vegetables to hot cooked fettucini in large bowl. Stir in cheese, butter, and cream. Toss to coat.

May also be served as first course for 10 persons.

158

VEGETABLE MEDLEY

Anne E. Alexander   *Yield: 8 servings*

1	package (10 oz.) frozen peas, thawed
1	package (8 oz.) frozen asparagus spears, thawed and cut into thirds
3	eggs, hard-cooked and chopped
½	cup chopped green pepper
½	cup chopped celery
	Salt and pepper to taste
½	pound sharp New York Cheddar cheese, grated
2	cans (10¾ oz. each) tomato soup

In bottom of greased 2-quart casserole, spread half of the green peas and asparagus, which have been gently mixed together. Mix eggs, green pepper, and celery and layer half over peas and asparagus. Add salt and pepper to taste. Add half of grated cheese and pour 1 can of tomato soup over all. Repeat layering, ending with second can of soup. Bake at 350 degrees for 45 minutes.

May be assembled ahead.

STERLING IDEAS

Entrées

To brown meats nicely in a skillet, first pat them dry with paper towels.

For a rich and robust gravy, add one or two teaspoons of instant coffee or 1/2 cup of strong cold coffee to the pan as the gravy thickens. The flavor will not be altered. Add to beef or lamb stew for a rich color.

Instant potato makes a good, non-lumpy thickener for stews and gravies.

Try adding a grated raw potato to each pound of ground meat for juicy hamburgers. Adding a raw egg will hold the patty together and prevent its sticking to the grill.

Always bring meats to be grilled to room temperature. This makes it easier to estimate cooking time and gives a more uniformly grilled meat.

For garlic-flavored steak, throw a few cloves of garlic on top of the hot briquets while barbecuing the steaks. Also, brushing steaks with melted butter before barbecuing adds to their flavor.

Use equal parts butter and vegetable oil when sautéeing meats to prevent the butter from burning.

Place chicken parts on cookie sheet to freeze. Then store in plastic bag. The desired amount can then be removed for cooking. Place on jelly roll pan, sprinkle with salt, and bake from frozen state at 375 degrees for one hour. The skin will be wonderfully crisp.

Freeze leftover chicken broth in ice cube trays. When frozen, store in plastic bag in freezer and add to gravies, soups, and frozen vegetables when needed.

Do not overcook fish. As a general rule, cook ten minutes per inch of thickness of fish. Cook only until flesh becomes white and opaque. Fish will be flakier and easier to bone.

To clarify butter, microwave one pound on high for two minutes. The clear layer will float on top, making it easy to pour off.

To cut down the odor of boiling shrimp, add celery leaves or vinegar.

Fish will not stick to your grill if the grill is very hot before the fish is broiled.

TERRIFIC TENDERLOIN

Steve Mason   *Yield: 6 servings*

Whole beef tenderloin (2½ lbs.), well trimmed
Salad oil
Seasoned salt

Grill tenderloin on outdoor grill to desired doneness, about 20-25 minutes for medium-rare, basting and turning often. At each turning, baste with salad oil and sprinkle liberally with seasoned salt. May be served hot or at room temperature.

STEAK DIANE

Kenneth H. Holloway   *Yield: 4 servings*

4   **sirloin strip steaks (6-8 oz. each)**
4   **tablespoons butter (divided)**
2   **tablespoons Dijon mustard**
⅛   **teaspoon ground black pepper**
2   **tablespoons Worcestershire sauce (divided)**
2   **cups sliced mushrooms**
4   **tablespoons minced shallots or onion**
¼   **cup brandy**
½   **cup beef bouillon**
1   **teaspoon chopped parsley**

Pound steaks between 2 pieces of waxed paper until ¼-inch thick. Trim well. Melt 2 tablespoons butter in large skillet, add steaks, and brown 1 minute on each side. Remove steaks to platter and spread both sides with mustard, pepper, and 1 tablespoon Worcestershire sauce; set aside. In same skillet, melt remaining butter and add mushrooms and shallots; sauté for 3 minutes. Add brandy and flame. Stir in bouillon and remainder of Worcestershire sauce. Stir and cook until hot. Return steaks to skillet and reheat. Sprinkle with parsley and serve.

STEAK AU ROQUEFORT

Bella Freeman   *Yield: 4 servings*

4	New York strip steaks
	Salt
	Pepper
	Garlic, minced
¾	cup brandy
½	pound Roquefort or bleu cheese, crumbled

Place steaks in 9x13-inch glass baking dish. Season with salt, pepper, and garlic to taste. Mix brandy and ¼ pound Roquefort and pour over steaks. Marinate 1-2 hours at room temperature, turning once to make sure both sides are coated with cheese. Grill or broil to desired doneness. During last few minutes of cooking, top with remaining cheese and allow cheese to melt slightly.

KITTY OWEN'S TENDERLOIN

Karen F. Perry   *Yield: 6 servings*

1	jar (9 oz.) Major Grey's Chutney
1	bottle (8 oz.) Italian dressing
1	bottle (8 oz.) French dressing
	Whole beef tenderloin (3 lbs.), trimmed of fat and "silver"

Combine chutney and dressings. Marinate tenderloin in mixture for 24 hours in refrigerator. Remove beef from marinade and grill over hot coals, turning once, to desired doneness. (Allow 15-25 minutes total cooking time.) Carve in 1½ to 2-inch slices and serve immediately.

Allow ½ pound per person. Freeze leftover marinade and use again.

MEATS

PEPPER STEAK

Mrs. John Finlay (Ann)   *Yield: 4-6 servings*

1½   **pounds top round steak, cut into strips**
½   **cup flour**
   Salt and pepper
¼   **cup cooking oil**
1   **can (8 oz.) tomatoes**
1-
1½   **cups water**
½   **cup chopped onion**
1   **small clove garlic, minced, or garlic powder to taste**
2   **cubes beef bouillon**
1½   **teaspoons Worcestershire sauce**
2   **green peppers, cut into strips**
   Hot cooked rice

Combine flour, salt, and pepper; coat meat strips. In large skillet, brown meat in oil. Add cut-up tomatoes and their liquid, water, onion, garlic, bouillon cubes, and Worcestershire sauce. Cover and simmer about an hour or until meat is tender. Add green pepper strips; simmer 5 minutes. (May thicken gravy with flour and water, if desired.) Serve over hot rice.

FRAGRANT POT ROAST

Nicki Thompson   *Yield: 6-8 servings*

   Pot roast (4 lb.)
3   **tablespoons oil**
1   **teaspoon salt**
⅛   **teaspoon pepper**
½   **cup ketchup**
½   **cup water**
1   **tablespoon vinegar**
1   **tablespoon sugar**
2   **tablespoons lemon juice**
1   **tablespoon Worcestershire sauce**
½   **teaspoon salt**
3   **medium onions, sliced**

Brown pot roast in oil. Pour off drippings. Season with salt and pepper. Mix remaining ingredients, except onions. Arrange onions on top and around sides of meat. Pour sauce over onions and meat. Cover tightly and simmer 3½-4 hours or until tender. Thicken liquid for gravy, if desired.

BUL-KOGI

Jane Corbly   *Yield: 4-6 servings*

½   cup soy sauce
1   tablespoon sesame seed oil
2   tablespoons vinegar
       Garlic powder to taste
2   tablespoons sugar
1   tablespoon sesame seed
2   pounds sirloin steak or
       rump roast (sliced as thin
       as possible)
1-2 bunches green onions,
       finely chopped (include
       tops)

Mix soy sauce, oil, vinegar, garlic powder, sugar, and sesame seed. Dip sliced meat into sauce and place in glass dish, alternating with layers of onions. Marinate several hours in refrigerator before cooking. Drain meat and onions and place on baking sheet with shallow sides. Broil to desired doneness. Serve with rice.

INDIVIDUAL ITALIAN MEAT LOAVES

Chris Saunders   *Yield: 6 servings*

¾   cup cracker crumbs
¾   cup milk
1½ pounds ground beef
2   eggs
¼   cup grated Romano or
       Parmesan cheese
¼   cup minced green pepper
¼   cup minced onion
1   tablespoon Worcestershire
       sauce
½   teaspoon salt
½   teaspoon garlic salt
¼   teaspoon basil
       Dash of pepper
       Ketchup
       Basil and grated cheese
       for garnish

Soak cracker crumbs in milk. Add remaining ingredients, except ketchup, and mix well. Shape into 6 individual loaves and place in shallow baking pan. Spread ketchup over loaves and sprinkle with additional basil and cheese. Bake at 350 degrees for 45 minutes.

SWEDISH MEATBALLS

Anna-May Jacobsen   *Yield: 6 servings*

1	medium onion, finely chopped
	Butter
½	pound ground beef
¼	pound ground pork
¼	pound ground veal
1	egg, beaten
½	cup milk
1	teaspoon salt
½	teaspoon pepper
½	cup dry bread crumbs

Sauté onion in a little butter until golden brown. Mix together meats, onion, egg, milk, salt, and pepper. Stir in bread crumbs and mix well. Refrigerate several hours or overnight. Shape into small meatballs and brown well in skillet, shaking pan to keep meatballs round. Place in pot with small amount of water in bottom. Cover and simmer about ½ hour (to ensure that all pork is cooked); drain liquid and reserve for gravy.

GRAVY

1	beef bouillon cube
1	cup boiling water
2	tablespoons flour
½	cup cream

Skim off and discard fat from meatball liquid. Add bouillon cube dissolved in boiling water. Slowly add flour mixed with cream, stirring constantly. Cook until thickened. Add meatballs. Serve over rice.

Meatballs may be frozen after cooking. Thaw and heat in sauce.

MARINATED FLANK STEAK

Marilyn Hoback   *Yield: 5-6 servings*

1	can (10¾ oz.) beef consommé
⅓	cup soy sauce
1½	teaspoons seasoned salt
¼	teaspoon onion powder
3	tablespoons lime juice
2	tablespoons brown sugar
3	pounds flank steak

Mix together consommé, soy sauce, seasoned salt, onion powder, lime juice, and brown sugar. Pour over steak and marinate for 24 hours in refrigerator. Remove from marinade and broil steak 7 minutes on 1 side and 5 on the other. Cut into 1-inch diagonal strips. Serve hot.

ROSE'S GREEK STEW

Catherine E. Baer *Yield: 8 servings*

3	pounds stew meat
¼-	
½	cup butter
	Salt and pepper
2½	pounds small onions (may use frozen)
1	can (6 oz.) tomato paste
⅓	cup red wine
1	tablespoon brown sugar
1	clove garlic, minced
1	bay leaf
1	small stick cinnamon or 1 teaspoon ground cinnamon
½	teaspoon whole cloves
2	tablespoons raisins

Melt butter in large covered casserole or skillet (oven proof). Coat meat with butter, but do not brown. Add salt and pepper to taste. Place onions on top of beef. Mix remaining ingredients and pour over onions. Bake at 275-300 degrees for 3 hours.

BLEU CHEESE FLANK STEAK

Karen F. Perry *Yield: 8 servings*

2	flank steaks (1-1½ lbs. each) with pockets
4	ounces bleu cheese, crumbled
1	package (1.1 oz.) bleu cheese dressing mix
¼	cup salad oil
¼	cup red wine
2	tablespoons red wine vinegar
	Dash of soy sauce

Stuff pocket of each flank steak with half of bleu cheese. Place steaks in shallow dish. Combine dressing mix, oil, wine, vinegar, and soy sauce. Pour over steaks. Marinate 4-6 hours in refrigerator. Remove from marinade and grill over charcoal or broil under preheated broiler 4 minutes per side or until done to taste. Slice thin on the diagonal.

This is also delicious served cold!

MEATS

PASTICCIO

Mary Houpis   *Yield: 10 servings*

1½   **pounds elbow macaroni**
2   **eggs, beaten**
1   **cup grated Parmesan cheese**
½   **cup melted butter**
¼   **teaspoon nutmeg**
      Parmesan cheese, grated (for topping)

Cook macaroni as package directs; do not overcook. Drain and put in large bowl. Add eggs, cheese, butter, and nutmeg; toss well. In buttered 13x15x1½-inch pan, spread half of macaroni mixture, all of meat sauce, and remaining macaroni. Cover with white sauce. Sprinkle top with Parmesan cheese. Bake at 350 degrees for 40-45 minutes or until golden brown. Cool slightly; cut into serving pieces.

MEAT SAUCE
1   **cup chopped onion**
½   **cup margarine**
1½   **pounds ground chuck**
½   **cup grated carrots**
1   **cup tomato sauce or 2 tablespoons tomato purée**
½   **cup red wine (optional)**
¼   **cup water**
      Salt
      Pepper

Sauté onion in margarine; add meat, stirring until well browned. Add carrots, tomato sauce, wine, water, and seasonings. Simmer until sauce thickens, about 30 minutes.

WHITE SAUCE
1   **stick butter**
1   **cup flour**
1   **teaspoon salt**
3   **cups milk**
3   **eggs**
1   **cup grated Parmesan cheese**

Melt butter over medium heat; stir in flour and salt. Slowly add milk, stirring constantly, until mixture begins to thicken. Add beaten eggs and cheese, stirring until mixture is thick enough to spread over macaroni.

169

CHIPPED BEEF CASSEROLE

Maureen K. Gilmore   *Yield: 4-6 servings*

1 cup elbow macaroni, uncooked
1 cup sharp cheese cubes
1 can (10¾ oz.) cream of mushroom soup
1 cup milk
¼ pound dried beef
2 hard-cooked eggs, chopped

Combine all ingredients. Let stand 4 hours or overnight, covered, in refrigerator. Bake, covered, at 350 degrees for 1 hour.

LASAGNA

Sally Forbes   *Yield: 10-12 servings*

2 tablespoons olive oil
2 medium onions, chopped
2 pounds bulk Italian sausage
1½ pounds ground chuck
2 cans (6 oz. each) tomato paste
1 can (28 oz.) Italian tomatoes
1½ teaspoons salt
1 teaspoon sugar
¼ teaspoon pepper
1 teaspoon oregano
1 package (8 oz.) lasagna noodles
½ pound mozzarella cheese
¾ pound ricotta cheese
½ cup Parmesan cheese

Heat oil in skillet. Sauté onions; add sausage and chuck and sauté until browned. Add tomato ingredients and seasonings; cover and simmer for 20 minutes. Meanwhile, cook noodles in salted water with a little olive oil to keep them from sticking together. Drain and rinse. Using half of each ingredient, arrange layers of noodles, sliced mozzarella, spoonfuls of ricotta, and tomato-meat sauce in rectangular 3-quart casserole; repeat layers. Sprinkle with Parmesan. Bake at 375 degrees for 25 minutes.

Flavor improves if assembled a day ahead and refrigerated. Tomato-meat sauce is excellent served with any pasta; it may be varied with clams or mushrooms.

NO-BOIL LASAGNA

Nancy Schuler   *Yield: 8 servings*

1	**pound ground beef**
1½	**tablespoons Italian seasoning**
1	**jar (32 oz.) spaghetti sauce (or homemade)**
1	**package (8 oz.) lasagna noodles, uncooked**
24	**ounces low-fat cottage cheese**
1	**pound mozzarella cheese, sliced**

Brown ground beef in skillet and drain off excess fat; add Italian seasoning and mix well. Into 9x13-inch metal pan, pour enough spaghetti sauce to cover bottom. Top with single layer of noodles. Spread with half of meat and half of cottage cheese. Top with ⅓ of mozzarella cheese. Add another layer of noodles and lightly cover with spaghetti sauce. Cover with remaining meat and cottage cheese and ⅓ of mozzarella. Add third layer of noodles and cover with remaining spaghetti sauce. Cover tightly with foil and bake at 350-375 degrees for 1 hour. Top with remaining slices of mozzarella cheese cut in small pieces. Replace foil and let stand for 10-15 minutes before serving.

May be made ahead and reheated or frozen. Heat some extra sauce in saucepan and ladle over top of each serving if lasagna seems too dry.

PIZZA BURGERS

Betty Sue Wydman   *Yield: 6 servings*

1	large onion, chopped
2	tablespoons oil
1½-	
2	pounds ground beef
1	can (15 oz.) tomato sauce
1	teaspoon oregano
1	teaspoon salt
6	hamburger buns, split and buttered
1	package (8 oz.) mozzarella cheese
	Stuffed green olives, sliced

Sauté onion in oil; add beef and brown. Stir in tomato sauce and seasonings; simmer 10 minutes. Broil hamburger buns until lightly toasted. Spoon sauce on buns. Cut cheese to fit tops of buns; arrange olive slices on cheese. Broil 3 minutes.

SARA'S MEATBALLS AND SAUCE

Gerry Meyer   *Yield: 8-10 servings*

1	medium onion, chopped
3	tablespoons olive oil
2½	pounds ground beef
1¼	pounds bulk Italian sausage
2	cans (12 oz. each) tomato paste and 3 cans water
1	can (28 oz.) tomato purée and 1 can water
1	cup dry red wine
3-4	teaspoons oregano
¾	teaspoon basil
1	tablespoon salt
2	bay leaves
1¼	cups cracker crumbs
½	cup grated Parmesan cheese
1	teaspoon garlic salt
2	teaspoons dried parsley
2	eggs
1	cup milk

Sauté onion in olive oil. Add ¾ pound ground beef and ¼ pound sausage and brown. Add tomato paste, tomato purée, water, wine, oregano, basil, salt, and bay leaves. Simmer, uncovered, 1½ hours. Mix remainder of meat with cracker crumbs, Parmesan cheese, garlic salt, parsley, eggs, and milk. Roll into balls (about 24) and drop into sauce; simmer 1 hour. Remove bay leaves. Serve over spaghetti.

Best made a day ahead. Skim off fat before reheating.

MEATBALLS WIKI WIKI

Lois Ross   *Yield: 6-8 servings*

2	pounds ground chuck
⅔	cup evaporated milk
½	cup finely chopped onion
⅔	cup corn flake crumbs
1	teaspoon seasoned salt

SAUCE

2	cups unsweetened pineapple juice
½	cup vinegar
¼	cup cornstarch
½	cup brown sugar
½	cup soy sauce
1	can (20 oz.) pineapple chunks, drained
1	green pepper, sliced

Combine all ingredients and form into 1-inch meatballs. Place on broiling pan and bake at 400 degrees for 20 minutes or until brown.

Combine all sauce ingredients, except pineapple and pepper, in saucepan and simmer until sauce thickens, stirring constantly. Pour sauce over meatballs and add pineapple chunks and green pepper slices. Serve with rice.

May be served with cocktail picks as hors d'oeuvre.

CHILLY DAYS CHILI

Sara Rendall   *Yield: 8-10 servings*

2	pounds ground beef
1	large onion, chopped
1	green pepper, diced
1	can (28 oz.) whole tomatoes
1	can (15 oz.) tomato sauce
1	bottle (12 oz.) chili sauce
1	cup water
1	package (1¼ oz.) chili seasoning
1	teaspoon chili powder
½	teaspoon pepper
1	teaspoon salt
½	teaspoon paprika
1	can (15 oz.) kidney beans
	Tabasco (optional)

Brown beef, onion, and green pepper; drain. Add all other ingredients, except beans. Bring to boil. Reduce heat. Simmer 2 hours, covered, or 1 hour, uncovered. Add beans and serve when heated through.

Great dish for tailgate parties or to serve after hayrides.

ENCHILADA

Martha B. Ordeman   *Yield: 10 servings*

2	**pounds ground beef**
1	**large onion, chopped**
1	**package (10 oz.) frozen chopped spinach, cooked and well drained**
1	**can (16 oz.) tomatoes**
	Salt and pepper
1	**can (10¾ oz.) cream of mushroom soup**
1	**can (10¾ oz.) golden mushroom soup**
8	**ounces sour cream**
¼	**cup milk**
¼	**teaspoon garlic powder**
12-16	**frozen tortillas, thawed**
½	**cup melted butter or margarine**
2	**small cans (4 oz. each) roasted green chilies, chopped**
1	**pound Cheddar cheese, grated**

Brown meat and drain off fat. Stir in onion, spinach, tomatoes, salt, and pepper. In bowl, combine soups, sour cream, milk, and garlic powder. Dip tortillas in butter and line the bottom and sides of 9x13-inch pan. Spoon in meat mixture; sprinkle with chilies and all but ½ cup cheese. Add another layer of tortillas dipped in butter. Pour soup mixture over tortillas and smooth out. Cover with foil and refrigerate overnight. Top with remaining ½ cup cheese before baking. Bake, uncovered, at 325 degrees for 35-45 minutes.

Freezes well.

BEEF AND CABBAGE CASSEROLE

Sue Lindquist (Mrs. Elden)   *Yield: 6-8 servings*

1   small head cabbage
1½   pounds ground beef
      Salt and pepper
1   small onion, minced
⅓   cup rice, uncooked
1   can (10¾ oz.) tomato soup
1   soup can water

Chop cabbage into bite-sized pieces and place in bottom of greased 9x13-inch casserole. Brown meat; drain and add salt and pepper to taste. Add onion and stir in rice. Place meat mixture over cabbage and cover with soup and water. Bake, uncovered, at 350 degrees for 20 minutes; cover and continue baking for another hour or until rice is tender.

This has the flavor of cabbage rolls without all the fuss; a low-calorie treat.

BEEF-ZUCCHINI CASSEROLE

Martha A. Gardner   *Yield: 10-12 servings*

2   packages (10 oz. each) frozen zucchini or 6 medium-sized fresh zucchini, sliced
½   cup water
1   teaspoon salt
1   pound ground beef
1   onion, chopped
1   cup instant rice, uncooked
1   teaspoon garlic salt
1   teaspoon crushed oregano
1   pint small curd cottage cheese
1   can (10¾ oz.) cream of celery soup
1   cup grated Cheddar cheese

Cook zucchini in water and salt until barely tender, about 5 minutes. Drain well. Brown beef and onion. Add rice and seasonings. Place ½ of zucchini in 2-quart shallow casserole. Cover with beef mixture and top with cottage cheese. Add remaining zucchini. Spread celery soup over all. Sprinkle with cheese. Bake, uncovered, at 350 degrees for 35-40 minutes or until bubbly.

CABBAGE ROLLS

Mrs. Robert Koenig (Patricia)   *Yield: 10-12 servings*

2   medium heads cabbage
2   pounds lean ground pork
1   pound ground chuck
¾   cup rice, uncooked
3   medium onions, diced
3   teaspoons salt
1   teaspoon black pepper
1   teaspoon red pepper
1   teaspoon garlic juice
1   package (32 oz.) sauer-
       kraut
2   cans (10¾ oz. each) tomato
       soup
1-2   pounds Kielbasa or Hun-
       garian sausage (optional)
       Sour cream

Core cabbage and dip into large kettle of boiling water. Remove leaves as they begin to separate. Mix meat, rice, onions, and seasonings. Place portion of meat mixture (according to size of leaf) in cup of leaf, roll once, fold in sides, and continue to roll. Place alternate layers of cabbage rolls (seam side down) and sauerkraut in large roasting pan. Cut up remaining cabbage when leaves get too small and spread over top layer. Spread with sauerkraut and cover with tomato soup. Bake, covered, at 325 degrees for 2 hours. May add browned Kielbasa or Hungarian sausage (cut into 2-inch pieces) last half hour of roasting. Serve with sour cream.

Make several days in advance to improve flavor. May be frozen.

BEEF AND EGGPLANT CASSEROLE

Angela D. Colaizzi   *Yield: 8 servings*

1   pound ground chuck
1   medium onion, chopped
1   clove garlic, crushed
     Salt and pepper
1   eggplant
2-3 cups spaghetti sauce
     Parmesan cheese
     Bread crumbs

Brown meat, onion, and garlic in large skillet. Salt and pepper to taste. Peel and slice eggplant lengthwise in ½-inch slices. Layer half of eggplant slices in 9x13-inch pan. Cover with half of meat mixture, then half of spaghetti sauce, and sprinkle liberally with Parmesan cheese; repeat layers. Top liberally with Parmesan cheese and bread crumbs. Cover with foil. (May be frozen at this point.) Pierce a few holes in foil to let steam escape. Bake at 350 degrees for 1 hour.

VEAL OF THE HOUSE

Patti D. Ballard   *Yield: 8 servings*

3   pounds lean veal, cut into
     1½-inch cubes
     Flour
     Salt
     Pepper
¼-
½   cup olive oil
6   cloves garlic, minced
4-6 medium onions, sliced
2   teaspoons rosemary
½-
¾   cup dry white wine
2   tablespoons tomato paste
2-3 cups chicken stock
1   pound mushrooms, sliced
     Chopped parsley

Dredge veal in flour, salt, and pepper. Heat oil in Dutch oven, add veal, and brown on all sides. Add garlic and onion and cook 2 minutes, stirring with wooden spoon. Add rosemary, wine, tomato paste, and enough stock to cover. Cover and bake at 300 degrees for 2 hours. Add mushrooms and bake another 15-20 minutes. Before serving, sprinkle with chopped parsley. Serve with long grain and wild rice.

SWEET-SOUR VEAL WITH RICE

Carole Woehrmyer   *Yield: 6 servings*

1½   pounds veal, cut in 1½-inch cubes
2   tablespoons cooking oil
1   cup celery slices
½   cup chopped onion
¾   teaspoon salt
      Dash of pepper
1   beef bouillon cube
½   cup hot water
1   can (20 oz.) pineapple tidbits, drained (reserve syrup)
1   can (16 oz.) bean sprouts, drained
1   can (3 oz.) sliced mushrooms, undrained
3   tablespoons cornstarch
3   tablespoons soy sauce
1   teaspoon monosodium glutamate
3   cups hot cooked rice

Brown veal in hot cooking oil. Add celery, onion, salt, pepper, bouillon cube dissolved in hot water, and reserved pineapple syrup. Cover and simmer 60-75 minutes or until meat is tender. Add pineapple, bean sprouts, mushrooms, and mushroom liquid. Blend cornstarch with soy sauce and monosodium glutamate; stir into hot mixture. Cook, stirring constantly, until thick. Serve over rice.

For an inexpensive version, use turkey cutlets.

GRILLED LAMB CHOPS

Sonnie Kasch (Mrs. William)   *Yield: 5 servings*

½   cup soy sauce
½   cup water
2   cloves garlic, minced
½   teaspoon ground ginger
10   lamb chops, ½-1 inch thick

Mix first 4 ingredients. Pour over chops, cover, and refrigerate several hours or overnight. Grill chops 5-8 minutes on each side.

LEG OF LAMB À LA GEORGE

Dorothy Dybvig   *Yield: 4-6 servings*

Leg of lamb (5-6 lbs.), boned and butterflied
1   package instant meat marinade
⅔   cup sherry
¼   teaspoon ground marjoram
2   tablespoons melted mint jelly
Garlic salt to taste
4   tablespoons currant jelly

Place lamb in shallow pan; pierce deeply all over. Combine meat marinade, sherry, marjoram, mint jelly, and garlic salt. Marinate meat for 30 minutes (no longer), turning several times. Drain; save marinade. Place lamb, fat side down, 3-4 inches above hot coals and broil for 10 minutes. Turn and broil until meat is sealed and browned. Reduce heat and roast with top of grill down for an additional 25 minutes. Add currant jelly to marinade and baste lamb during last 15 minutes. Carve diagonally into thin strips.

LEG OF LAMB À LA GREQUE

Mary Houpis   *Yield: 4-6 servings*

Leg of lamb (4½-5 lbs.)
Garlic salt
Salt
Pepper
Flour
¼   cup tomato sauce

Trim fat; place lamb in baking pan. Cut slits in meat and sprinkle garlic salt, salt, and pepper in slits. Sprinkle flour lightly over entire roast. Add tomato sauce. Cover and bake at 350 degrees for ½ hour per pound. Uncover last 20 minutes. Let cool slightly before slicing.

For another meal, mix leftover meat with cooked elbow macaroni; add more tomato sauce and water to leftover gravy. Mix gravy with meat and macaroni. Place all in casserole, top with grated cheese, heat, and serve.

179

VEAL ROLLS

Susan Mills   *Yield: 6 servings*

½ cup bread crumbs
¼ cup milk
¼ pound bulk pork sausage, cooked
¼ cup chopped onion
½ clove garlic, minced
2 slices bacon, cooked and diced
1 tablespoon minced parsley
1 egg yolk
6 veal cutlets, pounded ¼ inch thick
2 tablespoons shortening
1 cup beef bouillon
1 cup red wine
1 cup sliced mushrooms (optional)

Combine crumbs, milk, sausage, onion, garlic, bacon, parsley, and egg yolk. Toss lightly and spread on each piece of veal. Roll up and secure with string or toothpick. Brown in hot shortening and place in baking dish. Pour bouillon and ½ cup wine over meat. Bake, covered, at 350 degrees for 45-60 minutes. When meat is tender, remove and keep warm on serving platter. Thicken pan juices with mixture of flour and water. Add remaining wine and mushrooms and cook about 5 minutes. Pour over meat and serve.

Butterflied flank steak may be substituted for veal cutlets. Rolls may be prepared for cooking a day ahead. May be baked early and held in 200 degree oven for hours.

EASY MOUSSAKA

Ellen Jane Porter   *Yield: 6 servings*

1	medium eggplant
2	tablespoons oil
2	medium onions
1	pound ground lamb or beef
	Celery salt
	Garlic salt
1	can (8 oz.) tomato sauce
	Grated cheese

Peel and cut eggplant into ¾-inch slices. Put oil in 9x13-inch pan. Arrange slices in pan, turning once to coat both sides. Bake at 350 degrees until eggplant becomes transparent, about 7 minutes on each side. Chop onions, mix with ground meat, and cook until meat is just done. Season to taste with celery salt and garlic salt. Add tomato sauce. Spoon meat mixture over eggplant slices, cover with grated cheese, and bake until cheese melts.

Add sliced mushrooms with grated cheese for a company lunch.

NEW YEAR'S PORK FRY

Judge George J. Gounaris   *Yield: 4 servings*

6	tablespoons vegetable oil
4	tablespoons butter
1½	pounds pork loin or lean pork shoulder, cut into 1-inch cubes
	Oregano
	Garlic powder
	Salt and pepper
	Juice of 1 lemon
½	cup dry white wine
	Parsley

Heat oil and butter in large frying pan. Add meat and season with oregano, garlic powder, salt, and pepper to taste. Sauté, turning frequently until meat is done and golden brown. Pour lemon juice and wine over meat. Garnish with parsley.

This is a recipe enjoyed in certain parts of Greece during the New Year season. Excellent served with pilaf made with beef broth.

PORK LOIN WITH PLUM SAUCE

Sonnie Kasch (Mrs. William)   *Yield: 8-10 servings*

Pork loin (4-6 lbs.)
3   **tablespoons sherry**
¾   **cup soy sauce**
4   **tablespoons brown sugar**
2   **teaspoons salt**
1½ **teaspoons cinnamon**
¾   **teaspoon ground cloves**
¾   **teaspoon ground ginger**

P lace pork loin in glass loaf pan in which it fits closely. Mix remaining ingredients; pour over meat. Marinate in refrigerator at least 12 hours, turning meat occasionally. Put meat in broiler pan. Brown at 450 degrees for 10 minutes. Baste with marinade; turn oven to 325 degrees and roast for 1-2 hours or until meat thermometer reaches 165-170 degrees. Serve with sauce.

PLUM SAUCE
1   **jar (18 oz.) plum preserves**
1   **cup chutney**
2   **tablespoons vinegar**

Mix sauce ingredients in processor or blender until smooth. May be served hot or cold with pork.

Pork loin may also be cooked on a covered grill. Gauge time according to type of grill. (Meat thermometer should register 165-170 degrees.) Baste occasionally with marinade.

PORK MEDALLIONS

Sara Rendall   *Yield: 4 servings*

MEATS

2	tablespoons oil
12	slices pork tenderloin, ½ inch thick
½	teaspoon salt
¼	teaspoon pepper
¼	teaspoon allspice
¼	teaspoon thyme
1	clove garlic, finely chopped
3	green onions, finely chopped
1	cup white wine
1	cup whipping cream Parsley

Heat oil in skillet. Cook meat, a few pieces at a time, until brown, about 2 minutes on each side. Season with salt, pepper, allspice, and thyme. Return all meat to skillet; add garlic and green onion. Cover and cook over medium heat until tender, about 6 minutes. Transfer to platter. Add wine to skillet. Cook over high heat until mixture is reduced by half, about 5 minutes. Stir in cream; cook until slightly thickened. Return pork to skillet; baste with sauce. Cover and simmer over low heat until hot. Return pork to platter. Spoon sauce over pork and garnish with parsley.

Equally delicious made with veal.

HAM BALLS WITH CUMBERLAND SAUCE

Virginia Grice   *Yield: 8 servings*

1½   pounds ground ham
2   eggs, slightly beaten
1   cup dry bread crumbs
¾   cup milk
½   cup slivered almonds
      (optional)

Mix ham, eggs, crumbs, and milk; form into 25-30 balls. Place on greased baking pan and bake at 400 degrees until brown, about 20 minutes. Place in casserole; cover with Cumberland sauce and bake at 300 degrees for ½ hour. Add almonds, if desired, and serve.

CUMBERLAND SAUCE
¾   cup red wine
1   cup orange juice
1   tablespoon lemon juice
1   tablespoon cornstarch
½   teaspoon dry mustard
¼   teaspoon ground cloves
¼   teaspoon ground ginger
½   cup seedless raisins
⅔   cup currant jelly

Combine wine, orange juice, and lemon juice. Stir cornstarch, mustard, and ground spices into a small portion of liquid; add cornstarch mixture to liquid. Add raisins. Bring mixture to boil and allow to simmer for a few minutes. Remove from heat, add currant jelly, and stir to melt.

May be assembled ahead. Allow extra time for baking (1 hour total). Good with potato salad or scalloped potatoes.

MARINATED TURKEY BREAST

Nan C. Baird   *Yield: 6-8 servings*

1½   **cups soy sauce**
1½   **cups salad oil**
3   **cups sauterne**
      Garlic salt (regular salt
      or onion salt may be
      substituted)
      Pepper
1   **turkey breast**

Mix all ingredients, except turkey, in pot or bowl large enough to fit turkey. Marinate turkey breast in mixture 3-5 hours, turning occasionally. Cook on covered grill for 1-1½ hours (use drip pan to avoid flaming). Heat marinade in large saucepan; add cooked turkey breast and cook over low heat for 20 minutes. Slice turkey and serve with marinade used as French dip for bread.

FESTIVE CHICKEN

Ellie Shulman *Yield: 4-6 servings*

3   chicken breasts, halved
1-2 tablespoons melted butter
1   lemon, cut into 6 wedges
    Salt
    Pepper
    Paprika
12-
14 rings of sweet red, yellow,
    and green peppers
1   tablespoon butter

Place breasts in single layer, skin side up, in shallow roasting pan. Brush with melted butter, squeeze lemon juice on meat, and season to taste with salt, pepper, and enough paprika to entirely cover top surface. Roast at 450 degrees for 45 minutes. Baste several times during last 15 minutes. (Skin will become crisp and dark reddish-brown.) When chicken is almost done, sauté pepper rings in 1 tablespoon butter for 1-2 minutes and pour over chicken on serving platter.

BONELESS CHICKEN PARMESAN

Betty Sue Wydman *Yield: 4 servings*

8   pieces chicken (breast or
    thigh), boned and skinned
    Flour, seasoned with salt
    and pepper
1   stick butter (8 tablespoons)
½ cup chopped onion
3   cups canned tomatoes,
    drained and crushed
2   bay leaves
1   clove garlic
1   teaspoon oregano
1   teaspoon basil
    Salt and pepper
4   ounces mozzarella cheese,
    cut into 8 slices to fit
    chicken pieces
    Parmesan cheese

Roll chicken in seasoned flour. Sauté until golden brown in 3 tablespoons butter. Remove and place in baking dish. Remove excess fat from skillet. Add remaining 5 tablespoons butter; add onion and sauté until transparent. Add tomatoes, bay leaves, garlic, oregano, basil, salt, and pepper. Simmer until sauce cooks down and darkens in color, about ½ hour. Spoon sauce generously over each piece of chicken. Place slice of mozzarella on each piece. Sprinkle with Parmesan. Bake at 350 degrees for ½ hour.

SPINACH-CHEESE STUFFED CHICKEN

Susan Mills   *Yield: 4-6 servings*

1	pound fresh spinach, stems removed
½	cup margarine
⅓	cup low-fat cottage cheese or ricotta
⅓	cup grated Swiss cheese
¼	cup freshly grated Parmesan cheese
1	egg
⅛	teaspoon nutmeg
	Salt and pepper
	Whole chicken (3-3½ lbs.)
2	tablespoons margarine
	Paprika
½	teaspoon oregano
¼	teaspoon thyme
¼	teaspoon marjoram

Cook spinach until wilted. Cool and squeeze out excess moisture. Chop and combine with ½ cup margarine, cheeses, and egg, mixing well. Add nutmeg, salt, and pepper to taste. Lift skin of chicken breast gently to create pocket. Stuff pocket with spinach mixture. Oil roasting pan. Combine 2 tablespoons margarine with enough paprika to give a rosy color. Combine herbs. Coat chicken with margarine and sprinkle both sides with herb mixture. Tuck wings under body of chicken and bake at 375 degrees for 1 hour or until chicken is golden brown and tender, basting frequently with pan drippings.

To really impress your guests, remove breast bone from inside before making pocket for stuffing, being careful not to tear skin.

WEEZIE'S BAKED CHICKEN

Mrs. Edward C. McGinnis   *Yield: 6 servings*

2	cups chopped cooked chicken
2	cups chopped celery
⅓	cup chopped peanuts
2	tablespoons minced onion
¾	cup mayonnaise
2	tablespoons lemon juice
1	cup shredded Cheddar cheese
1	cup crushed potato chips

Combine chicken, celery, peanuts, onion, mayonnaise, and lemon juice. Place mixture in 2-quart casserole. Sprinkle with cheese and potato chips. Bake at 350 degrees for 25-30 minutes.

CHICKEN L'ORANGE

Mrs. Hugh J. Lynch   *Yield: 6-8 servings*

3-4	chicken breasts, halved and boned
	Flour
	Salt
	Pepper
	Paprika
	Margarine or butter
2	cups orange juice
2	tablespoons grated orange rind
1	teaspoon salt
2	tablespoons packed brown sugar (may substitute 2 tablespoons orange marmalade)
¼-½	cup sherry
3	tablespoons water
2	tablespoons cornstarch
1	can (16 oz.) artichoke hearts, drained
1	jar (4½ oz.) whole mushrooms, drained

Coat chicken with mixture of flour, salt, pepper, and paprika. Sauté in margarine until lightly browned. Place in 9x13-inch casserole. Put orange juice and rind, salt, sugar, and sherry in saucepan and heat to boiling. Mix water and cornstarch and add to sauce. Stir until thickened; cool. Place artichokes and mushrooms on chicken. Pour sauce over all; cover and refrigerate or freeze. When ready to cook, uncover and bake at 350 degrees for 45 minutes to 1 hour.

DELUXE CHICKEN DIJON

Todd Marinoff   *Yield: 4-6 servings*

3 chicken breasts, halved,
   skinned, and boned
   Kosher salt
1 jar (8 oz.) Dijon mustard
   Freshly prepared bread
   crumbs (1 large loaf
   French bread)
   Olive oil
1 stick unsalted butter

Sprinkle chicken breasts lightly with salt and spread liberally with Dijon mustard, covering completely. Dip chicken pieces into fresh bread crumbs and place in baking pan oiled with olive oil. Melt butter and drizzle over prepared chicken breasts. Bake, uncovered, at 350 degrees for 45 minutes.

This may be assembled early in the day and refrigerated until ready to bake.

CHICKEN SAUTERNE

Bettie Howdieshell   *Yield: 8 servings*

5   chicken breasts, halved
    and boned
8   ounces spaghetti
5   ounces fresh mushrooms
    Butter
½   cup dry sauterne
1½-
2   cups sour cream
1   clove garlic, minced
1   teaspoon salt
¼   teaspoon pepper
½   teaspoon oregano
1   can (16 oz.) stewed
    tomatoes
½   cup chopped onion
8   ounces mozzarella cheese,
    sliced

Brown chicken breasts and set aside. Cook and drain spaghetti. Brown mushrooms in butter. Add sauterne to sour cream and blend in garlic, salt, pepper, and oregano. Toss spaghetti with seasoned sour cream, mushrooms, stewed tomatoes, and chopped onion. Turn into large greased baking dish and top with chicken and mozzarella cheese. Bake at 325 degrees for 1 hour.

DRESSED CHICKEN

Letitia Johnson   *Yield: 4-6 servings*

4	chicken breasts, halved and boned
8	ounces Swiss cheese, sliced
1	can (10¾ oz.) cream of mushroom soup
2	cans (3 oz. each) chopped mushrooms, drained
⅓	cup white wine
1	cup herb-seasoned stuffing mix
½	cup melted butter

Place chicken breasts in greased 9x13-inch casserole; top with Swiss cheese. Mix soup, drained mushrooms, and wine. Pour over chicken and cheese. Sprinkle with stuffing and drizzle with melted butter. Cover tightly and bake at 350 degrees for 1½ hours.

ARTICHOKE-CHICKEN CASSEROLE

Jean N. Vesper   *Yield: 6 servings*

3	chicken breasts, halved and boned
3	tablespoons oil
¼	pound mushrooms, cut up
1	can (16 oz.) artichoke hearts, drained and cut up
1	can (8 oz.) sliced water chestnuts
1	jar (2 oz.) chopped pimentos or ½ cup sliced green olives

Sauté chicken in oil. Add mushrooms and artichoke hearts and cook briefly. Arrange in buttered 9x13-inch casserole. Add water chestnuts and pimentos or sliced olives. Make cream sauce and pour over contents of casserole. Bake, uncovered, at 350 degrees for 45 minutes. Serve over rice or noodles.

CREAM SAUCE

3	tablespoons butter
3	tablespoons flour
2	cups chicken bouillon
3	tablespoons cooking sherry

Melt butter in saucepan; add flour and stir. Pour in bouillon, stirring constantly to prevent lumping. Cook until thickened; add sherry.

CHICKEN IN PUFF PASTRY

Mrs. Donald Adams (Patch)   *Yield: 4 servings*

2	chicken breasts, halved, skinned, and boned
4	tablespoons butter
	Salt
	Pepper
1-2	tablespoons lemon juice
2	cups finely chopped mushrooms
¼	teaspoon crushed rosemary
1	egg yolk, beaten
1	tablespoon water
4	frozen patty shells, thawed in refrigerator

Flatten chicken slightly. Sauté in 2 tablespoons butter for 2 minutes on each side. Season with salt, pepper, and lemon juice and chill at least 30 minutes. Sauté mushrooms in 2 tablespoons butter for 5 minutes. Add rosemary and cook 2 minutes more; chill. Mix egg yolk and water for egg wash. Roll out each patty shell into rectangle to fit size of chicken breast; spread 1 tablespoon mushroom mixture on each patty shell and place chicken on top. Fold as a turnover, sealing with fork. Brush with egg wash. Place on ungreased cookie sheet and bake at 400 degrees for 10 minutes. Lower heat to 350 degrees and bake 20 minutes longer or until golden.

SAUCE

¾	cup cream
1	package (¾ oz.) gravy mix
¼	cup sherry
½	cup sautéed mushrooms

Heat cream; stir in gravy mix and sherry; mix well. Add mushrooms and stir until heated through. Spoon over pastry at table.

Chicken and mushroom mixture may be prepared a day ahead or entire recipe (except sauce) may be completely assembled and frozen. Thaw in refrigerator prior to cooking.

MICROWAVE COMPANY CHICKEN

Pam Treimann   *Yield: 6-8 servings*

2½ **pounds chicken breasts,
    halved**
¼   **teaspoon each of sage,
    thyme, marjoram**
1   **carrot stick**
1   **celery stick**
¾   **pound broccoli or
    asparagus**
½   **cup sliced large mushrooms**
½   **cup long grain and wild rice**

SAUCE
2   **tablespoons butter**
1   **tablespoon finely chopped
    onion**
3   **tablespoons flour**
½   **teaspoon salt (optional)
    Pinch of white pepper**
1½ **cups chicken broth or
    2% milk**
½   **cup white wine**
½   **cup grated extra-sharp
    Cheddar cheese**
½   **cup grated Parmesan
    cheese**

Cook chicken with spices, carrot, and celery in 2 cups water for 15 minutes in pressure cooker or 30 minutes by conventional method; remove bones. Wash broccoli and cut into serving-sized pieces. Microwave on high 5 minutes in 2 tablespoons water. Cover broccoli with chicken pieces and sliced mushrooms. Prepare sauce. Pour over chicken and vegetables. Store in refrigerator. Prepare rice according to package directions and hold in oiled, ovenproof casserole in warm oven until needed. When ready to serve, microwave chicken mixture on high for 15-18 minutes (longer if casserole is frozen). Serve chicken over rice.

In large glass casserole, microwave butter with onion for 1 minute on high. Stir in flour, salt, and pepper. Add liquid all at once, stir, and cook uncovered on high for 1½ minutes. Stir 5 times while cooking additional 5 minutes. Add cheeses.

May be prepared a day in advance or frozen.

CHICKEN SPINACH DELIGHT

Bea Sides   *Yield: 6-8 servings*

2   packages (10 oz. each)
     frozen chopped spinach,
     thawed and well drained
4-6 chicken breasts, halved,
     skinned, and boned
1   cup mayonnaise
2   cans (10¾ oz. each) cream
     of chicken soup
1   teaspoon curry powder
1   tablespoon lemon juice
½   cup grated extra-sharp
     Cheddar cheese
½   cup buttered fresh bread
     crumbs

Spread spinach in greased 8x12-inch casserole. Place chicken breasts on top in single layer. Mix mayonnaise, soup, curry, and lemon juice and spread over chicken. Sprinkle with cheese and bread crumbs. Bake at 350 degrees for 1 hour.

May be made ahead and frozen. Thaw before baking.

CHICKEN WITH SOUR CREAM SAUCE

Myrna Eyre   *Yield: 4 servings*

2   chicken breasts, halved
6   tablespoons butter
½   cup white table wine
     Pinch of tarragon leaves
1   small onion, finely chopped
¾-1 cup sour cream
     Salt and pepper
     Parsley

Remove skin from chicken. In heavy skillet, brown breast halves lightly in 4 tablespoons butter, turning occasionally. Sprinkle half of wine over chicken. Sprinkle with tarragon as desired. Cover and simmer 20 minutes or until tender. Meanwhile, melt 2 tablespoons butter in saucepan. Add onion and cook until soft, not browned. Add remaining wine; slowly stir in sour cream. Season with salt and pepper. Heat just enough to warm cream. Place chicken on serving dish and pour sauce over. Garnish with parsley.

ASPARAGUS AND CHICKEN MORNAY

Barbara Neff   *Yield: 12 servings*

½   cup onion, chopped
⅓   cup butter
1   can (8 oz.) chopped mushrooms, with liquid
1   can (10¾ oz.) cream of mushroom soup
1   can (10¾ oz.) cream of chicken soup
1   can (5½ oz.) evaporated milk
1   tablespoon soy sauce
¼   teaspoon freshly ground pepper
1   teaspoon monosodium glutamate
½   pound sharp cheese, grated
2   packages (9 oz. each) frozen asparagus spears, cooked, drained, cut in thirds
6   cups cooked chicken or turkey, in bite-sized pieces
½   cup slivered almonds

Sauté onion in butter, add next 8 ingredients, and simmer just until cheese melts. Add asparagus and chicken and mix well. Put in 3-quart casserole. Sprinkle with almonds. Bake at 350 degrees for 30 minutes or until bubbly.

May be refrigerated or frozen before baking. If frozen, thaw in refrigerator overnight. Leftovers also freeze well. Add extra cooking time if baked after refrigerating.

194

OLD-FASHIONED CHICKEN SQUARES

Virginia Grice   *Yield: 10 servings*

2	cups cooked macaroni
2	cups fine, dry bread crumbs
2	cups chopped cooked chicken
1	tablespoon chopped parsley
1	tablespoon chopped onion
1	tablespoon chopped green pepper
1	tablespoon chopped pimento
1	teaspoon salt
6	eggs, beaten very lightly
½	cup melted butter or margarine
1	pint whipping cream Paprika

SAUCE

¼	cup milk
1	can (10¾ oz.) cream of mushroom soup
¼	cup chopped pimento
1	cup sour cream

Grind cooked macaroni in grinder or food processor. Mix together all ingredients except cream and paprika. Whip cream and fold in. Place in greased 9x13-inch baking dish. Sprinkle with paprika. Set in another pan containing hot water. Bake at 350 degrees for 1 hour or until set. Cut in squares and serve with sauce.

Combine sauce ingredients and heat.

This recipe may be prepared in advance (except whipped cream) and refrigerated. Whip cream and fold in just before baking.

ROAST STUFFED GAME HENS

Bette Huter   *Yield: 8 servings*

8	frozen game hens
4	apples, unpeeled
10	buttery crackers
1	cup raisins

Thaw, wash, and prepare birds for roasting according to package directions. Dice apples, crumble crackers, and mix with raisins. Stuff birds and roast at 350 degrees for 1 hour.

195

CHICKEN CRÊPES

Lynn J. Olive   *Yield: 24 crêpes*

6	eggs, beaten
1	cup milk
1	cup pancake mix

Combine eggs and milk. Add pancake mix. Use crêpe-maker according to directions or cook in 6-inch skillet, brushing with melted butter between crêpes. Stack crêpes between sheets of waxed paper.

SAUCE

4	tablespoons margarine or butter
¼	cup finely chopped onion
4	cups sliced mushrooms
1	cup flour
1	cup grated Parmesan cheese
1	teaspoon paprika
3½	cups rich chicken broth
1	can (13 oz.) evaporated milk
4	drops yellow food coloring
	Salt and pepper to taste
½-	
¾	cup sherry
6	cups diced cooked chicken
½	cup slivered almonds
	Paprika
	Parsley

Use 4-quart pan or Dutch oven. Sauté onion and mushrooms in margarine. Sprinkle with flour, ½ cup cheese, and paprika and mix well. Add heated liquids gradually, stirring constantly. Add coloring and seasoning. Simmer until thickened. Remove from heat and add sherry. Mix well. Reserve 2 cups of sauce. Add chicken to remaining sauce. To assemble, put ⅓ cup of chicken mixture across center of each crêpe, roll up, and place seam side down in glass casserole. Pour reserved sauce down center of crêpes; sprinkle sauce with ½ cup cheese, almonds, and paprika. Bake at 350 degrees for 20-30 minutes. Garnish with parsley.

Crêpes may be frozen before or after filling. Thaw in refrigerator before filling or baking.

MY OWN SPAGHETTI CARUSO

Betty Arnold   *Yield: 4 servings*

½   cup chopped onion
½   cup chopped green pepper
1   tablespoon olive oil combined with 1 tablespoon melted margarine
1   can (16 oz.) tomatoes
1   teaspoon dried basil
1   teaspoon slivered lemon peel
2   tablespoons dried parsley
    Salt and pepper
¾   pound spaghetti
1   pound chicken livers
½   pound fresh mushrooms, sliced
½   stick margarine

Sauté onion and green pepper in combined oil and margarine. Add tomatoes, basil, lemon peel, parsley, salt, and pepper. Simmer about 15 minutes. Meanwhile, cook spaghetti according to package directions. Sauté livers and mushrooms in margarine. Mix sauce into drained spaghetti, place in serving dish, and top with livers and mushrooms.

ESCALLOPED CHICKEN

Mrs. Robert Pretzinger   *Yield: 8 servings*

5   slices white bread, cut into cubes
3   eggs, beaten
1   can (10¾ oz.) cream of mushroom soup
1   cup sliced mushrooms
1   small onion, chopped
2   cups diced cooked chicken
1   cup cubed Cheddar cheese or 2 cups shredded cheese
1¾ cups mayonnaise
½   cup chopped celery

Mix all ingredients. Bake in well-greased 2-quart casserole at 350 degrees for 45-50 minutes.

CHICKEN TETRAZZINI

Diane W. Colaizzi *Yield: 8 servings*

4	whole chicken breasts
1	onion, chopped
2	stalks celery, chopped
	Salt
½	pound spaghetti (broken in half)
1	can (10¾ oz.) cream of chicken soup
8	ounces Cheddar cheese, grated
1	cup sour cream
½	cup dry sherry or white wine or ¼ cup of each
¼	teaspoon freshly ground pepper
1	pint fresh mushrooms, sliced
½	cup freshly grated Parmesan cheese
½	cup herb-seasoned bread crumbs

Cook chicken with onion and celery in salted water until tender, 30-45 minutes. Reserve onion, celery, and broth. Cube chicken. Cook spaghetti in boiling salted water. Drain and rinse. Combine soup, cheese, sour cream, sherry, and pepper in saucepan and heat (do not boil). Cook mushrooms in chicken broth for a few minutes. Add mushrooms, reserved onion and celery, and 1 cup chicken broth to sauce. Stir in spaghetti and chicken and blend well. Pour mixture into greased 9x13-inch baking dish or 3-quart casserole. Sprinkle with Parmesan cheese and bread crumbs. Bake at 350 degrees for 30 minutes.

CHICKEN WITH RICE AND WALNUTS

Judy Beriss *Yield: 4 servings*

½	cup chopped onion
½	cup butter or margarine
3	cups diced cooked chicken
1	cup uncooked rice
2½	cups chicken broth
½-1	cup drained, chopped, canned tomatoes
	Salt and pepper to taste
¼	teaspoon garlic salt
½	teaspoon ground thyme
½	cup chopped walnuts

In large, heavy skillet, sauté onion in butter until light brown. Stir in remaining ingredients, except nuts. Cover and simmer for 30 minutes, stirring occasionally. Stir in nuts before serving.

CHICKEN-SAUSAGE SUPREME

Nancy D. Hardy   *Yield: 12-14 servings*

1   **pound pork sausage**
2   **boxes (6 oz. each) long grain and wild rice mix**
3-4 **chicken breasts, cooked, boned, and cubed**
2   **cups diced celery**
1   **can (8 oz.) water chestnuts, cut into halves or quarters (optional)**
1   **cup sliced black olives (optional)**
2   **cans (10¾ oz. each) cream of mushroom soup**

Cook and drain sausage; crumble. Cook rice according to package directions. Combine sausage and rice; add chicken, celery, chestnuts, and olives. Add soup and mix well. Bake at 350 degrees for 30-40 minutes.

Freezes well.

CHICKEN SAUTÉ

Susan T. Sauer   *Yield: 4 servings*

2   **chicken breasts, halved**
     Butter
½-
¾   **cup dry white wine**
3   **tablespoons of any of the following mixtures: tarragon and parsley tarragon, parsley, and chives parsley and rosemary parsley and chervil parsley, chives, and dill**

Brown chicken breast halves in a little butter. Add wine and herbs. Cover and simmer until done, 20-30 minutes.

ROAST CHICKEN WITH HERBS

Susan T. Sauer   *Yield: 4 servings*

	Whole chicken (3-3½ lbs.)
4	**cloves garlic**
2	**bay leaves**
6	**tablespoons melted butter**
1½	**teaspoons salt**
1	**teaspoon pepper**
½	**teaspoon thyme**
½	**teaspoon sage**
½	**teaspoon oregano**
½	**teaspoon marjoram**
½	**teaspoon basil**

Rinse chicken and pat dry. Rub skin with cut clove of garlic. Stuff cavity with bay leaves and garlic (including cut clove). Add seasonings and dry herbs to butter. Put 1 tablespoon of herb mixture in cavity of chicken; brush outside generously with mixture. Place breast side down in baking pan. Place in cold oven; turn temperature to 425 degrees. Bake 45 minutes. Turn bird over and bake 30-40 minutes longer. Baste occasionally. Serve hot or cold.

A foil tent placed loosely over the chicken helps control spattering.

STUFFED QUAIL

Mrs. Carl Skoggard (Dorothy)   *Yield: 4 servings*

8	**quail, cleaned**
1	**cup stuffing mix**
¾	**cup water**
2	**tablespoons melted butter**
1	**package (¾ oz.) brown gravy mix**
½	**cup apricot preserves**
	Dash of ground cloves
	Currant jelly

Prepare quail for stuffing. Make stuffing with mix, ¼ cup water, and butter. Generously stuff each quail. Place in single layer in casserole. In saucepan, combine gravy mix, ½ cup water, preserves, and cloves. Bring to boil and pour over birds. Bake, uncovered, at 350 degrees for 1-1½ hours; baste occasionally. To hold, turn oven to 150 degrees and cover. Serve with currant jelly.

SAUTÉED RED SNAPPER

Patricia Hickernell Donese   *Yield: 2-4 servings*

1	**stick butter (no substitutes)**
1	**teaspoon dried parsley**
	Juice of 1 lemon
	Dash of Worcestershire sauce
2	**red snapper fillets (8 oz. each)**
⅓	**cup milk**
¼	**cup flour**
	Salt
	Pepper
1	**tablespoon shortening**

Warm butter in saucepan on medium-low heat until golden brown. Add parsley, lemon juice, and Worcestershire sauce. Mix lightly; keep warm over low heat. Dip fillets in milk, then into flour, salt, and pepper mixture. Melt shortening in non-stick fry pan. Sauté snapper on both sides until golden brown. Place on serving plate. Pour brown butter sauce over fillets.

SEAFOOD

BAKED TROUT

Carol Dickerson   *Yield: 1 serving*

**Whole rainbow trout
(about ½ pound)
Salt
Pepper
Powdered bouillon
Paprika
Parsley**

Rinse fish in cold water. Sprinkle outside surface and cavity with seasonings. Wrap fish in heavy-duty foil and bake at 325 degrees for 30 minutes.

SHRIMP JAMBALAYA

Rosalind Venable   *Yield: 8-10 servings*

½	**pound smoked sausage, sliced**
½	**pound ham, cubed**
¼	**cup oil**
1	**cup chopped onion**
1	**cup chopped green pepper**
1	**cup chopped celery**
1	**cup chopped green onion**
2	**cloves garlic, minced**
1	**can (16 oz.) tomatoes (drain and save liquid)**
1	**teaspoon thyme**
1	**teaspoon black pepper**
¼	**teaspoon cayenne pepper**
1	**teaspoon salt**
1	**cup rice, uncooked**
1½	**cups chicken stock**
1½	**tablespoons Worcestershire sauce**
2	**pounds peeled shrimp, uncooked**

In large pan, sauté sausage and ham in oil until lightly brown. Remove from pot. Sauté onion, green pepper, celery, green onion, and garlic in meat drippings until tender. Add tomatoes, thyme, black pepper, cayenne, and salt. Cook 5 minutes. Stir in rice. Mix together liquid from tomatoes, chicken stock, and Worcestershire sauce to equal 2½ cups. Add to vegetable mixture. Bring to boil and reduce heat to simmer. Add shrimp, ham, and sausage. Cook, uncovered, for 30 minutes, stirring occasionally, until shrimp and rice are done.

202

SEAFOOD

SHRIMP CREOLE

Carol Dickerson   *Yield: 4 servings*

2	tablespoons butter
2	onions, chopped
1	small green pepper, minced
4	stalks celery, chopped
1	cup water
2	tablespoons flour
1	teaspoon salt
	Pepper to taste
1	teaspoon chili powder or mace
6	green olives, sliced
2	cups chopped tomatoes
1	tablespoon vinegar
1	teaspoon sugar
½	teaspoon thyme
2	cups shrimp, cooked
3	cups cooked rice

Combine butter, onions, green pepper, and celery. Cook slowly until tender, about 10 minutes Combine water, flour, salt, pepper, and chili powder. Add slowly to onion mixture, stirring until smooth. Add olives, tomatoes, vinegar, sugar, and thyme. Simmer 10 minutes. Add shrimp; cook until hot, no more than 5 minutes. Serve over rice.

BAKED LEMON SOLE

Mary Houpis   *Yield: 4 servings*

¼	cup oil
¼	cup lemon juice
1	pound sole fillets
	Paprika
	Parmesan cheese, grated
	Cheddar cheese, sliced thin
	Bread crumbs

Mix oil and lemon juice and pour into pyrex dish. Add fish and turn to cover with oil mixture. Sprinkle with paprika. Top with cheese and bread crumbs. Bake at 350 degrees for 15-20 minutes.

To reduce caloric content, eliminate Cheddar cheese.

FISH IN SOUR CREAM

Susan Smith   *Yield: 3 servings*

1	pound fish fillets (sole or flounder)
1	stick butter, melted
1	tablespoon white wine
1	tablespoon lemon juice
1	tablespoon grated onion
2	tablespoons grated Parmesan cheese
¾	teaspoon dill weed
1	cup sour cream
¼	cup bread crumbs or corn flakes, crushed

Drain fish fillets well; set aside. Mix butter, wine, lemon juice, onion, and cheese. Dip fish in mixture; arrange in 9x13-inch dish. Pour remaining mixture over fillets. Sprinkle with dill. Spread fillets with sour cream and top with crumbs. Bake at 350 degrees for 25-30 minutes or until flaky.

GREEK SHRIMP PASTA

Lou Mason   *Yield: 12 servings*

1	pound shrimp, cooked, shelled, and deveined
1	pound Feta cheese, rinsed, dried, and crumbled
6	green onions, sliced thin
2	cans (14½ oz. each) tomato wedges, drained and chopped
1½	teaspoons dried oregano, crumbled
	Freshly ground pepper
1	pound vermicelli, broken in thirds, cooked, and drained

Combine first six ingredients in large bowl. Let stand at room temperature 1 hour. Add hot cooked vermicelli, toss well, and serve.

Vermicelli may be cooked ahead, drained well, and stored in plastic bag in refrigerator. Place in colander, run under hot tap water, and drain well before serving. This method can be used with any pasta.

GROUPER RENOISE

Stephen K. Dowe *Yield: 6 servings*

3   **pounds grouper (or any flaky white fish)**
2   **frozen lobster tails (7-8 oz. each), shelled**
1   **pint heavy cream**
    Salt and pepper
2   **lemons**
1   **egg yolk**
1   **stick sweet butter**
¼   **cup chopped shallots**
1   **cup dry white wine**
½   **pint fish velouté**
½   **ounce caviar, fine American Parsley**

FISH VELOUTÉ
2   **tablespoons butter**
2   **tablespoons flour**
¼   **teaspoon salt**
    Few grains of pepper
1   **cup fish stock (or use chicken stock)**

Cut grouper into 6 steaks, each about 6 ounces in size. In blender, mix trimmings from grouper, meat from 1 lobster tail, and ½ pint cream to make mousseline. (Add cream slowly.) Season with salt and pepper; add juice of ½ lemon and egg yolk. Make slit in each steak and stuff with mousseline. Heat an oven-proof skillet; add half the butter and lightly sauté shallots. Add seasoned steaks and cook for 1 minute; turn and cook for 1 minute more. Pour in wine, cover, and bake at 350 degrees for 10-15 minutes. Meanwhile, heat remaining cream and poach remaining lobster tail. Remove lobster from cream and slice into 6 equal slices. Reduce cream until it starts to thicken. Prepare velouté, add to cream, and simmer. Cover bottom of platter with ⅓ of velouté. Place cooked fish steaks on platter, forming a circle. Whip remaining softened butter into remaining velouté, and coat fish steaks. Cut remaining lemon into 6 slices. Place 1 slice of lemon and 1 slice of lobster on top of each steak. Garnish slices with caviar. Put parsley sprigs in center of platter.

Melt butter in pan; add flour mixed with seasonings. Stir until well blended. Add stock gradually, stirring constantly. (Wire whisk works well.) Continue cooking until slightly thickened.

Stephen Dowe, executive chef of Kiawah Island in South Carolina, is the recipient of many culinary awards.

DESTIN SHRIMP

Ann C. Karter   *Yield: 10-12 servings*

7-8   **pounds uncooked shrimp (in the shell)**
1   **pound butter**
1   **pound margarine**
6   **ounces Worcestershire sauce**
6-8   **tablespoons black pepper**
1   **teaspoon rosemary**
2   **tablespoons lemon juice**
1   **teaspoon Tabasco**
4   **teaspoons salt**
       Sliced French bread

Spread shrimp in single layer on 3-4 jelly roll pans. In saucepan, melt butter and margarine; add Worcestershire, pepper, rosemary, lemon juice, Tabasco, and salt. Mix well. Pour butter mixture over shrimp on pans. Bake at 400 degrees for 20 minutes. Use bread to dip into butter sauce.

CRAB-SHRIMP CASSEROLE

Doris H. Ponitz   *Yield: 6-8 servings*

1-2   **cups shrimp, cooked**
1   **cup crab meat, cooked (canned or fresh)**
2   **cups cooked wild rice**
1   **cup cooked white rice**
1¼   **cups finely chopped celery**
1   **medium onion, finely chopped**
1   **green pepper, chopped**
1   **jar (2 oz.) pimentos, chopped**
3   **cans (10¾ oz. each) cream of mushroom soup**
1   **pound fresh mushrooms, sliced**
       Butter

Mix 1 cup of shrimp with crab meat, wild and white rice, celery, onion, green pepper, pimentos, and 1½ cans of soup. (If too dry, add a little water.) Bake, covered, at 350 degrees for 1½ hours. To make sauce, heat remaining soup in double boiler. (Thin with cream, if too thick.) Add mushrooms, browned in butter, and remaining shrimp to soup. Serve with generous spoonfuls of sauce.

May be made ahead, refrigerated, and reheated.

SARASOTA SCALLOP SAUTÉ

Valerie J. Doll   *Yield: 2-4 servings*

4	tablespoons butter
1	clove garlic, minced
½	teaspoon salt
⅛	teaspoon pepper
½	teaspoon paprika
1	pound bay scallops
2	tablespoons fresh parsley
3	tablespoons lemon juice

I n large skillet, heat 2 tablespoons butter with garlic, salt, pepper, and paprika. Add enough scallops to cover bottom of skillet without crowding. Cook quickly on high heat, stirring occasionally, until golden, about 5-7 minutes. (Repeat until all scallops are cooked, keeping cooked ones warm.) In same skillet, heat parsley, lemon juice, and remaining butter; pour over scallops and serve.

May be served as appetizer for 4-6 persons. Serve on slices of toasted French bread or in scallop shells.

SHRIMP IN BEER

Jane Poe   *Yield: 4 servings*

2	pounds large raw shrimp
2	bottles of beer
1	clove garlic, peeled
2	teaspoons salt
½	teaspoon thyme
2	bay leaves
	Juice of 1 lemon
1	teaspoon celery seed
	Dash of Tabasco
1	tablespoon chopped parsley
	Butter, melted

W ash shrimp, but do not remove shells. Combine remaining ingredients, except butter, and heat to boiling. Add shrimp and return to boil. Reduce heat and simmer, uncovered, until pink, 2-5 minutes; drain. Peel and serve with melted butter.

Add dash of Tabasco and garlic powder to melted butter for extra flavor.

EASY WOK DINNER

Sally Hawthorne   *Yield: 4 servings*

2-3 cups bite-sized
     vegetables (any combina-
     tion of broccoli, celery,
     onion, cauliflower, snow
     peas, green beans, water
     chestnuts)
1   tablespoon peanut oil
     Soy sauce
2   cups bay scallops, washed
     and drained, or boned
     chicken breasts, sliced
     Black pepper
     Cashews or almonds
     (optional)
     Bean sprouts (optional)

Sauté vegetables in peanut oil in hot wok or skillet 2-3 minutes for crisp vegetables, 5-6 minutes for softer vegetables. Sprinkle with soy sauce to taste. In separate skillet (non-stick) quickly sauté scallops or chicken. (Add a little water with chicken; scallops need none.) Season with pepper. Add to vegetables and toss quickly. Sprinkle with cashews or almonds and bean sprouts, if desired.

Good alone or with bread sticks or fried rice.

SCALLOP CRÊPES

Jane Corbly   *Yield: 10-12 servings*

24   crêpes
1   pound bay scallops or sea
     scallops, cut into small
     pieces
1   can (10¾ oz.) cream of
     mushroom soup
1⅓ cups sour cream
⅓   cup dry white wine
1½   tablespoons minced onion
½   teaspoon dried tarragon
1   cup sliced fresh mush-
     rooms (optional)
     Salt and pepper to taste
½   pound Colby or Cheddar
     cheese, sliced julienne
½   pound Swiss cheese, sliced
     julienne
     Grated Parmesan cheese

Use basic recipe for crêpes (see Index) or make crêpes from your favorite recipe. Place scallops in boiling water for 3 minutes until tender; drain. Do not overcook. Combine soup, sour cream, wine, onion, tarragon, mushrooms, salt, and pepper; mix thoroughly. Put dollop of soup mixture on each crêpe; add a few pieces of scallops, a slice of Swiss cheese, a slice of Colby cheese, and a sprinkling of Parmesan cheese. Roll crêpes, tucking in ends, and place on jelly roll pan. Bake at 325 degrees for 20 minutes.

SEAFOOD

BAKED SCALLOPS

Mrs. William R. Thompson   *Yield: 1 serving*

4-6 ounces bay scallops or
     sea scallops, cut up
1   tablespoon sherry
2   ounces Monterey Jack
     cheese
1   tablespoon bread crumbs
1   tablespoon butter or
     margarine

Put scallops in au gratin dish or other small oven-proof casserole. Sprinkle sherry over scallops. Slice cheese about ⅛ inch thick and place on scallops. Sprinkle with bread crumbs. Dot with butter. Bake at 500 degrees for 10 minutes. Do not overcook or scallops will become tough.

CIOPPINO

Susan T. Sauer   *Yield: 8 servings*

2   cups chopped onion
½   cup chopped green pepper
6   cloves garlic, minced
½   cup olive oil
1   can (28 oz.) Italian
     tomatoes
1   can (6 oz.) tomato paste
2   cups dry red wine
1   lemon, thinly sliced
1   cup chopped parsley
1   teaspoon basil
1   teaspoon oregano
1   teaspoon salt
     Freshly ground black
     pepper
2   pounds halibut filets (or
     other firm fish), cut into
     2-inch chunks
4-8 lobster tails, shelled
2   pounds shrimp, shelled
     and cleaned
1   pound scallops

In large kettle, combine onion, green pepper, and garlic in olive oil. Cook over low heat for 10 minutes, stirring occasionally. Add tomatoes, tomato paste, wine, lemon, ½ cup parsley, and all other seasonings. Bring to boil; reduce heat, cover, and simmer for 20 minutes. Add halibut and lobster tails; simmer, covered, 15 minutes. Add shrimp and scallops and simmer 10 more minutes or until all seafood is done. Serve sprinkled with remaining chopped parsley.

Wonderful with French bread.

CRABMEAT GRUYÈRE

Ann C. Karter   *Yield: 6 servings*

¼ pound sliced fresh mush-
    rooms
7 tablespoons butter
6 tablespoons flour
3 cups half-and-half
¼ cup chopped onion
3 tablespoons chopped
    pimento
1⅓ cups shredded Gruyère
    cheese
1 cup freshly grated Par-
    mesan cheese
8 ounces fresh or frozen
    crabmeat (thawed)

Sauté mushrooms in 1 table-spoon butter; set aside. In saucepan, melt 6 tablespoons butter and blend in flour until smooth. Gradually add half-and-half and cook, stirring constantly, until sauce is thickened. Add onion, pimento, Gruyère, and Parmesan. Stir until cheeses are melted. Add mushrooms and crabmeat. Heat until thoroughly warmed. Serve over patty shells, toasted rusks, or toast points.

May be made ahead, refrigerated, and reheated.

FISH RAGOUT

Charlye Maloney   *Yield: 6-8 servings*

½ cup chopped onion
1 clove garlic, minced
¼ cup chopped green pepper
3 stalks celery, sliced
    diagonally
3 carrots, cut julienne
2 tablespoons oil
2 cans (16 oz. each) toma-
    toes, undrained
2 chicken bouillon cubes
1 teaspoon salt
¼ teaspoon thyme
⅛ teaspoon pepper
¼ teaspoon basil
3 tablespoons minced parsley
2 pounds fish (fresh or
    frozen sole, cod, or
    flounder), cut into 1-inch
    pieces

Sauté onion, garlic, green pepper, celery, and carrots in oil for 5 minutes. Add other ingredients, except fish, and 1 table-spoon parsley. Cover and cook for 20 minutes. Add fish. Simmer 5-10 minutes or until fish is cooked. Sprinkle with remaining parsley. Serve in bowls or on rice.

STERLING IDEAS

Brunch & Lunch

To bake a casserole ahead, deduct 20 minutes from the specified time. Cool and store casserole, covered, in the refrigerator. Finish by baking 30 minutes more (ten minutes for rewarming plus the last 20 minutes specified).

When using glass baking pans, always lower the oven temperature by 25 degrees.

Always add curry powder and chili powder when you are browning ingredients; do not add directly to a sauce. Browning removes the bitter taste of the curry or chili powder.

When food boils over in the oven, sprinkle the burned surface with a little salt. This will stop the smoking and neutralize the burned odor. It also will make the spot easier to clean later.

When a recipe calls for a quantity of melted butter, always measure the butter after melting, not before. The butter expands when heated.

Keep cans of grated Parmesan or Romano cheese on a cool, dry kitchen shelf. The cheese will not lump as it does in the refrigerator.

Macaroni doubles itself when cooked. Noodles increase by a third when cooked.

A generous pinch of basil in the boiling water before spaghetti is added will give the spaghetti an excellent flavor.

To distinguish a hard-cooked egg from an uncooked egg, spin the egg on its side. If it is hard-cooked, the egg will spin like a top; if it is raw, it will wobble but not spin.

Freeze leftover egg whites in ice cube tray, one per cube; then remove and store in a plastic bag in the freezer. Thaw as needed and use like fresh egg whites.

CHEESE SOUFFLÉ

Sally Forbes   *Yield: 4 servings*

¼	cup butter
½	cup flour
1	teaspoon salt
	Dash of cayenne pepper
1	pint milk
1	cup grated Parmesan cheese
6	eggs, separated

Melt butter over low heat. Add flour, salt, and cayenne. Stir until well blended. Gradually pour in milk, mixing with rotary beater. Boil 2 minutes or cook 10 minutes in double boiler. Mixture will be very thick. Add cheese; stir until melted. Remove from heat; stir a little cheese mixture into slightly beaten egg yolks. Stir egg yolk mixture into cheese base. Beat egg whites until very stiff, but not dry. Fold carefully into egg yolk-cheese mixture. Pour into ungreased 1½-quart casserole, leaving at least 1 inch at the top. Bake at 325 degrees for 50 minutes. Serve immediately.

MARYLEE'S DISH

Mary Houpis   *Yield: 6 servings*

1	can (15 oz.) tomato sauce
¼	cup butter
6	slices American cheese
6	ounces cooked ham, cubed
5	eggs

Heat tomato sauce with butter until slightly thickened. Spread evenly in 9x13-inch pan. Place cheese slices over tomato sauce and top with ham. Scramble eggs just until they begin to set and pour over ham. Pour white sauce over eggs, covering completely. Bake at 350 degrees for ½ hour. Cool 5 minutes before cutting into serving pieces.

WHITE SAUCE

4	tablespoons butter or margarine
3-4	tablespoons flour
2	cups milk

Melt butter; add flour, stirring constantly. Slowly add milk; cook and stir until thickened.

STEAMED CHEESE PUDDING

Maggie Spriggs   *Yield: 4-6 servings*

6   eggs, separated
¼   cup flour
1   cup milk
¼   teaspoon salt
¼   teaspoon pepper
1   teaspoon minced bouquet garni (Fines Herbes)
¾   cup grated Parmesan cheese
¼   cup grated Romano cheese

SAUCE
1   clove garlic, minced
1   teaspoon oil
2   cups tomato sauce
   Salt and pepper

Beat egg whites until stiff; set aside. Beat egg yolks. Blend flour with a little milk until smooth; add remaining milk and cook, stirring constantly, until thickened. Slowly stir warm mixture into egg yolks. Return mixture to pan and cook a little longer. Stir in salt, pepper, herbs, and cheeses. Fold in egg whites. Pour into greased 1½-quart mold, cover tightly with greased lid or foil, and place on rack in kettle. Add enough boiling water to come halfway up side of mold. Cover kettle and steam 45 minutes. Unmold and serve with hot tomato sauce.

Sauté garlic in oil, add tomato sauce, and heat. Season to taste with salt and pepper.

HAM AND CHEESE BAKE

Kathy Cavers   *Yield: 12-14 servings*

12   slices bread, cubed
½   pound Cheddar cheese, grated
2   cups cubed ham
7   eggs
1¼   cups milk
2   tablespoons minced onion
2   dashes of Tabasco

In greased 9x13-inch pan, layer bread cubes, cheese, and ham. Mix eggs and milk in blender on medium speed for 20 seconds. Add onion and Tabasco; pour over bread mixture. Refrigerate overnight. Bake at 325 degrees for 40 minutes, covered, and 15-20 minutes, uncovered.

SAVORY CHEESE-FILLED PASTRIES

JoAnn Saunders Maness   *Yield: 6 servings*

6	frozen patty shells
1	tablespoon butter
1	cup sliced fresh mush-rooms
¼	cup chopped cooked ham
2	eggs
⅓	cup half-and-half
1	cup shredded Danish samsoe, danbo, or tybo cheese, firmly packed (If none of these is available, Muenster may be used.)
½	teaspoon cornstarch
	Dash of cayenne

Bake patty shells until crisp, according to package directions. Sauté mushrooms in butter until golden brown; stir in ham and set aside. Lightly beat eggs and half-and-half together. Add cheese, cornstarch, and cayenne; mix well. Place baked patty shells on baking sheet. Partially fill shells with ham and mushrooms; add cheese mixture until shells are full. Bake at 400 degrees for 20 minutes. Heat remaining sauce just until hot and spoon over baked shells just before serving.

Delicious served with fruit for special brunch or luncheon.

BRUNCH PIZZA

Lois Ross   *Yield: 6-8 servings*

1	pound pork sausage
1	package (8 count) refrigerator crescent rolls
1	cup frozen loose-pack hashed brown potatoes, thawed
1	cup shredded cheese (Cheddar or Monterey Jack)
5	eggs
¼	cup milk
½	teaspoon salt
⅛	teaspoon pepper
2	tablespoons grated Parmesan cheese

Cook and drain sausage. Separate crescent dough into 8 triangles. Place on ungreased 12-inch pizza pan with points toward center. Press dough over bottom and sides of pan to form crust. Spoon sausage over crust. Sprinkle with potatoes and top with shredded cheese. Beat eggs, milk, salt, and pepper; pour over cheese layer. Sprinkle with Parmesan cheese. Bake at 375 degrees for 25-30 minutes.

DEVILED EGGS DIVINE

Jean Perry   *Yield: 6-8 servings*

1	package (10 oz.) frozen broccoli spears
6-8	hard-cooked eggs
1	can (4½ oz.) deviled ham
¼	teaspoon Worcestershire sauce
½	teaspoon grated onion
¼	teaspoon salt
½	teaspoon dry mustard
½	teaspoon curry powder
1	tablespoon mayonnaise
	Paprika
1½	cups soft bread crumbs
1	tablespoon melted butter

SAUCE

1½	tablespoons butter
2	tablespoons flour
½	teaspoon dry mustard
½	teaspoon salt
1	cup milk
1	cup grated Cheddar cheese

Cook broccoli according to package directions. Slice eggs lengthwise and remove yolks. Mash yolks and add deviled ham, Worcestershire sauce, onion, salt, mustard, curry, and mayonnaise. Mix well and fill egg whites. Place broccoli in buttered 7x11-inch pan; place eggs on top. Sprinkle with paprika. Prepare sauce and pour over eggs. Top with bread crumbs mixed with butter. Bake at 350 degrees for 25 minutes.

In saucepan, melt butter and blend in flour and seasonings; slowly add milk and stir. Add cheese. Heat until thick and smooth.

DUTCH CHEESE TART

Becki Sammons   *Yield: 6 servings*

10	ounces Edam or Gouda cheese
5	tablespoons melted butter or margarine
1	cup soft bread crumbs
3	medium tomatoes, sliced
6-8	small mushroom caps or 1 can (4 oz.), drained

Shred 4 ounces cheese (1 cup). Cut remaining cheese into thin strips. Blend shredded cheese, 4 tablespoons melted butter, and bread crumbs; press firmly on bottom and sides of well-greased 9-inch pie pan. Cover with layer of sliced cheese, then tomato slices. Top with mushroom caps. Brush with remaining 1 tablespoon melted butter. Bake at 350 degrees for 20 minutes.

BRUNCH EGGS

Mrs. Ed Rodabaugh   *Yield: 8 servings*

¾-1 **pound Monterey Jack cheese, grated**
24 **ounces cottage cheese**
½ **teaspoon salt**
¼ **teaspoon cayenne pepper**
6 **eggs, beaten**
¼ **cup melted margarine or butter**
1 **cup milk**
1 **cup Bisquick**
½ **cup of one of the following: canned seeded green chilies; chopped cooked bacon; sliced mushrooms; canned French fried onions**

Mix cheeses, salt, pepper, eggs, margarine, milk, and Bisquick and pour into greased 9x13-inch pan. Add green chilies or optional choice. (Press into mixture; do not stir.) Bake at 350 degrees for 35-40 minutes until mixture is solid and begins to brown around edge.

SLIM SPINACH QUICHE

Mrs. Thomas Johnson   *Yield: 4-6 servings*

CRUST
2 **cups cooked brown rice**
1 **egg**
⅔ **cup grated Parmesan cheese**

Mix rice, egg, and cheese; press in buttered 10-inch pie pan and refrigerate.

FILLING
3 **eggs**
1 **cup milk**
½ **teaspoon salt**
¼ **teaspoon nutmeg**
½ **cup shredded Swiss cheese**
1 **package (10 oz.) frozen chopped spinach, thawed and drained**

Place eggs, milk, salt, and nutmeg in blender and blend. Add Swiss cheese and spinach and blend until smooth. Pour into prepared rice crust. Bake at 350 degrees for 45-60 minutes. Let stand about 5 minutes before cutting. If crust browns too quickly, cover with foil.

CURRIED EGGS WITH SHRIMP SAUCE

Betty Arnold   *Yield: 8 servings*

8   hard-cooked eggs
½   teaspoon salt
½   teaspoon paprika
½   teaspoon curry powder
¼   teaspoon dry mustard
⅓   cup mayonnaise
1   cup soft bread crumbs
2   tablespoons butter or
       margarine, melted

SHRIMP SAUCE
2   tablespoons butter or
       margarine
2   tablespoons flour
1   cup milk
1   can (10¾ oz.) cream of
       shrimp soup
½   cup shredded Cheddar
       cheese
1   can (4½ oz.) shrimp,
       drained

Cut eggs in half and combine yolks with seasonings and mayonnaise. Stuff egg whites with mixture. Arrange eggs in flat baking dish and pour shrimp sauce over eggs. Sprinkle with crumbs mixed with butter. Bake at 350 degrees for 20-25 minutes or until heated through and crumbs are crisp.

Stir flour into melted butter in pan and cook until bubbly. Slowly add milk, stirring constantly until thickened. Blend soup into white sauce. Add cheese and stir until melted. Add shrimp.

CHIPPED BEEF AND ARTICHOKES

Chris Saunders   *Yield: 6 servings*

1   carton (16 oz.) sour cream
¼   cup white wine or
       vermouth
1   tablespoon grated
       Parmesan cheese
1   teaspoon arrowroot
       Dash of Tabasco
3   packages (2½ oz. each)
       chipped beef, frizzled in
       butter or margarine
1   can (14 oz.) artichoke
       hearts, cut in half
6   toast cups or patty shells

Put sour cream, wine, cheese, arrowroot, and Tabasco in double boiler. Heat until hot and thickened. Gently fold in chipped beef and artichoke hearts. Serve in toast cups or patty shells.

CRÊPES À LA FLORENTINE

Mrs. Paul W. Wheaton   *Yield: 12 crêpes*

CRÊPES
½   cup cold water
½   cup cold milk
2   large eggs
¼   teaspoon salt
1   cup sifted all-purpose flour
2   tablespoons melted butter

Put crêpe ingredients in blender and blend at high speed 1 minute. Refrigerate at least 2 hours. Use scant ¼ cup of batter to make each crêpe. Cook quickly in buttered crêpe pan or frying pan. Makes 12 crêpes, 6½-inch diameter. (Crêpes may be frozen between waxed paper.)

SAUCE
4   tablespoons butter
5   tablespoons flour
2¾   cups milk
¼   cup whipping cream
     Salt and pepper
     Nutmeg
1   cup grated Swiss cheese
     (reserve ½ for topping)

Melt butter; add flour and heat until bubbly. Gradually add milk and whipping cream; stir until thickened. Add salt, pepper, and nutmeg to taste. Add ½ cup cheese and stir until blended.

FILLING
2   tablespoons butter
1   cup sliced fresh mush-
     rooms
6   green onions (with tops),
     chopped
1   package (10 oz.) frozen
     chopped spinach, thawed
     and well drained
1   cup cottage cheese
1   egg

Sauté mushrooms and green onions in butter; drain. Combine with spinach, cottage cheese, and egg. Add ½ cup sauce.

To assemble: Place equal portions of filling on each crêpe, roll, and place in 9x13-inch pan. Top with remaining sauce and sprinkle with remaining cheese. Bake at 350 degrees for 20 minutes or until cheese melts and crêpes are heated through.

LEMON PEPPER SANDWICH LOAF

Kate Whitehead   *Yield: 6 servings*

1	loaf (1 lb.) unsliced white bread
½	cup lemon pepper butter (see recipe below)
1	tablespoon prepared mustard
2	teaspoons poppy seed
8	slices Swiss cheese
8	slices bacon, cooked and crumbled

C ut bread loaf almost through into 9 slices. Combine lemon pepper butter, mustard, and poppy seed; mix well. Set aside 3 tablespoons mixture. Spread remainder on cut surfaces of bread. Place 1 slice of cheese in each cut; sprinkle bacon over cheese. Spread reserved lemon pepper butter on top and sides of bread. Bake on ungreased baking sheet at 350 degrees for 15-20 minutes.

LEMON PEPPER BUTTER

1	pound butter
¼	cup snipped chives
1½	teaspoons grated lemon peel
2	tablespoons lemon juice
½	teaspoon freshly ground pepper

Cream butter until light and fluffy. Add chives, lemon peel, lemon juice, and pepper. Mix and store in refrigerator.

SAUSAGE SQUARES

Shirlee O'Loughlin   *Yield: 10-12 servings*

1	cup Bisquick
⅓	cup milk
3	tablespoons mayonnaise
1	pound hot sausage (or ½ hot, ½ regular)
1	large onion, chopped
1	egg
2	cups grated cheese
2	cans (4 oz. each) chopped green chilies

M ix Bisquick, milk, and 2 tablespoons mayonnaise; place in well-greased 9x13-inch casserole and pat down. Sauté sausage and onion; drain well. Spread sausage and onion on top of Bisquick mixture. Mix egg, 1 tablespoon mayonnaise, cheese, and chilies, and pour over sausage. Bake at 400 degrees for 30 minutes. Cut into squares and serve.

May be cut into smaller squares and served as appetizer.

MAKE-AHEAD SAUSAGE CASSEROLE

Susan S. Seyfarth   *Yield: 10-12 servings*

1	pound pork sausage
2	packages (10 oz. each) frozen chopped spinach
2	packages (10 oz. each) frozen chopped broccoli
1	can (10¾ oz.) cream of mushroom soup
½	cup mayonnaise
½	teaspoon dill weed
½	teaspoon pepper
½	teaspoon Beau Monde seasoning
	Seasoned salt to taste
1	teaspoon grated lemon rind
3	tablespoons lemon juice
½	cup chopped walnuts
1	cup shredded Cheddar cheese
2	large tomatoes, peeled and diced
1	can (2.8 oz.) fried onion rings

Cook sausage and drain off fat. Thaw vegetables and drain well. Combine all ingredients, except cheese, tomatoes, and onion rings, and put in 9x13-inch casserole. This can be done a day or so ahead. Before baking, place cheese and tomatoes on top. Bake at 350 degrees for ½ hour. Sprinkle onions on top and bake 15 minutes longer.

QUESO FUNDIDO

Sandy Krieger   *Yield: 4-6 servings*

2	pounds stew meat
2	tablespoons shortening
1¾	cups water
¼	cup chili powder, California mild
¼	cup chili powder, New Mexico hot
2	tablespoons barbecue sauce
1	tablespoon bouillon granules (mixed in water)
5	garlic cloves, finely chopped
1	onion, finely chopped
1	tablespoon vegetable oil
1	tablespoon flour
2	teaspoons oregano
¼	teaspoon ground cumin
	Salt to taste
	Flour tortillas
1-1½	pounds Monterey Jack cheese, shredded
	Paprika
	Lime wedges
	Sour cream

Cube meat; brown in shortening. Add water and simmer, covered, 1 hour or more. Add chili powders, barbecue sauce, more water if needed, and bouillon. Sauté garlic and onion in oil until tender, but not browned. Add flour and cook 1 minute. Add garlic mixture, oregano, and cumin to meat mixture. Cover and simmer 2 hours. Salt to taste. Sprinkle water between flour tortillas; wrap in foil and heat in oven. Divide shredded cheese equally, covering half of each serving plate; sprinkle with paprika. Cover remaining half of each plate with equal serving of meat mixture. Microwave each plate until cheese melts and sauce is hot, ½-1 minute. Spoon cheese on warm tortillas and top with meat sauce. Squeeze juice of lime over meat sauce, add sour cream, and roll up.

This is a great dish for a casual, fun occasion. Give each guest a plate and let him make his own. Messy, but delicious!

SAUSAGE ROLL

Jane Poe   *Yield: 2 loaves*

1	**package dry yeast**
1½	**cups warm water**
1½	**teaspoons sugar**
1½	**teaspoons salt**
4	**tablespoons oil**
4-5	**cups all-purpose flour**
1	**large onion, chopped**
1½	**pounds bulk Italian sausage**
4	**eggs**
1	**pound mozzarella cheese, shredded**

Dissolve yeast in water; stir in sugar, salt, oil, and 2 cups flour. Beat until smooth. Stir in remaining flour and knead for 5 minutes. Place in greased bowl (turning to grease all surfaces of dough) and let rise about 45 minutes. Punch down and divide for 2 loaves. Sauté onion and sausage; remove from heat and add 2 lightly beaten eggs plus 2 egg whites (reserve yolks). Roll out 1 piece of dough to size of cookie sheet. Spread with half of sausage mixture and sprinkle with half of cheese. Roll, starting at long side, and place, seam up, on ungreased cookie sheet. Repeat with second piece of dough. Brush with lightly beaten egg yolks and bake at 350 degrees for 25-30 minutes. Slice and serve.

MACARONI DELUXE

Lois Ann Gerhard   *Yield: 8 servings*

1   package (8 oz.) macaroni, uncooked
2   cups milk
2   cans (10¾ oz. each) cream of mushroom soup
1   small onion, chopped
4   hard-cooked eggs, diced
2   cups diced cooked chicken or turkey
½   pound Velveeta cheese, cubed
2   cans (4 oz. each) mushroom stems and pieces, drained
    Buttered bread crumbs
    Grated Parmesan cheese

Mix all ingredients, except bread crumbs and Parmesan cheese. Place in 2-quart casserole, cover, and let stand in refrigerator overnight. Sprinkle with buttered crumbs and Parmesan cheese. Bake at 350 degrees for 1 hour.

VIII | Desserts & Sweets

STERLING IDEAS

Desserts & Sweets

For easy handling, bake children's cupcakes in flat-bottomed ice cream cones.

To melt chocolate squares, place them in their wrappers, seam side up, on a plate and microwave on medium for one minute per square. Transfer directly to mixing bowl. To bring out the chocolate flavor, add a little salt.

Protect vanilla and all extracts from light and excessive heat by keeping the bottle in the box in which it comes.

To keep juice from overflowing fruit pies, insert a small cornucopia of paper into the center of the pie, twice the height of the pie.

Tart shells can more easily be formed on the bottoms of overturned tart or muffin pans.

When baking white or brown sugar cookies, substitute a cup of applesauce for sour milk. The flavor is better and the cookies keep moist longer.

A pinch of salt added to the sugar in icings will prevent graining.

Heavy cream doubles in volume when whipped. Freeze dollops of whipped cream on a cookie sheet, then transfer to a plastic bag. Handy for instant garnish.

To obtain maximum volume, egg whites for meringue should be brought to room temperature before beating. Remember not to tap the beaters on bowl, as jarring will deflate the egg whites.

For black frosting for Halloween cakes, add blue food coloring to chocolate frosting.

To warm liqueur for flaming, microwave 1/4 cup on high, uncovered, for 15 seconds.

To soften brown sugar, cover tightly with plastic wrap and microwave on high for 30 seconds.

If a portion of egg yolk falls into separated egg whites, moisten a cloth with cold water and touch to the yolk; yolk will adhere to the cloth.

PERFECT PIE CRUST

Blanche J. Palmeter   *Yield: 2 crusts (9-inch)*

2   **cups flour**
1   **teaspoon salt**
⅔   **cup shortening**
6-7 **tablespoons ice water**

Measure flour into large bowl; add salt. Cut ½ of shortening into flour with pastry blender until mixture is coarse-textured. Cut remaining shortening into flour until mixture is finely blended. (Mixture should be crumbly.) Add ice water, a little at a time, and mix gently and quickly with fork until mixture is just moist. Form 2 equal balls of dough and place on floured surface. Flatten balls slightly with palm of hand, turn to cover both sides with flour, and roll out with quick, short motions. (Keep rolling pin well floured.) When desired size, place bottom crust carefully in pan. Add filling. Cut slits or design into top crust and place over filling in pan. Seal pastry edges together by pressing gently with fork tines or rounded edge of knife handle. Run sharp edge of knife around rim of pie to trim excess dough. Pie is ready for oven. (Children love to cover excess dough with a little milk, sugar, and cinnamon and bake along with mother's pie for 10-15 minutes or until golden brown. A great snack, warm from oven, with glass of milk.)

This pie crust is rich and flaky; it will steal attention from pie filling. For best results, do not roll too thin and do not handle more than necessary. For 1-crust pie, use 1½ cups flour and adjust ingredients accordingly. To make pie shell, prick crust in many places and bake at 425 degrees for 15 minutes or until lightly browned.

APPLE CREAM PIE

Jan Rudd   *Yield: 8 servings*

1   tablespoon cornstarch
½   cup sugar
¼   cup heavy cream
3   tablespoons butter
1   tablespoon lemon juice
1   can (1 lb. 4 oz.) sliced
     pie apples
     Pie shell (9-inch), baked

TOPPING
1   package (8 oz.) cream
     cheese
⅓   cup sugar
1   egg
½   cup chopped walnuts
½   cup grated coconut

Combine cornstarch and sugar in saucepan; stir in cream and mix well. Cook over medium heat until boiling; stir in butter and lemon juice. Add drained apples and simmer for 10 minutes, stirring occasionally. Cool. Spoon into baked crust.

Beat cream cheese and sugar until fluffy. Beat in egg only until well mixed. Spoon over apple filling and sprinkle with walnuts and coconut. Bake at 350 degrees for 15-20 minutes or until topping is brown. Cool before serving.

OLD-FASHIONED RAISIN PIE

Josephine F. Bishop   *Yield: 6 servings*

2   cups seedless raisins
2   cups water
1   teaspoon grated lemon rind
½   cup granulated sugar
2   tablespoons cornstarch
½   teaspoon salt
2   tablespoons lemon juice
1   tablespoon butter or
     margarine
     Pastry for two-crust pie
     (8-inch)

Combine raisins with water and lemon rind; cook 5 minutes. Blend sugar, cornstarch, and salt. Slowly stir a little of raisin liquid into sugar mixture. Stir sugar mixture into raisin mixture. Cook until thick and clear, stirring constantly. Remove from heat and blend in lemon juice and butter. Pour into pastry-lined 8-inch pie pan. Cover with lattice crust. Bake at 450 degrees for 25 minutes. Cool before cutting.

FRESH BLUEBERRY PIE

Doris J. Conway   *Yield: 8 servings*

1   pint fresh blueberries
     Prepared graham cracker
     crust (8-inch)
1   jar (8 oz.) currant jelly
1   cup sour cream

Wash blueberries; put in crust. Heat currant jelly slowly until melted and pour over blueberries. Spread sour cream over top. Refrigerate.

To make special dessert for Fourth of July, garnish each slice of blueberry pie with a strawberry.

PUMPKIN-APPLE PIE

Jean Collins   *Yield: 8 servings*

½   cup packed brown sugar
1   tablespoon cornstarch
1   teaspoon cinnamon
½   teaspoon salt
½   cup water
2   tablespoons butter
4   tart medium apples (4
     cups), peeled, cored, and
     sliced
1   tablespoon lemon juice
     Pie shell (9-inch), unbaked
1   egg, beaten
1   cup canned pumpkin
½   cup sugar
¼   teaspoon salt
½   teaspoon ground ginger
⅛   teaspoon ground cloves
1   can (5⅓ oz.) evaporated
     milk
     Whipped cream

In medium saucepan, combine brown sugar, cornstarch, cinnamon, ¼ teaspoon salt, water, and butter; stir and mix over medium heat until boiling. Add apples, cover, and cook 5 minutes, stirring occasionally, until crisp-tender. Remove from heat and add lemon juice. Spread hot apples evenly in unbaked pie shell. Combine egg, pumpkin, sugar, remaining salt, and spices; blend in evaporated milk. Carefully pour over apples. (Edges must be high on pie crust; this is a full pie.) Bake at 375 degrees for 40-45 minutes, until pumpkin is just set. Cool and serve with whipped cream.

229

STRAWBERRIES AND CREAM PIE

Laurie Wilderman (Mrs. John G.)   *Yield: 6-8 servings*

½   cup powdered sugar, sifted
½   teaspoon vanilla
¼   teaspoon almond extract
1   package (3 oz.) cream cheese
½   cup whipping cream, whipped
   Pie shell (9 or 10-inch), baked
2-3   cups fresh whole or halved strawberries

GLAZE
1   cup crushed strawberries
1   cup sugar
   Pinch of salt
½   cup water
3   tablespoons cornstarch dissolved in ¼ cup cold water
3-5   drops red food coloring (optional)
1   tablespoon lemon juice

Beat sugar, extracts, and cream cheese until creamy. Fold in whipped cream. Spread evenly over bottom of pie shell. Chill. Arrange strawberries on cream layer. Carefully cover with cooled glaze. Chill several hours or overnight.

Combine crushed strawberries, sugar, salt, and water in saucepan. Bring to a boil. Add cornstarch mixture, stirring constantly, and cook until clear and thickened. Strain; add food coloring, if desired. Stir in lemon juice. Cool.

PEANUT BUTTER CHEESE PIE

Ann McGhee   *Yield: 6-8 servings*

2   packages (3 oz. each) cream cheese, softened
¾   cup powdered sugar, sifted
½   cup peanut butter (smooth)
2   tablespoons milk
1   envelope dessert topping mix
   Graham cracker pie shell (8-inch)

In small mixer bowl, beat cream cheese and sugar until light and fluffy. Add peanut butter and milk, beating until smooth and creamy. Prepare dessert topping according to package directions. Fold into peanut butter mixture. Turn into prepared crust. Chill 5-6 hours or overnight.

RUSSIAN APRICOT PASTRIES

Kathleen Dixon   *Yield: 5-6 dozen*

PASTRY

4	cups flour
1½	cups margarine
1	package dry yeast
½	cup warm water
4	egg yolks
¼	cup milk

Blend sifted flour with margarine until mealy. Dissolve yeast in water (105-115 degrees F.) until bubbly. Add egg yolks and milk to yeast mixture; add to flour mixture and mix until dough pulls away from bowl. Knead on floured board for 3 minutes. Cut into 3 equal portions. Between waxed paper, roll out 1 piece of dough large enough (about 11x16 inches) to line greased 10x15-inch pan, bringing dough halfway up sides of pan.

FILLINGS

4	cups ground walnuts
1	cup sugar
2	teaspoons cinnamon
1	can (12 oz.) apricot cake filling

Mix walnuts, sugar, and cinnamon. Spread over pastry in pan, reserving ½ cup for topping. Roll second piece of dough large enough (10x15 inches) to cover layer of nuts; place on top of nuts and spread with apricot filling. Roll third piece of dough (10x15 inches) and place on top of apricot filling. Bake at 350 degrees for 30 minutes.

TOPPING

4	egg whites
10	tablespoons sugar

Beat egg whites until stiff. Gradually add sugar. Frost top of pastry with egg white mixture and sprinkle with remaining ½ cup nuts. Return to oven and bake at 425 degrees for 5-10 minutes longer or until browned. Cut into diamonds while hot. Leave in pan until cool.

PUMPKIN CHIFFON PIE

Mrs. Robert (Stevie) Schriber   *Yield: 8 servings*

2   envelopes unflavored
    gelatin
⅓   cup light brown sugar,
    firmly packed
½   teaspoon salt
1   teaspoon cinnamon
1½ tablespoons dark molasses
3   eggs, separated
½   cup milk
1   can (1 lb.) pumpkin
½   cup sugar
1   cup whipping cream,
    whipped
    Pie shell (9-inch), baked

In medium saucepan, combine gelatin, brown sugar, salt, and cinnamon; mix well. Add molasses, slightly beaten yolks, milk, and pumpkin, stirring until well combined. Bring to a boil, stirring constantly. Remove from heat; turn into large bowl, cover, and chill until firm, 1½-2 hours. In large bowl of electric mixer, beat egg whites at high speed until foamy. Add sugar, 2 tablespoons at a time, beating after each addition. Continue to beat until stiff peaks form. Using electric mixer, beat pumpkin mixture until smooth. With wire whisk or rubber scraper, gently fold egg white mixture and whipped cream into pumpkin mixture. Chill 10 minutes. Turn into pie shell, mounding high in center. Refrigerate until firm.

ARIZONA PIE

Kay Staley   *Yield: 8 servings*

¾   cup juice of Arizona
    sour oranges or ½ cup
    orange juice and ¼ cup
    lemon juice
1   can (14 oz.) sweetened
    condensed milk
1   container (8 oz.) frozen
    whipped topping, thawed
    Graham cracker crust
    (8-inch)
    Grated orange peel

Mix juice, condensed milk, and whipped topping. Spoon into prepared crust. Garnish with orange peel and refrigerate until ready to serve.

This is an easy, rich dessert; cut servings slightly smaller than usual.

THE BEST PECAN PIE

Mrs. Robert (Debby) Goldenberg   *Yield: 8 servings*

1	stick butter
1	cup light corn syrup
1	cup sugar
3	large eggs, beaten
½	teaspoon lemon juice
1	teaspoon vanilla
	Dash of salt
2	cups chopped pecans
12	pecan halves
	Pie shell (10-inch), unbaked

Heat butter in saucepan until golden brown (do not burn); cool. In separate bowl, place next 7 ingredients in order listed; stir. Blend in browned butter. Pour into unbaked pie shell and decorate top with pecan halves. Bake at 425 degrees for 10 minutes; lower temperature to 325 degrees and bake for 40 minutes.

LEMON CHIFFON PIE

Helen Swart   *Yield: 6-8 servings*

1	large lemon
3	tablespoons water
3	eggs, separated
¾-1	cup sugar
	Pie shell (9-inch), baked

Grate lemon rind into double boiler top, being careful not to cut too deeply. Add juice of lemon, water, and egg yolks. Beat lightly; add ½ cup sugar and stir thoroughly. Cook over hot water until eggs are cooked and mixture thickens slightly. (This may be done more rapidly in a saucepan over direct heat, but constant stirring is needed.) Set aside to cool, about 15 minutes. Beat egg whites until stiff. Gradually add remaining ¼-½ cup sugar to taste, fold in lemon custard, and fill shell with resulting chiffon. Brown very lightly in preheated 475 degree oven.

For best results, serve pie within 4-5 hours. Sugar may be eliminated from recipe for special diets; pie will be tart, but tasty.

FRUIT CREAM PIE

Mrs. Charles Skipton   *Yield: 6-8 servings*

1	stick margarine
6	tablespoons chopped pecans
1	cup all-purpose flour
1¼	teaspoons baking powder
⅛	teaspoon salt

FILLING

4	ounces cream cheese, softened
1	container (8 oz.) frozen whipped topping, thawed
1½	cups powdered sugar
½	teaspoon rum
1	can (16 oz.) fruit pie filling (any flavor)

Melt margarine; mix with nuts, flour, baking powder, and salt. Press into 9-inch pie pan. Bake at 300 degrees for 20 minutes, until golden brown. Cool completely.

Mix cream cheese, whipped topping, and sugar and put in crust. Add rum to fruit pie filling and pour evenly over cheese layer. Chill well before serving.

PECAN TARTS

Susan M. Falter   *Yield: 2 dozen*

CRUST

½	cup butter or margarine, softened
3	ounces cream cheese, softened
1	cup sifted flour

FILLING

1	egg
¾	cup light brown sugar
1	tablespoon soft butter
1	teaspoon vanilla
	Dash of salt
¾	cup coarsely broken pecans

Cream butter and cheese. Cut in flour; chill 1 hour. Shape into 2 dozen 1-inch balls. Place in miniature muffin pans, pressing dough to fit bottom and sides of cups.

Beat together egg, sugar, butter, vanilla, and salt just until smooth. Divide half the pecans among pastry-lined cups. Add egg mixture and top with remaining pecans. Bake at 325 degrees for 25 minutes.

MOTHER'S CHESS PIE

Jane Corbly   *Yield: 8 servings*

2   eggs, beaten
1   cup brown sugar
½   cup white sugar
¼   cup milk
¾   stick margarine
1   teaspoon vinegar
1   tablespoon vanilla
1   tablespoon corn meal
1   tablespoon flour
     Pie crust (9-inch), unbaked

Mix all ingredients well. Place in pie shell. Cover edges with foil. Bake at 400 degrees for 20 minutes; remove foil. Bake 20-25 minutes longer, until filling is firm. Cool before cutting.

LIZZIE'S LEMON PIES

Betty Arnold   *Yield: 36 servings*

     Pie crust dough (enough
     for 3 single crusts)
½   stick butter or margarine
3   cups plus 2 tablespoons
     sugar
4   eggs, separated
2   tablespoons (heaping) flour
2   tablespoons (heaping) corn
     meal
⅔   cup milk
     Juice and grated rind of
     2 lemons

Prepare pastry (see Perfect Pie Crust) and line tart pans for 36 tarts (3 inch). Cream butter and sugar. Add egg yolks. Mix flour and corn meal and add to butter mixture. Add milk, lemon juice, and grated rind. Beat egg whites until stiff and fold a little into lemon mixture; fold lemon mixture into whites. Fill unbaked tart shells and bake at 350 degrees for 25-30 minutes.

Tarts keep well in freezer for 2 weeks.

CHOCOLATE-CHEESE MOUSSE PIE

Pam Kramer   *Yield: 8 servings*

¼   cup skim milk
1   envelope unflavored gelatin
⅔   cup skim milk
2   eggs, separated
6   tablespoons sugar
1   tablespoon unsweetened
    cocoa
1   teaspoon vanilla
1½ cups low-fat cottage cheese
⅓   cup graham cracker
    crumbs
⅛   teaspoon cinnamon

Pour ¼ cup skim milk into blender container; sprinkle gelatin over milk; allow to soften 5 minutes. Heat ⅔ cup skim milk to boiling point. Pour into blender and blend until gelatin dissolves. Add egg yolks, 4 tablespoons sugar, cocoa, and vanilla. Blend at medium speed until well mixed. Add cottage cheese and blend until smooth. Refrigerate until thick. Beat egg whites; add remaining sugar and fold into chocolate mixture. Mix crumbs and cinnamon and place in 8-inch pie pan. Carefully pour in chocolate mixture and refrigerate.

Only 105 calories per serving!

CHOCOLATE POUND CAKE

Lou Mason   *Yield: 15-20 servings*

1	cup butter or margarine, softened
½	cup shortening
3	cups sugar
5	eggs
3	cups flour
½	teaspoon baking powder
¼	teaspoon salt
¼	cup cocoa
1	cup milk
1	teaspoon vanilla

Cream butter, shortening, and sugar well. Add eggs, 1 at a time, beating well after each. Sift together flour, baking powder, salt, and cocoa. Mix milk and vanilla. Add dry ingredients alternately with milk mixture in 3 or 4 additions of each, beating well after each addition. Pour into greased 10-inch tube pan with removable bottom. Bake at 325 degrees for 1¼ hours. Cool in pan on rack. Remove to cake plate and frost.

FROSTING

1	pound powdered sugar, sifted
¼	cup cocoa
½	cup butter
4-5	tablespoons milk

Combine all frosting ingredients and beat until smooth and creamy.

Best made 1 day ahead. Will keep several days in airtight container.

SOUR CREAM POUND CAKE

Sudie A. Fulford   *Yield: 16-20 servings*

2	sticks butter, softened
3	cups sugar
6	eggs
1	cup sour cream
3	cups flour, sifted twice
¼	teaspoon baking soda
1	teaspoon vanilla
1	teaspoon butter flavoring
1	teaspoon lemon flavoring

Cream butter and sugar. Beat in eggs, 1 at a time. Add sour cream; beat well. Add flour and soda; beat well. Stir in flavorings. Pour into greased 10-inch tube pan with removable bottom. Bake at 300 degrees for 1 hour, 40 minutes. Cool in pan. Serve plain, or with frosting or sweetened fruit.

HAWAIIAN ANGEL CAKE

Jan Rudd   *Yield: 8 servings*

1   angel food cake
1   can (8 oz.) crushed pine-
    apple
1   cup diced orange sections
1   cup hot liquid (fruit juices
    and enough water to make
    1 cup)
1   package (3¼ oz.) orange
    gelatin
1   pint vanilla ice cream

FROSTING
½   teaspoon grated orange
    rind
2   tablespoons sugar
½   pint whipping cream,
    whipped
1   can (20 oz.) sliced pine-
    apple

Cut angel food cake in half crosswise to make 2 layers. Drain pineapple and orange sections, reserving liquid. Dissolve gelatin in hot liquid. Add ice cream and blend thoroughly. Chill until mixture begins to set; stir in drained fruit. Spread half of fruit mixture over bottom layer of cake and cover with top layer. Fill center of cake with remaining mixture. Chill thoroughly.

Fold orange rind and sugar into whipped cream. Spread frosting on sides and top of cake, covering fruit filling. Make 8 cuts about 1 inch deep at even intervals around edge of cake top. Cut pineapple slices to open rings; insert 1 end of pineapple slice in each cut in top of cake and bring other end down side of cake. Chill. Cut cake in wedges between pineapple slices.

CHOCOLATE CHERRY CAKE

Betty Arnold   *Yield: 18-24 servings*

1   **package devil's food cake mix or chocolate cake mix without pudding**
2   **eggs**
1   **can (20 oz.) cherry pie filling (lightly sweetened)**
1   **teaspoon vanilla**

Mix all ingredients in mixer on medium speed for 2 minutes. Pour into greased and floured pan (9x13-inch or two 8x8-inch). Bake at 350 degrees for 30-35 minutes.

FROSTING
1   **cup sugar**
5   **tablespoons margarine**
⅓   **cup milk**
6   **ounces chocolate chips**

Boil first 3 ingredients. Remove from heat and stir in chocolate chips. Cool until proper consistency to spread on cake.

BLANCHIE'S JELLY ROLL

Blanche J. Palmeter   *Yield: 8-10 servings*

1   **cup flour**
2   **teaspoons baking powder**
    Pinch of salt
3   **eggs, separated**
¾   **cup sugar**
¼   **cup water**
½   **teaspoon lemon flavoring**
    Powdered sugar
1   **jar (10 oz.) jelly (elderberry or currant)**

Sift together flour, baking powder, and salt. Combine lightly beaten egg yolks, sugar, and water and add to dry ingredients. Mix well. Add lemon flavoring. Fold in beaten egg whites. Pour batter into 10x15-inch jelly roll pan which has been thoroughly greased and fitted with waxed paper. Bake at 350 degrees for 20-25 minutes. Remove from oven and allow to sweat in pan for 10 minutes. Turn cake out onto board or clean cloth sprinkled generously with powdered sugar. Remove paper and spread cake with jelly. Roll cake from narrow end and wrap in waxed paper until ready to slice and serve.

COUNTRY PECAN CAKE

Laurie Wilderman (Mrs. John G.)   *Yield: 8-10 servings*

4	eggs, separated
1	cup sugar
¼	cup water
1	teaspoon vanilla
1	cup cake flour
2	teaspoons baking powder
¼	teaspoon salt
1	tablespoon sugar
¼	cup finely chopped pecans

Beat egg whites in small, deep bowl until foamy. Gradually beat in ½ cup sugar; beat until stiff and glossy. In large bowl, beat egg yolks until light. Gradually beat in ½ cup sugar, water, and vanilla. Sift in flour, baking powder, and salt. Beat ½ minute on low speed, then 2 minutes on high speed. Carefully fold egg white mixture into egg yolk mixture. Pour into 2 greased and floured 9-inch cake pans. Sprinkle sugar and pecans over batter in 1 pan. Bake at 325 degrees for 30 minutes. Cool.

CREAM FILLING

1	package (3¼ oz.) instant vanilla pudding, prepared as directed
1	cup frozen whipped topping, thawed

Fold pudding and whipped topping together. Split cake layers, reserving sugared layer for top. Fill three layers with pudding mixture. Top with sugared layer. Refrigerate up to 24 hours.

GENERAL'S GOLDEN FRUIT CAKE

Gwendolyn McCausland   *Yield: 2 cakes*

1½   cups butter or margarine
2   cups sugar
6   eggs, separated
1   cup milk
3   tablespoons brandy extract
2   tablespoons vanilla
3½   cups flour
½   teaspoon salt
2   cups golden raisins
1   cup chopped dried apricots
1   cup chopped dates
1   cup fruit cake mix
1½   cups coarsely chopped
     walnuts
½   teaspoon cream of tartar

Cream butter and sugar, beating until fluffy. Add beaten egg yolks. Combine milk, brandy, and vanilla. Mix flour and salt together. Alternately add milk mixture and flour mixture to butter mixture. Fold in fruits and nuts. Beat egg whites with cream of tartar until stiff. Fold whites into batter. Pour mixture into 2 greased and floured molds (approximately 6 cups each). Bake at 275 degrees for 2½ hours. Cool; unmold. Wrap in cheesecloth soaked in orange juice and wrap in foil. Store in refrigerator 2-3 weeks. Keep cheesecloth moist.

COCONUT CRUNCH TORTE

Mrs. George Albrecht   *Yield: 8 servings*

1   cup graham cracker
     crumbs
½   cup coconut
½   cup pecans
4   egg whites
¼   teaspoon salt
1   teaspoon vanilla
1   cup sugar
1   pint vanilla ice cream
     Chocolate shavings

Combine graham cracker crumbs, coconut, and pecans; set aside. Beat egg whites with salt and vanilla until foamy; gradually add sugar and continue beating until egg whites form stiff peaks. Fold in graham cracker mixture. Spread in well-greased 9-inch pie pan. Bake at 350 degrees for 30 minutes. Cool. Cut into wedges and top with ice cream and chocolate shavings.

QUICK BANANA CAKE

Lois Ross   *Yield: 12 servings*

1	package yellow cake mix
⅛	teaspoon baking soda
⅓	cup water
1	cup mashed bananas
2	eggs

Grease two 8-inch cake pans (or one 9x13-inch pan). Place cake mix in large mixer bowl; add baking soda and stir well. Add water and ½ cup mashed bananas; beat 2 minutes at medium speed. Add eggs and beat 1 minute. On low speed, gradually blend in remaining bananas. Beat on low speed 1 minute; pour into prepared pans. Bake at 350 degrees for 25-30 minutes. Cool on rack and frost.

LEMON BUTTER FROSTING

½	cup butter
1	pound powdered sugar, sifted
	Pinch of salt
1	teaspoon grated lemon rind
1	egg
3-4	tablespoons lemon juice

Cream butter with half of sugar. Add remaining sugar. Add remaining ingredients, and beat with electric mixer until fluffy.

RASPBERRY TORTE

Linda Bossi Wegley   *Yield: 8-10 servings*

½	pound butter, softened
2	cups sugar
2	egg yolks
2	cups flour
1	teaspoon cinnamon
½	teaspoon salt
	Grated rind of 1 lemon
	Juice of 1 lemon
3	cups ground almonds
1	jar (12 oz.) raspberry jam
	Whipped cream or ice cream

Mix all ingredients, except raspberry jam. Spread ¾ of dough in well-greased springform pan. Starting at outer edge of dough, spread jam to 1 inch from center, leaving small circle in center without jam. With remaining dough, make crisscross design for top. Bake at 325 degrees for 1 hour. Serve with whipped cream or ice cream.

PUMPKIN ROLL

Sue Hallin   *Yield: 16 slices*

3	eggs
1	cup sugar
⅔	cup pumpkin
1	tablespoon lemon juice
¾	cup flour
1	teaspoon baking powder
½	teaspoon salt
2	teaspoons cinnamon
1	teaspoon ginger
1	cup chopped pecans

Beat eggs in mixer at highest speed for 5 minutes. Add sugar, pumpkin, and lemon juice. In another bowl, sift together dry ingredients and add to pumpkin mixture. Add nuts. Pour mixture into greased and floured 10x15-inch jelly roll pan. Bake at 375 degrees for 15 minutes (no longer). Sprinkle cotton tea towel with powdered sugar. Turn hot cake onto towel. Roll up from narrow end with towel and allow to cool. Prepare filling. Unroll cooled cake, remove towel, and spread cake with filling. Roll up again and refrigerate. Slice when chilled for easy handling. Allow to stand 10 minutes before serving.

FILLING

1	cup powdered sugar, sifted
4	tablespoons butter
6	ounces cream cheese, softened
¾	teaspoon vanilla

Combine ingredients and beat until creamy.

Follow directions exactly for beating eggs and baking. Best to use timer. Cake freezes well.

243

TERRI'S POPPY SEED CAKE

Mrs. Leon A. Whitney   *Yield: 12-15 servings*

1	package yellow cake mix
1	package (4 oz.) instant vanilla pudding
1	cup sour cream
½	cup cocktail sherry
½	cup vegetable oil
4	eggs
⅓	cup canned poppy seed filling

GLAZE

½	cup powdered sugar
1	tablespoon butter or margarine
2	tablespoons sherry
	Grated lemon peel
	Powdered sugar

Place cake mix, pudding mix, sour cream, sherry, oil, eggs, and poppy seed filling in large bowl of electric mixer. Beat 3 minutes at medium speed. Bake in greased bundt pan at 350 degrees for 50-60 minutes. Cool in pan 10 minutes. Remove from pan and cool on rack.

Mix well ½ cup sugar, butter, and sherry, and drizzle on warm cake. Before serving, garnish with grated lemon peel and powdered sugar.

Cake freezes well.

FROZEN MOCHA CREAM ROLL

Jeane Marinoff   *Yield: 8-10 servings*

5   eggs, separated (room
     temperature)
1   cup powdered sugar
3   tablespoons cocoa
     Dash of salt

Grease 10x15-inch jelly roll pan and line with waxed paper; grease and flour paper. Beat egg whites until soft peaks form, gradually adding ½ cup powdered sugar. Beat until glossy peaks form and sugar is dissolved. In small bowl, beat egg yolks until thick and lemon-colored. At low speed, beat in ½ cup powdered sugar, cocoa, and salt. Gently fold yolk mixture into whites. Spread batter evenly in pan; bake at 400 degrees for 15 minutes or until "springy." Invert cake on towel sprinkled with cocoa. Peel waxed paper from cake. Roll with towel from narrow end. Cool completely, seam side down, on wire rack. Unroll, remove towel, and spread with filling. Roll cake again from same end. Wrap and freeze.

MOCHA CREAM FILLING
⅓   cup packed light brown
     sugar
2   tablespoons instant coffee
2   cups whipping cream

Combine filling ingredients and beat until soft peaks form.

Cake will keep well in freezer as long as 1 month.

MOCHA TORTE

Sally J. Thompson   *Yield: 10-12 servings*

4	eggs, separated
1	cup sugar
	Pinch of salt
2	tablespoons mocha extract*
¾	cup flour
2	teaspoons baking powder

Beat egg yolks and add sugar, salt, and mocha extract. Gradually add flour and baking powder. Beat egg whites until stiff and fold into batter. Bake at 350 degrees for 15-20 minutes in 2 ungreased 9-inch cake pans. Cool on rack. Remove cakes from pans when completely cool.

FILLING

1	pint whipping cream
	Sugar to taste (approximately ¼ cup)
4	teaspoons mocha extract*

Whip cream until stiff. Add sugar and mocha extract. Spread filling between layers of cooled cake. (Cakes may be split into 4 layers).

FROSTING

1½	tablespoons butter
1	cup powdered sugar
1	tablespoon milk
1	tablespoon mocha extract*

Mix all frosting ingredients until smooth and creamy. Spread on cake. Refrigerate overnight before serving.

*MOCHA EXTRACT

4	tablespoons cocoa
3-4	tablespoons strong coffee

Mix together to make a paste-like mixture.

PUMPKIN TORTE

Sara Rendall   *Yield: 12 servings*

CRUST

1⅔ cups graham cracker
    crumbs
⅓   cup sugar
½   cup butter, melted

Mix graham cracker crumbs, sugar, and butter thoroughly. Press in bottom of 9x13-inch pan.

CREAM CHEESE BASE

1   package (8 oz.) cream
    cheese, softened
2   eggs
¾   cup sugar

Beat cheese in small bowl of electric mixer until light and fluffy. Add eggs and sugar. Beat until blended. Spoon over crust. Bake at 350 degrees for 20 minutes. Cool.

PUMPKIN FILLING

1   tablespoon unflavored
    gelatin
¼   cup cold water
1   can (16 oz.) pumpkin
3   eggs, separated
¾   cup sugar
½   cup milk
1   teaspoon cinnamon
½   teaspoon salt
    Whipped cream for garnish

Soften gelatin in cold water. Cook pumpkin, egg yolks, ½ cup sugar, milk, cinnamon, and salt in heavy pan, stirring constantly, until slightly thickened. Remove from heat. Add gelatin and stir until dissolved; cool. Beat egg whites until stiff but not dry. Gradually beat in remaining sugar. Fold into pumpkin mixture. Pour over cheese layer. Chill overnight. Garnish each serving with dollop of whipped cream.

CHEESECAKE EXTRAORDINAIRE

Judy D. McCormick   *Yield: 16 servings*

CRUST
1⅔ cups graham cracker
    crumbs
¼ cup finely chopped walnuts
½ teaspoon cinnamon
2 tablespoons sugar
⅓ cup butter, melted

FILLING
3 eggs, separated
1 cup sugar
2 packages (8 oz. each)
    cream cheese
¼ teaspoon salt
2 teaspoons vanilla
½ teaspoon almond extract
3 cups sour cream

Mix crust ingredients. Reserve 3 tablespoons for topping. Press remaining mixture on bottom and sides of 9-inch springform pan and chill.

Combine egg yolks, sugar, cream cheese, salt, and flavorings. Beat until smooth. Blend in sour cream; fold in beaten egg whites. Put filling in crust. Sprinkle reserved crumbs on top. Bake at 375 degrees for 45-50 minutes or until set. Filling will be soft in center. Cool; refrigerate until firm.

Delicious plain or topped with kiwi slices, strawberries, or boysenberry sauce.

OUTSTANDING CHEESECAKE

Barbara Weprin   *Yield: 10-12 servings*

CRUST

1½   cups graham cracker
     crumbs
3   tablespoons powdered
     sugar
2   tablespoons butter, melted

Mix crust ingredients and press into well-greased 10-inch springform pan. Chill for several hours.

FILLING

3   packages (8 oz. each)
     cream cheese
1   cup sugar
4   eggs
1   teaspoon vanilla

In mixer bowl, combine filling ingredients and beat at medium-high speed for 25-30 minutes. Pour into chilled crust and bake at 350 degrees for 40 minutes. Turn off oven, open oven door, and leave cake in oven for 30 minutes. Remove from oven and cool an additional 30 minutes.

TOPPING

16   ounces sour cream
¾   cup sugar
1   teaspoon vanilla
     Canned fruit pie filling
     (optional)

Mix sour cream, sugar, and vanilla; pour on cheesecake. Bake at 475 degrees for 7 minutes. Cool. Top with pie filling, if desired.

APPLE CHEESECAKE

Mrs. Kenneth E. Huff   *Yield: 12 servings*

2	cups graham cracker crumbs
⅓	cup packed light brown sugar
½	cup butter, melted
1	tablespoon cinnamon
3	medium cooking apples
4	eggs
¾	cup sugar
8	ounces ricotta cheese
8	ounces cream cheese
2	teaspoons vanilla
8	ounces whipping cream
	Cinnamon for topping

Mix graham cracker crumbs, brown sugar, 4 tablespoons melted butter, and cinnamon. Press on bottom and sides of 9-inch springform pan. Peel and core apples. Slice into 12 rings. Sauté on both sides in remaining 4 tablespoons butter. Arrange 6 slices on crust. Beat eggs, sugar, ricotta cheese, cream cheese, and vanilla until smooth, scraping bottom of bowl several times. Add cream and blend. Place springform pan on foil-lined cookie sheet to catch drips. Pour cheese mixture into pan. Arrange remaining 6 apple rings on top. Press apples lightly under mixture. Sprinkle heavily with cinnamon. Bake at 450 degrees for 10 minutes; reduce heat to 300 degrees and bake for 55 minutes. Cool 30 minutes; refrigerate overnight.

Best prepared day before serving.

JAM SQUARES

Nancy Abbott   *Yield: 16 squares*

2   cups oatmeal, quick or old-fashioned
1   cup margarine
1¾   cups flour
1   cup firmly packed brown sugar
½   cup chopped nuts
1   teaspoon cinnamon
¾   teaspoon salt
½   teaspoon baking soda
¾   cup preserves

Combine all ingredients, except preserves, in large mixing bowl; beat at low speed until mixture is crumbly. Reserve 2 cups of mixture; press remaining mixture into bottom of greased 9x13-inch baking pan. Spread preserves evenly over base. Sprinkle with remaining mixture. Bake at 400 degrees for 25-30 minutes or until golden brown. Cool and cut into squares.

For variation, combine 1 cup applesauce, ¾ cup raisins, and ½ cup nuts and substitute for preserves. Squares freeze well.

CHOCOLATE PECAN CAKE COOKIES

Carol B. Reed   *Yield: 4 dozen large cookies*

3¼   cups flour
1½   teaspoons baking soda
1   teaspoon salt
1   cup butter, melted
¾   cup sugar
¾   cup firmly packed brown sugar
2   teaspoons vanilla
2   eggs
1   package (12 oz.) semi-sweet chocolate chips
1   package (6¼ oz.) pecan halves (do not chop)

Combine flour, baking soda, and salt and set aside. Combine butter, sugar, brown sugar, and vanilla. Beat in eggs. Add flour mixture and mix well. Stir in chocolate chips and pecan halves. (Dough will be sticky.) Refrigerate for at least ½ hour. Shape into large balls and place on ungreased cookie sheet (1 dozen on each sheet). Bake at 375 degrees for 8-10 minutes or until light brown. Watch closely.

May be made days ahead; freeze well.

CHESS BROWNIES

Nancy L. Abbott   *Yield: 15-18 squares*

1	stick margarine
1	package (18 oz.) yellow or chocolate cake mix
1	egg
1	box (1 lb.) powdered sugar
1	package (8 oz.) cream cheese, softened
2	eggs

Melt margarine; mix with cake mix and egg. Press in bottom of 9x13-inch pan. Mix sugar, cream cheese, and eggs thoroughly by hand or with electric mixer. Pour on top of cake mixture. Bake at 325 degrees for 45 minutes. Cool before cutting into squares.

Very rich and very easy.

PEANUT BUTTER MAPLE COOKIES

Pam Kramer   *Yield: 6-7 dozen*

2	cups flour
¾	cup oatmeal
1	teaspoon baking soda
1½	teaspoons baking powder
1	teaspoon salt
1	cup margarine
1	cup sugar
1	cup brown sugar
2	eggs
½	cup peanut butter
1	tablespoon maple syrup
2	teaspoons vanilla
1	package (12 oz.) peanut butter chips

Combine dry ingredients; set aside. Mix margarine, sugars, eggs, peanut butter, syrup, and vanilla. Add dry ingredients and mix thoroughly. Add peanut butter chips and drop by teaspoon on lightly greased cookie sheet. Bake at 325 degrees for 6-8 minutes.

BLUSHING BLONDES

Rosemary Collins   *Yield: 4 dozen*

⅔   cup shortening
2¼ cups brown sugar
3   eggs
2¾ cups flour
2½ teaspoons baking powder
½   teaspoon salt
1   package (6 oz.) butter-
    scotch bits
1   cup chopped nuts
1   teaspoon vanilla

PINK FROSTING
2   cups powdered sugar, sifted
3   tablespoons butter,
    softened
1½ tablespoons milk
    Red food coloring

Cream shortening and sugar. Add eggs, 1 at a time. Sift together flour, baking powder, and salt. Blend into creamed mixture. Stir in butterscotch bits, nuts, and vanilla. Turn into greased 10x15-inch pan. Bake at 350 degrees for 25-30 minutes. Frost when cool and cut into squares.

Blend ½ cup powdered sugar with butter. Add remaining sugar alternately with milk. Add food coloring to make pretty pink frosting.

DUNKIN' PLATTERS

Marilyn Hoback   *Yield: 5 dozen*

1   cup butter or margarine,
    melted
1   cup packed brown sugar
1   cup sugar
2   eggs, beaten
1   teaspoon vanilla
1   cup quick oatmeal
1   cup corn flakes
2   cups flour
1   teaspoon baking soda
1   teaspoon baking powder
1   cup raisins
½   cup coconut (optional)

Blend butter and sugars; add eggs and vanilla. Mix oatmeal and corn flakes and add to mixture. Sift dry ingredients and add to mixture with raisins and coconut. Drop by teaspoonfuls on ungreased cookie sheet. Bake at 350 degrees for 8-10 minutes.

BUTTERSCOTCH CHEWIES

Marie Kindrick   *Yield: 4 dozen*

½   **pound butter or margarine**
1   **pound brown sugar**
2   **cups flour**
2   **eggs**
1   **teaspoon vanilla**
1   **cup chopped English walnuts**

Melt butter and add brown sugar; heat until bubbly and thoroughly mixed. Remove from heat; add flour and mix thoroughly. Add 1 egg at a time, beating well. Add vanilla and nuts. Spread in 9x13-inch greased and floured pan. Bake at 325 degrees for 25-30 minutes (until cake pulls away from sides of pan). Cool about 10 minutes; cut into squares and cool on rack.

Better made a day or two ahead.

TIGER STRIPES

Virginia Grice   *Yield: 5 dozen*

1   **cup semi-sweet chocolate chips**
1   **cup butter or margarine, softened**
1   **cup sugar**
2   **eggs**
1   **teaspoon vanilla**
2   **cups sifted flour**
1   **teaspoon baking soda**
½   **teaspoon salt**
3   **cups sugar-frosted corn flakes, partially crushed**

Melt chocolate over low heat, stirring constantly. Remove from heat; set aside. In large bowl, cream butter and sugar until light and fluffy. Add eggs and vanilla; beat well. Add sifted dry ingredients; mix thoroughly. Fold in corn flakes. Swirl warm melted chocolate through batter, leaving "tiger stripes." Drop by teaspoonfuls onto ungreased baking sheets. Bake at 375 degrees for 12 minutes. Cool thoroughly on wire rack.

CHOCOLATE MERINGUE BARS

Becki Sammons   *Yield: 3-4 dozen*

BATTER
1	cup shortening
½	cup brown sugar
½	cup sugar
3	egg yolks
2	cups flour
¼	teaspoon salt
¼	teaspoon baking soda
1	tablespoon cold water
1	teaspoon vanilla
1	cup chocolate chips

Cream shortening; add sugars and egg yolks and beat well. Sift dry ingredients together and stir into batter with water and vanilla. Spread batter in greased 9x13-inch pan. Sprinkle with chocolate chips.

MERINGUE
3	egg whites
1	cup brown sugar
1	cup chopped nuts

Beat egg whites until stiff and gradually add brown sugar. Spread over batter. Sprinkle with nuts. Bake at 350 degrees for 25 minutes. Cool in pan and cut into bars.

NORWEGIAN CROWNS

Helen Marinoff   *Yield: 4 dozen*

1	cup butter
4	hard-cooked egg yolks
½	cup sugar
2	cups sifted flour
½	teaspoon almond extract

Cream butter in electric mixer. Put egg yolks through sieve or grind in processor. Add to creamed butter and mix thoroughly. Gradually add sugar and continue creaming until well blended. Add sifted flour and extract. Chill dough 15-20 minutes. Force dough through cookie press, using desired shapes, onto chilled cookie sheet. Bake at 375 degrees for 10-12 minutes. May be decorated with candied cherries or colored sugars.

PEANUT BUTTER TEMPTATIONS

Cindy Gesme   *Yield: 4 dozen*

½	**cup butter**
½	**cup peanut butter**
½	**cup sugar**
½	**cup brown sugar**
1	**egg**
½	**teaspoon vanilla**
1¼	**cups flour**
¾	**teaspoon baking soda**
¼	**teaspoon salt**
48	**miniature peanut butter cup candies**

Cream butter, peanut butter, and sugars; add egg and vanilla. Beat until creamy. Stir in dry ingredients until blended. Shape dough into 1-inch balls. Press into 1½-inch muffin tins. (Paper liners may be used.) Bake at 350 degrees for 12 minutes. Remove from oven and immediately press 1 miniature peanut butter cup candy into each hot cookie crust. Allow to cool.

JELLY SANDWICH COOKIES

Linda Bossi Wegley   *Yield: 10 dozen*

2	**cups sugar**
2	**cups plus 6 tablespoons butter, softened**
2	**teaspoons vanilla**
4	**cups ground almonds**
5	**cups flour**
2	**jars (10 oz. each) currant jelly**

In large mixing bowl, mix sugar and butter. Add vanilla and almonds; mix well. Stir in 1 cup flour at a time until well blended. On floured board, roll dough ⅛ inch thick. Cut cookies (1½-inch) with round cookie cutter. Place on ungreased cookie sheets. Bake at 350 degrees for 10-15 minutes. While still warm, spread half the cookies with currant jelly (½ teaspoon each). Top with remaining cookies, forming sandwich. Store in airtight containers.

Cookies get better the longer you keep them.

256

TREASURE BARS

Theda Roup   *Yield: 2 dozen*

2	cups flour
1½	teaspoons baking powder
½	teaspoon salt
½	cup brown sugar
½	cup sugar
1	stick butter
2	eggs, well-beaten
1	teaspoon vanilla
¾	cup milk
¼-	
½	cup chopped walnuts
1	cup maraschino cherries, drained and halved
6	ounces chocolate chips

Sift together flour, baking powder, and salt. Set aside. Cream together sugars and butter; add eggs and vanilla. Add milk alternately with flour to creamed ingredients, beating after each addition. Fold in walnuts, cherries, and chocolate chips. Spread mixture in greased 10x15-inch pan. Bake at 325 degrees for 25-30 minutes.

FROSTING

¼	cup butter, browned
2	cups powdered sugar
2	tablespoons milk
1	teaspoon (scant) vanilla

Mix frosting ingredients and spread on warm cake. Cut cake into bars when cool.

PEANUT BUTTER CRUNCHIES

Dustie Mackay   *Yield: 4 dozen*

2	cups graham cracker crumbs
2	cups powdered sugar, sifted
1	cup smooth peanut butter
1	cup butter, melted
1	package (11½ oz.) milk chocolate chips

Combine crumbs and sugar in large bowl. Melt peanut butter and butter together and add to dry mixture. Place in bottom of greased 9x13-inch pan. Melt chocolate chips and spread on top. Refrigerate several hours. Cut into squares and serve.

May be frozen.

HOMEMADE FIG NEWTONS

Marylizabeth Grefe   *Yield: 4-5 dozen*

1   **cup chopped pitted dates**
1   **cup raisins**
1   **cup chopped dried figs**
1   **cup chopped pitted prunes**
    Orange juice
    Honey graham crackers

Grind all fruit in food grinder or processor, or chop fine. Add enough orange juice to fruit to make mixture spreadable. Spread between crackers.

Make only the number of fig newtons needed at one time. Store the remaining mixture in refrigerator until needed. If mixture hardens, add more orange juice. Tastes just like fig newtons from the store!

BUTTERFINGERS

Beverly F. Johnson   *Yield: 5 dozen*

3   **sticks butter or margarine**
⅓   **cup shortening**
¾   **cup powdered sugar (additional sugar for rolling baked cookies)**
4   **cups flour**
4   **tablespoons ice water**
1   **teaspoon vanilla**
2   **cups chopped nuts**

Cream butter, shortening, and sugar until smooth. Alternately add flour and water. Stir in vanilla and fold in nuts. Shape into finger-sized cookies. Bake at 350 degrees for 10-15 minutes (until slightly browned). When cool, roll in powdered sugar. Store in airtight container or freeze.

BISCOTTI (ITALIAN COOKIE-TOAST)

Marie Kindrick   *Yield: 1½ dozen*

4   **eggs**
¾   **cup sugar**
2   **cups flour**
2   **teaspoons ground anise**
       seed

Beat eggs until fluffy. Slowly add sugar. Add flour and anise seed and continue beating until thoroughly blended. Divide batter and place in 2 greased 5x9-inch pans. Bake at 350 degrees approximately 20 minutes (test with cake tester). Remove from pans immediately. Slice and place on buttered baking sheet. Return to oven for 5-10 minutes. Turn each piece and bake 5-10 minutes longer. Cool and store in airtight container.

Delicious with fruit or ice cream, or served with tea.

HUMDINGERS

Mrs. Jim Murray (Jo-Ann Ryan)   *Yield: 3-3½ dozen*

¼   **cup margarine**
1   **package (8 oz.) pitted**
       dates, chopped
1   **cup chopped nuts (walnuts**
       or pecans)
1   **cup sugar**
1   **teaspoon vanilla**
1½   **cups crisp rice cereal**
½   **cup powdered sugar, sifted**

Melt margarine in large sauce pan. Add dates, nuts, and sugar. Cook 8 minutes over low heat, stirring often. Remove from heat; add vanilla and cereal. Mix well. Cool until mixture can be worked with hands. Shape into small balls. Roll in powdered sugar and store in airtight container.

259

FRENCH MINT BARS

Chris Saunders   *Yield: 6½ dozen*

BROWNIES
½ cup margarine
½ cup shortening
4   squares (1 oz. each)
    unsweetened chocolate
4   eggs
½ teaspoon salt
2   cups sugar
½ teaspoon peppermint
    extract
1   cup flour

Melt margarine, shortening, and chocolate in double boiler or microwave; cool. In large bowl, beat eggs until light and foamy; add salt, sugar, and flavoring and mix well. Blend chocolate mixture into egg mixture. Stir in flour. Pour into greased 9x13-inch pan. Bake at 375 degrees for 15-20 minutes (do not overbake) and cool thoroughly.

FROSTING
4   tablespoons margarine
2   cups powdered sugar, sifted
2   tablespoons cream or milk
½ teaspoon peppermint
    extract
1-3 drops green food coloring

Beat margarine until soft. Gradually add powdered sugar and blend until creamy. Slowly add cream until frosting is spreading consistency. Add peppermint extract and food coloring. Spread on cooled brownies. Set in refrigerator 20 minutes.

GLAZE
2   tablespoons margarine
1   square (1 oz.)
    unsweetened chocolate

Melt margarine and chocolate in double boiler or microwave. While still warm, swirl on top of green frosting, leaving portions of green showing. Cool and cut into 1x1½-inch bars.

Bars freeze well.

DATE CRUMBLE

Alice Thomason   *Yield: 6 servings*

2	**eggs, beaten**
¾	**cup sugar**
1	**teaspoon baking powder**
1	**tablespoon flour**
¾	**cup chopped nuts**
¾	**cup chopped dates**
½	**pint whipping cream**

Mix all ingredients, except whipping cream, and spread on well-greased jelly roll pan, covering entire pan. Bake at 325 degrees for 20 minutes. Let cool slightly; remove from pan and crumble. Whip cream and fold in crumbled mixture. Spoon into individual dishes and serve.

Date crumbs may be made ahead and stored in airtight container.

UPSIDE-DOWN DATE PUDDING

Susan M. Falter   *Yield: 9 servings*

1	**cup pitted dates, cut up**
1	**cup boiling water**
½	**cup sugar**
½	**cup brown sugar**
1	**egg**
2	**tablespoons butter or margarine, melted**
1½	**cups sifted flour**
1	**teaspoon baking soda**
½	**teaspoon baking powder**
½	**teaspoon salt**
1	**cup chopped walnuts**
	Whipped cream

Combine dates and water. Blend sugars, egg, and butter. Sift together flour, soda, baking powder, and salt; add to sugar mixture. Stir in nuts and cooled date mixture. Pour into 7x11-inch baking dish. Cover with brown sugar sauce. Bake at 375 degrees about 40 minutes. Cut into squares; invert on plates. Serve warm with whipped cream.

BROWN SUGAR SAUCE

1½	**cups brown sugar**
1	**tablespoon butter or margarine**
1½	**cups boiling water**

In bowl, combine sugar and butter. Pour boiling water over sugar-butter mixture; stir until sugar dissolves.

261

STEAMED CRANBERRY PUDDING

Barbara Neroni   *Yield: 8-10 servings*

2	cups cranberries, washed and dried
2	tablespoons butter
½	cup sugar
½	cup molasses
1	cup boiling water
1½	cups flour
1	teaspoon baking powder
1½	teaspoons baking soda
½	teaspoon salt

Mix cranberries, butter, sugar, and molasses in large bowl and add boiling water. Sift dry ingredients and stir into cranberry mixture. Pour into large buttered bread tin or mold. Cover tightly with buttered foil. Place in larger pan with 1½ inches hot water. Bake at 350 degrees for 2 hours, adding water to larger pan if necessary. (Baking time may vary; toothpick will come out clean when pudding is done.)

SAUCE

1	cup sugar
1	cup whipping cream plus 1 cup water or 1 pint half-and-half
1	stick butter
2	tablespoons cornstarch Bourbon, rum, or brandy to taste (optional)

Mix ingredients in saucepan and cook until thickened, stirring constantly. If desired, add liquor. Serve sauce warm on warm pudding.

May be made days ahead and refrigerated or frozen; bring to room temperature before serving or warm in microwave briefly. Double the recipe and make in small foil bread tins for gifts, attaching sauce recipe. Wonderful holiday dessert, easy and rich!

NEW ORLEANS BREAD PUDDING

Faye Martin   *Yield: 8 servings*

1	loaf French bread, cubed
1	quart milk
3	eggs
2	cups sugar
1	tablespoon vanilla
1	cup raisins
3	tablespoons margarine, melted

Soak bread in milk until soft. Add eggs, sugar, vanilla, and raisins and stir well. Spread margarine in bottom of baking dish and add mixed ingredients. Bake at 350 degrees until very firm, approximately 1 hour; cool. Cube pudding and put in individual oven-proof dishes. When ready to serve, add sauce and heat under broiler or in microwave.

BOURBON SAUCE

1	cup sugar
1	stick butter or margarine
1	egg
	Bourbon

Cook sugar and butter in double boiler until very hot and well dissolved. Add well-beaten egg and whip quickly so egg does not curdle. Cool and add bourbon to taste.

LEMON-LIME SOUFFLÉ

Rachel Sperry   *Yield: 8 servings*

2	tablespoons unflavored gelatin
1	cup cold water
1½	cups sugar
1½	cups boiling water
	Pinch of salt
2	tablespoons grated lemon peel
½	cup lemon juice
½	cup lime juice
1	cup whipping cream, whipped
3	egg whites
2	tablespoons sugar

Sprinkle gelatin over cold water to soften. Add 1½ cups sugar, boiling water, and salt and stir until gelatin is dissolved. Stir in lemon peel, lemon juice, and lime juice. Refrigerate until slightly thickened. Fold whipped cream into lemon-lime mixture. Beat egg whites with 2 tablespoons sugar until stiff but not dry. Fold into lemon-lime mixture. Turn into 2-quart soufflé dish. Chill until firm. Serve plain or with strawberries or raspberries.

COLD GRAND MARNIER SOUFFLÉ

Annabelle Cummings   *Yield: 10 servings*

1	tablespoon unflavored gelatin
¼	cup cold water
3	eggs, separated
1	cup sugar
	Dash of salt
⅓	cup lemon juice
	Grated rind of 1 lemon
3	ounces Grand Marnier
2	cups whipping cream, whipped

Variation: For Cold Lemon Soufflé, eliminate liqueur and garnish with slivered lemon peel.

Soak gelatin in cold water in small metal container. Set container in pan of hot water until gelatin is clear and liquid. Beat egg yolks, adding sugar slowly. Mixture should be thick and pale yellow. Beat egg whites with salt until stiff. Add lemon juice and rind, Grand Marnier, and melted gelatin to yolks. Using whisk, carefully fold mixture into whites, adding whipped cream at the same time. Pile lightly into soufflé dish and chill several hours. (Individual soufflé dishes work well.)

Bonus for the busy cook! This soufflé may be made a day in advance; may be frozen as long as 3 months, if carefully covered.

A DIETER'S BAVARIAN CREAM

Constance Klarer   *Yield: 6-8 servings*

2	eggs, separated
½	cup sugar
	Pinch of salt
1	pint milk, scalded
1	envelope gelatin, softened in ¼ cup cold milk
1½	teaspoons vanilla

Combine egg yolks, sugar, and salt. Add a little warm milk and mix. Add remaining milk to yolk mixture. Stir over medium heat for 5 minutes. Add gelatin mixture and cook 5 more minutes. Remove from heat and add stiffly beaten whites and vanilla. Refrigerate until set; whisk mixture to prevent separation, and refrigerate again until ready to serve.

For non-dieters, serve with whipped cream.

GALATOBOURIKO (CUSTARD PASTRY)

Mary Houpis   *Yield: 1 dozen*

2	**quarts milk**
¾	**cup cream of wheat**
6	**eggs, beaten**
1	**cup sugar**
1	**teaspoon vanilla**
2	**tablespoons butter**
½	**pound butter or margarine**
1	**pound filo or strudel sheets (will not use entire package; freeze remaining sheets)**

Heat milk in large pan, but do not scald. Add cream of wheat, stirring constantly until slightly thickened. Beat eggs in another bowl; add sugar. Slowly spoon some milk mixture into egg mixture; add egg mixture to milk mixture, stirring constantly. Add vanilla and 2 tablespoons butter and continue to cook over low heat until mixture is slightly thickened. Remove from heat and cool. Melt ½ pound butter. With pastry brush, generously butter 10x15-inch pan. Unwrap filo and cover with damp cloth. Remove each sheet as needed, place in pan, and brush generously with melted butter. Repeat this process until there are 7 pastry sheets in pan. Pour cooled milk mixture into pan. Add 7 or 8 more pastry sheets (brushing each with melted butter). Bake at 350 degrees for ½ hour. Pour cooled syrup evenly over hot pastry immediately upon removing from oven. Cool before cutting into squares.

SYRUP

3	**cups sugar**
2	**cups water**
1	**teaspoon vanilla**

Boil sugar with water until thickened. Remove from heat and add vanilla. Cool.

This recipe originated in Asia Minor.

265

SWEET DREAM MERINGUE

Ellen Jane Porter   *Yield: 6 servings*

3	egg whites
½	teaspoon baking powder
	Pinch of salt
1	teaspoon vanilla
1	teaspoon water
1	teaspoon vinegar
1	cup sugar, sifted

In large mixer bowl, combine all ingredients, except sugar, and beat until stiff. While still beating, slowly add sugar. Place mixture on large, ungreased cookie sheet. With spatula, spread mixture into large circle or oval 1 inch thick, with raised rim. Bake at 275 degrees for 1 hour. When done, run a long knife between meringue and cookie sheet and gently slide meringue onto platter. Fill with any combination of fruit, ice cream, and chocolate or custard sauce.

For an elegant and beautiful dessert, fill meringue with vanilla ice cream, sliced fresh peaches, and blueberries. Serve with flavored custard sauce.

ALMOND FLAN

Penny Haddick   *Yield: 6 servings*

1½	cups milk
½	cup whipping cream
½	cup sugar
¼	cup ground blanched almonds
1	tablespoon cognac
4	egg whites
⅛	teaspoon salt
	Butter
	Slivered almonds, toasted

Bring milk and cream to boil; add sugar and ground almonds. Cook over low heat for 15 minutes; cool. Stir in cognac. Beat egg whites until foamy; add salt and beat until whites form firm peaks. Gently fold egg whites into almond-milk mixture. Pour into buttered 2-quart mold, cover with foil, and place mold in pan with 1½ inches of hot water. Bake at 325 degrees for 1 hour or until silver knife comes out clean. Chill. To serve, unmold onto platter and garnish with toasted almonds.

ICE CREAM SQUARES

Carol Dickerson   *Yield: 12 servings*

1	stick butter or margarine
7	ounces coconut
6	ounces slivered almonds
¾-1	cup brown sugar
½	gallon ice cream, softened

Melt butter in saucepan; add coconut and almonds; brown. Add brown sugar, stirring until melted. Line 9x13-inch pan with ½ of mixture. Spread with ice cream; top with remaining mixture; freeze. Cut into squares and serve.

CHOCOLATE ORANGE CUPS

Sonnie Kasch (Mrs. William)   *Yield: 8 servings*

3	squares (1 oz. each) unsweetened chocolate
¾	cup sugar
1	tablespoon orange juice
1½	tablespoons orange liqueur
2	teaspoons grated orange peel
3	egg yolks, beaten
3	egg whites (room temperature)
½	cup whipping cream, whipped
8	medium orange cups with saw-toothed rims

Melt chocolate in top of double boiler over hot water; stir in ½ cup sugar. Blend in orange juice, liqueur, and orange peel. Stir in egg yolks and mix thoroughly. Allow mixture to cool. Beat egg whites until soft peaks form. Gradually add remaining sugar and beat until stiff and glossy. Gently fold into chocolate mixture. Whip cream and fold into mixture. Spoon into orange cups and chill overnight. Serve with dollop of whipped cream or top with meringue.

MERINGUE

2	egg whites
¼	teaspoon cream of tartar
3	tablespoons sugar
½	teaspoon vanilla

Beat egg whites until frothy and add cream of tartar. Continue to beat until soft peaks form. Gradually add sugar and vanilla, and beat until stiff and glossy. Spread on top of each orange cup (be sure to seal edges). Carefully broil until golden.

ALMOND CREAM CRÊPES

Lou Mason   *Yield: 8 servings*

1	package (3½ oz.) instant vanilla pudding
1¼	cups milk
¾	cup sour cream
1	teaspoon almond extract
8	6-inch crêpes (see Index for recipe)

Mix pudding and milk as package directs; chill. Add sour cream and almond extract and mix well. Spoon filling down middle of crêpes and fold sides over so they overlap. Place crêpes in 9x13-inch baking dish. Spoon sauce over crêpes; cover with plastic wrap and microwave on high 1 minute (or may be heated in oven at 300 degrees for 5 minutes). If made ahead, fill crêpes and refrigerate. Add sauce just before heating.

SAUCE

2	tablespoons butter
¼	cup sliced almonds
¼	cup honey

Microwave butter and almonds in glass container covered with plastic wrap for 3 minutes on high (or sauté on top of stove until light brown). Stir in honey.

AMARETTO ICE CREAM

Judy Cook   *Yield: 1½ quarts*

2	egg yolks
1	can (14 oz.) sweetened condensed milk
¼	cup Amaretto liqueur
¼	teaspoon almond extract
2	cups whipping cream
½	cup slivered almonds, toasted

Beat egg yolks well. Add condensed milk, Amaretto, and almond extract; mix well. Beat whipping cream until very stiff. Fold into liqueur mixture along with toasted almonds. Freeze in 2-quart container.

EASY BAKED ALASKA

Jeane Marinoff   *Yield: 12-15 servings*

1   **package (18½ oz.) choc-
     olate cake mix or brownie
     mix, following directions
     for cake-like brownies**
½   **gallon ice cream, any flavor**
5   **egg whites, room
     temperature
     Pinch of salt**
1   **jar (7 oz.) marshmallow
     cream**

Prepare cake mix as directed and bake in two 8-inch layers. Cool, wrap individually, and freeze. (Only 1 layer is used for 1 recipe.) Firmly pack softened ice cream into foil-lined 1½-quart mixing bowl (7-8 inch diameter). Cover with plastic wrap; freeze thoroughly at least 2 hours or overnight. Cover top of wooden board or baking sheet with 12-inch square of heavy brown paper. Center cake layer on paper. Unmold ice cream from bowl and place on top of cake. Cover with plastic wrap. Refreeze at least 1 hour. Beat egg whites with salt in large mixer bowl until soft peaks form. Gradually add marshmallow cream and beat until stiff peaks form. Remove Alaska from freezer. Spread meringue evenly over top and sides of ice cream and cake (about 1-1½ inches thick), sealing cake to brown paper. Bake at 450 degrees for 3-5 minutes or until lightly browned. Remove from oven, cut into wedges, and serve immediately. Cover leftovers and refreeze. Serve within a few days.

May be assembled (including meringue) 24 hours in advance of serving and placed in freezer. Cover with plastic wrap after Alaska freezes. When ready to serve, remove from freezer and bake as directed.

MOTHER'S SHORTCAKE

Chris Saunders   *Yield: 8 servings*

2   cups flour
1   teaspoon salt
4   teaspoons baking powder
⅛-
¼   cup sugar
¼   cup butter or margarine
¾   cup milk (more if needed)
     Strawberries or rasp-
     berries, sweetened and
     partially crushed
     Half-and-half

Sift dry ingredients. Add butter, cutting in with knives or pastry blender until coarse-textured. Mix in milk with knife. Turn dough onto floured board and knead lightly for ½ minute. Pat to ¼-inch thickness on bottoms of 2 upside-down buttered 8-inch cake pans. Bake at 450 degrees for 10-12 minutes or until crisp and golden brown. While hot, spread bottoms of short-cakes with butter. When ready to serve, place 1 layer, buttered side up, on plate. Top with strawberries or raspberries. Top with second layer, buttered side down. At table, cut in portions and serve in bowls. Pass a pitcher of half-and-half.

STRAWBERRY FREEZE

Lou Mason   *Yield: 8 servings*

6   cups strawberries
2   cups sugar
1½   cups orange juice
½   cup lemon juice

Blend all ingredients in blender or processor until smooth (⅓ at a time). Freeze in 9x13-inch pan. Remove from pan and beat with electric mixer until smooth; refreeze in same pan. Remove from freezer 10 minutes before serving. Scoop into dessert dishes.

May be made with frozen berries. If sweetened berries are used, adjust sugar to taste. A light and very attractive dessert.

FRUIT SLUSH

Mrs. Sherman B. Lyon   *Yield: 12-18 servings*

3	cups sugar
3	cups water
	Juice of 3 large oranges
	Juice of 3 large lemons
1	can (20 oz.) crushed pineapple
6	bananas, mashed (optional)
	Maraschino cherries

Mix sugar and water, stirring until sugar dissolves. Add juice from oranges and lemons. Add crushed pineapple; stir well. Place in freezer until mixture is partially frozen; remove and add bananas. Return to freezer. Ten minutes before serving, remove from freezer and garnish with maraschino cherries.

May be frozen in 1 large container or in separate cups.

KEY LIME BAKED ALASKA

Jocelyn Feeman   *Yield: 8 servings*

4	egg yolks
1	can (14 oz.) sweetened condensed milk
½	cup fresh lime juice
½	gallon vanilla ice cream

Beat egg yolks. Add milk and mix thoroughly. Add lime juice; mix well. Spread ½ of ice cream in bottom of loaf pan. Pour lime mixture over ice cream to make second layer; freeze until hard. Add remaining ice cream and freeze. Un-mold frozen loaf on foil-covered wooden board. Cover loaf with me-ringue. Return to freezer until ready to serve. Place in 500-degree oven for approximately 2 minutes until browned. Slice and serve immediately.

MERINGUE

4	egg whites
½	teaspoon cream of tartar
1	cup sugar

Combine egg whites and cream of tartar; beat well. Gradually add sugar, beating until stiff.

271

MILLIONAIRE PIE

Sue F. Strother   *Yield: 16 servings*

6   Heath bars
2-3 cups crushed macaroons
½   gallon butter brickle ice
     cream (or butter pecan,
     English toffee, butter
     crunch)

CHOCOLATE SAUCE
6   squares (1 oz. each)
     unsweetened chocolate
3   tablespoons butter
1½   cups sugar
1   cup coffee cream
1½   teaspoons vanilla

Freeze Heath bars; chop fine. Lightly butter 10-inch spring-form pan. Place ½ of maca-roons, Heath bars, and ice cream in layers in pan. Repeat layers. Freeze. Let stand 10 minutes before cutting. Serve with chocolate sauce.

Melt chocolate and butter over low heat. Mix in sugar. Slowly stir in coffee cream. Remove from heat. Add vanilla and refrigerate until ready to use.

ECSTATIC MOMENTS DESSERT

Louise French   *Yield: 9 servings*

5   egg whites
1½   cups sugar
     Pinch of cream of tartar
     Pinch of salt
1   cup whipping cream,
     whipped
     Sweetened fresh fruit

Beat egg whites and sugar 15 minutes with electric mixer, adding cream of tartar and salt after first few minutes. Start on high and lower speed as mixture thickens. Shape mixture into 9-inch circle on waxed paper on cookie sheet and bake at 375 degrees for 5 minutes. Turn off oven. Leave in oven with door closed 1 hour. Cover with whipped cream and refrigerate at least 4 hours. Cut into 9 wedges and serve topped with fruit.

For Fourth of July, top with straw-berries and blueberries.

FRUIT MEDLEY

Constance Klarer   *Yield: 9 servings*

2	cups sliced fresh peaches or canned unsweetened peaches, drained
1	can (15¼ oz.) pineapple tidbits with juice
1½	cups chopped dried apricots
1	teaspoon mace
½	teaspoon ground cardamon
2	tablespoons butter

TOPPING

1	cup sugar
1	cup flour
½	teaspoon cinnamon
1	stick butter

Mix fruits and place in greased 9x9-inch pan. Sprinkle spices over fruit and dot with butter. Sprinkle topping over fruit and bake, uncovered, at 350 degrees for 30 minutes or until fruit is soft.

Mix sugar, flour, and cinnamon. Cut in butter.

Recipe may be varied by adding ½ cup raisins and/or ½ cup chopped nuts. Delicious served with cream or ice cream.

AVOCADO AND STRAWBERRY CREAM

Narcisa Hirsch   *Yield: 8 servings*

4	large ripe avocados
1	quart fresh strawberries (reserve some for garnish) or 2 boxes (10 oz. each) frozen strawberries
½	cup sugar (if using fresh berries)
	Juice of 1 lemon
1½	cups whipping cream
1-3	drops red food coloring (optional)

Cut avocados in half and scoop out meat. Save shells. Blend avocado and strawberries in blender or processor. Add sugar and lemon juice. Whip 1 cup cream until stiff. Fold into strawberry/avocado mixture and spoon into avocado shells. Chill 2-3 hours and serve, garnished with remaining cream, whipped, and fresh strawberries. (If not served within 2-3 hours, freeze to prevent avocado from turning brown.)

This is a favorite light summer dessert or appetizer in Argentina.

273

TURKISH CREAM GOURMET PEARS

Susan S. Seyfarth   *Yield: 6 servings*

6   ripe pears
2   cups water
1   lemon slice
1   cup sugar
1   teaspoon ground ginger
      Crystallized ginger,
      chopped

TURKISH CREAM
1   cup whipping cream
2   tablespoons sugar

Pare and core pears. Poach in water with lemon slice, sugar, and ground ginger until pears are tender, but firm. Remove pears and reduce syrup slightly. Return pears to syrup and chill. Drain pears. Spoon Turkish cream over pears and sprinkle with chopped crystallized ginger.

Simmer (do not boil) whipping cream and sugar until reduced to ½ quantity. Cool at room temperature (do not refrigerate).

CRANBERRY-PEAR SORBET

Jocelyn Feeman   *Yield: 1 quart*

⅔   cup sugar
⅔   cup water
3   cups fresh or frozen whole
      cranberries, puréed
2   ripe pears, peeled, cored,
      and puréed
2   tablespoons Kirsch
      Rind of 2 oranges, grated
1   egg white

Combine sugar and water in small pan over medium-high heat and stir until sugar is dissolved. Just before it boils, remove from heat. Allow to cool; cover and chill. Combine syrup, cranberries, pears, Kirsch, and orange rind and blend well in processor. Turn into 9x13-inch metal pan and freeze. Thaw partially, put into processor, and process until smooth and fluffy. Add egg white and continue processing until well blended, about 5 minutes. Refreeze. Store in airtight container. If frozen solid, place container in refrigerator 1 hour before serving.

BLENDER CHOCOLATE MOUSSE

Rita Vlahos   *Yield: 3 servings*

1   **cup chocolate chips**
1   **egg, beaten**
2   **tablespoons sugar**
¾   **cup hot milk**
1   **teaspoon vanilla**
    Whipped cream
    Shaved chocolate

Place all ingredients, except cream and shaved chocolate, in blender; blend for 1 minute. Pour into 3 individual glasses or cups. Chill overnight. Top with whipped cream and shaved chocolate.

A make-ahead dessert that is quick, easy, and elegant.

ITALIAN MERINGUE (TORTONI)

Diane Colaizzi   *Yield: 6-8 servings*

2   **cups whipping cream**
1   **tablespoon vanilla**
2   **teaspoons sugar**
4   **egg whites (room temperature)**
⅛   **teaspoon cream of tartar**
⅛   **teaspoon salt**
¼   **cup sugar**
1   **package (6 oz.) milk chocolate morsels**
½   **cup slivered almonds, toasted**

Chill bowl and beaters. Beat cream until thick; add vanilla and 2 teaspoons sugar. Beat egg whites until foamy; add cream of tartar and salt. Continue beating until soft peaks form; gradually add ¼ cup sugar. (Egg whites and cream should be same consistency.) Fold cream into egg whites and place in freezer until crystals form. Melt chocolate. Remove cream mixture from freezer. Working quickly, fold hot melted chocolate and almonds into cream mixture. Spoon into sherbets and return to freezer. Remove from freezer 1 hour before serving.

DANISH RUM PUDDING

Carol Pettit   *Yield: 6 servings*

3   egg yolks
6   tablespoons sugar
2   tablespoons rum
1   envelope unflavored gelatin
¾   cup cold water
1   cup whipping cream,
    whipped, or 1 container
    (8 oz.) frozen topping,
    thawed

FRUIT SAUCE
¼   cup sugar
1½ teaspoons cornstarch
1   can (16 oz.) sour cherries
    or other fruit

Beat egg yolks and sugar well; add rum. Soak gelatin in cold water to soften; dissolve over heat. Cool gelatin and add to egg mixture. Chill mixture until it begins to thicken. Watch carefully, as it thickens very quickly (15-20 minutes). Slowly beat in whipped cream or frozen topping. Put into 4-cup mold and chill. Serve with fruit sauce.

Mix sugar and cornstarch together and add to cherries. Heat until juice thickens. Chill.

CARAMEL FROSTING

Sudie A. Fulford   *Yield: 3 cups (will frost 2-layer cake)*

3⅓ cups sugar
⅓ cup water
1 cup milk
1 stick butter
½ teaspoon baking soda

Brown ⅓ cup sugar until caramelized. Add water carefully to prevent excessive spattering. (Sugar will form a hard mass, but will dissolve when stirred.) In 3-quart saucepan, heat remaining sugar, milk, butter, and soda together until sugar melts. Add caramelized sugar mixture. Cook about 10-15 minutes or until mixture forms a soft ball (240 degrees on candy thermometer). Cool about ½ hour (until you can put hand on bottom of pan). Beat until thick enough to spread. Frosting will be runny, but will solidify quickly when spread on cake.

May be used as sauce as well as frosting. Store in suitable container and reheat before serving.

"CRACKER JACK" POPCORN

Marylizabeth Grefe   *Yield: 7 quarts*

2 cups brown sugar
½ cup light corn syrup
2 sticks margarine
1 teaspoon vanilla
½ teaspoon baking soda
½ pound dry roasted peanuts
7 quarts popped popcorn
   (1½ cups unpopped)

In 9-quart pan, mix brown sugar, corn syrup, and margarine. Boil 2-3 minutes and remove from heat. Stir in vanilla and baking soda until blended (mixture will foam). Stir in peanuts. Add popped corn, stirring to coat. Place on 2-3 buttered jelly roll pans. Bake at 250 degrees for 1 hour. Cool and break apart. Store in airtight container.

FABULOUS HOT FUDGE SAUCE

Linda L. Marshall (Mrs. Bruce)　　　　　*Yield: 12-18 servings*

1½　cups sugar
1¼　sticks butter or margarine
4　　squares (1 oz. each)
　　　unsweetened chocolate
½　　cup cocoa
1　　teaspoon vanilla
1　　cup light cream or milk

Place sugar, butter, chocolate, and cocoa in top of double boiler over hot water. Simmer for 45 minutes, stirring once or twice. Add vanilla and cream; stir to blend. Cook another 10 minutes.

Great over ice cream. Sauce keeps 2-3 weeks in refrigerator. Before serving, reheat over hot water or in microwave.

OHIO BUCKEYES

Susan M. Falter　　　　　　　　　*Yield: 250 candies*

1　　pound margarine
3　　pounds powdered sugar
2　　pounds peanut butter
12　ounces chocolate chips
⅔　　block of paraffin

Melt margarine and cool. Add powdered sugar and peanut butter and mix well. Roll into 1-inch balls; chill. Melt chocolate chips and paraffin in double boiler. Pick up chilled peanut butter balls with toothpicks and dip in chocolate, leaving tops uncovered. Press toothpick holes with thumb to cover holes. Place on waxed paper, peanut butter side up. When chocolate hardens, store in airtight containers in refrigerator.

Buckeyes freeze well.

CAROL'S CARAMELS

Carol C. Pohl   *Yield: 5 dozen caramels*

1   cup whipping cream
1   cup half-and-half
2   cups sugar
1½   cups light corn syrup
2   tablespoons margarine
1   teaspoon vanilla

Mix creams together in bowl. In heavy 5-quart pan, heat sugar, syrup, and ¼ cup cream to 238 degrees, stirring constantly with wooden spoon. Add another ¼ cup cream and reheat, stirring constantly, to 238 degrees. Continue stirring, add remaining cream, and bring mixture to 240 degrees. Remove from heat and stir in margarine and vanilla. Pour into well-greased 10x15-inch jelly roll pan. Cool until solid enough to hold shape, ½-1 hour. Cut into 1-inch squares and wrap in 3x6-inch pieces of waxed paper. Twist both ends of paper loosely. Store in refrigerator.

FLORENTINES FROM ENGLAND

Joyce Payne-Butler   *Yield: 12 candies*

¼   pound semi-sweet choco-
     late
1   egg
¼   cup sugar
¼   cup currants
½   cup Sultanas or golden
     raisins
¼   cup glacé cherries or half
     fruit cake mix and half
     cherries, cut up
¾   cup chopped nuts
¼   cup flaked coconut

Line 5x9-inch pan with foil. Melt chocolate and place in pan; allow to harden. Beat egg with sugar; add currants, raisins, cherries, nuts, and coconut. Spread over chocolate. Bake in middle of oven at 300-325 degrees about 20 minutes, until golden (do not overcook). Chill until hardened. Remove foil and cut into small squares.

PARTY WORKSHEET

1. Occasion/Event/Reason for Party _____

2. Date _____ Time _____

3. Type of Party (brunch, luncheon, open house, etc.) _____

4. Guest List

_____   _____

_____   _____

_____   _____

_____   _____

5.   Menu   Amount   Preparation Time   Presentation

_____   _____   _____   _____

_____   _____   _____   _____

_____   _____   _____   _____

_____   _____   _____   _____

6. Logistics

    Coats/Umbrellas   Food:

    Parking   Tables

    Bar: Chairs

       Location   Cloths

       Glasses   Napkins

       Liquor   Dishes

       Mix, Ice   Silver

       Equipment   Glassware

       Napkins, Coasters   Centerpieces

                             Wine

                             Candles

  Extra kitchen or bar equipment _____

  Help _____ Phone _____

7. Ambience

  Music _____ Entertainment _____

  Color scheme _____

  Flowers/Decorations _____

PARTY PLANNING

Joan D. Siebenthaler

Many of us dream of presiding at a beautiful dinner party for eight, with exquisite food and stimulating conversation, while mood music plays softly in the background. It sounds lovely, but how do you create such an affair? How do you pull together all the details? How do you avoid last-minute panic? How do you manage to be ready to sit down, smiling and unruffled, at the head of that beautiful table?

There are two basic answers to these questions. First, plan ahead, and, second, plan what you are comfortable with. Other elements, of course, go into creating a memorable party—an interesting mix of guests, an imaginative menu, a lovely setting—but they are all a part of planning. And planning is easiest if you put it all down on paper in a business-like manner.

Opposite is a tried and true worksheet that will help you think through your party carefully. It will help you organize your preparations so that you are in control throughout, so that you are, indeed, a smiling and unruffled hostess.

Buy looseleaf paper and a notebook, and use this sample as a guide. Write down everything. Writing out details forces you to think through your plans. The pages can then be posted on your refrigerator or bulletin board for guidance during the party. If you keep records like this for each party you give, and then file them in a notebook, in a few years you will have an invaluable source book of amounts to prepare, menus that work well, serving dishes to use with what, and things not to try again. Picture yourself as a professional caterer, and let's go through the worksheet step-by-step.

1. **The Occasion, Event, Reason for the Party.** If you have an obvious reason for a party—a holiday, a business obligation, a bridal shower—this is easy. But if you have a lengthy list of social obligations or just want to have a party, this takes some thought. It is easier to build a party around an event or theme, even if you have to invent one. Is Super Bowl Sunday coming or a special performance of an opera or symphony? Is your garden bursting with flowers or have you just built a backyard skating rink? If so, take advantage of such occasions. Or pick a historical date, such as the discovery of gold in California, or the first walk on the moon, and have a gold rush or a moonscape party. Make sure you keep your guests in mind, though, and don't over-reach them. If they are sports-minded, and you have planned an evening of chamber music and dessert, you have two strikes against you. A theme party is fun to plan, and is a good icebreaker if your guests do not know each other well.

2. **Date and Time.** Give yourself as much time as possible to plan and prepare for a party. Send or extend invitations three to four weeks ahead for a large affair or a party during the holiday season. For small, informal parties, two or three weeks is enough time for planning and inviting guests.

3. **Type of Party (brunch, luncheon, open house, etc.).** Decide what kind of party you want to give. Luncheons and dinners are usually small sit-down affairs and, therefore, limited in number of guests, location, and menu. Warmth, fine food, and conviviality are the hallmarks of the small luncheon or dinner. The larger, noisier affairs, the coffees, brunches, cocktail parties, and buffet suppers, offer more flexibility, accommodate more people, and give you a wider range of menu and decorating possibilities.

Carefully think through your resources before deciding on what kind of party you will give. Do you have enough dishes, seating space, serving space, oven and refrigerator space for a large buffet supper or would a cocktail party be better? Some shortages or handicaps can be overcome by renting or borrowing equipment, moving outside in summer, or using a bedroom or den for seating, but a too small kitchen or a single bathroom is an obstacle difficult to overcome. It is better to settle on several smaller suppers or a staggered-time cocktail party than to cram everyone you know into space that is too small.

4. **Guest List.** Often the hardest part of having a party is deciding whom to invite so that you have an interesting, well-balanced guest list. Your guests are the most important elements of your party. You are having it for them, after all, and you want to please them. It is the interaction of your guests that will make your party memorable, run-of-the-mill, or dull. Mixing your guest list is important. Bring fresh faces and fresh ideas into a group; mix generations; balance talkers and listeners. Just remember that if half the people don't know the others, you must act as the catalyst that brings them all together and helps them find a common ground.

The size of your guest list probably will dictate whether you send invitations or telephone. Make a complete list and note the acceptances and regrets. Do not be afraid to call those you have not heard from.

5. **Menu and Food Preparation.** Again, carefully assess your time, energy, and resources when planning your menu. If time and budget limit you to fettucine Alfredo and red table wine, so be it. Such an evening can be warm and exciting. If the sky is the limit and you feel like tackling a Roman feast complete with costumes and a staff of servants, try it. Just do what you are comfortable with. Don't include dishes demanding split-second timing or last-minute attention. If you are constantly bobbing up and down at the table or disappearing for long stints in the kitchen, your guests will feel that they have caused too much trouble.

Keep the season in mind and feature fresh fruits or vegetables whenever possible. Picture how your choices will look on the plate to be sure you have color and texture contrasts. Beware of sauces that cover indiscriminately.

After you have selected a tentative menu, figure out and write down how far ahead each dish can be made, how much you need of each one, and how long it realistically will take you to make them. Make sure you have enough space in your refrigerator or freezer to store make-aheads. Now is the time to simplify. Lastly, decide what tableware you will use to serve each dish. After the party, it is helpful to update these lists: How long did it take to make each dish? How much was left over, etc.?

6. **Logistics.** This is the nitty-gritty. Walk through your party on paper. Where will you have guests put their coats? What about umbrellas or boots if it is raining or snowing? Decide where you will place your bar and your food table. Plan your traffic pattern so you don't create a bottleneck in the front hall.

The logistics for a sit-down luncheon or dinner are fairly simple. Decide on dishes, linens, centerpiece, color scheme, and music or entertainment and you have it. Plan no more than 45 minutes to an hour for cocktails before dinner and always go easy on the hors d'oeuvres. They are meant to whet the appetite, not kill it.

For a small to medium-sized cocktail party, coffee, or tea, the logistics are also fairly simple. Decide where you will serve your drinks and what bar supplies you will need, plan a table or area for food service, and buy, rent, or borrow enough glasses, cups, napkins, and so forth.

As you add more people or decide on a more complicated event, you must assess your resources more carefully. You may want to consider hiring extra help to tend bar or assist in the kitchen. If you are doing a brunch or buffet supper, you need to look for space for everyone to sit down, if not at tables, at least on stair steps or cushions on the floor. It is impossible to eat standing up with a plate in one hand and a drink in the other. You also need to plan your buffet service carefully; holding a plate in one hand limits you severely. Tossed salads are especially hard to scoop with one spoon and meats are impossible to carve. It is always a good idea to test serving arrangements by setting your table several days ahead with the dishes you will use. Then, if your plan works, mark each spot with the name of the dish on a slip of paper.

If you can possibly set up tables and chairs for dining, your guests will be much more comfortable. Look over your house with a fresh eye. Do you have room corners big enough for a card table and chairs? Can you put cushions around a coffee table or put a cloth on an end table? Could you use a bedroom if beds were pushed aside?

Be careful, however, not to isolate a few guests from the main party. In warm weather, it is tempting to invite more people than you can handle indoors, but be sure you have a rain plan.

Investigate rental outlets, party shops, and linen supply stores in your area and see what they have available in the way of tables, chairs, cloths, napkins, dishes, silver, serving pieces, etc. They can be a life-saver, or at least a party-saver, and can often give you a fresh idea for a color scheme or a party theme.

PARTY PLANNING *(continued)*

7. **Ambience.** These are the creative touches, the thoughtful details that make a party memorable. Use your imagination, be yourself, do what pleases you, and what you hope, therefore, will please your guests. Use light, music, pattern, color, to create effect and carry out the theme of, or reason for, your party.

A mime greeting guests at the front door, a collection of windup toys or antique dolls on display, scooped-out vegetables from the garden used as serving dishes, a huge centerpiece of perfect strawberries—all signal a creative and thoughtful hostess. The details of your party reflect your personality and your interests and add a personal dimension.

Always keep in mind that you are responsible for your guests' well-being. But that does not mean you cannot relax and enjoy your party. If you are enjoying the party and the company of your guests, chances are they are too.

After-the-Party Hints   *Mary S. Martin*

Do not throw away the water in which eggs have been boiled; use it to water house plants. It contains many minerals.

A solution of crushed cigarettes or a cigar stub added to one quart of water will perk up new-cut foliage and prolong its freshness.

Stale club soda is good for watering plants. The chemicals add vigor and color to greenery.

Pour leftover tea in the saucer of African violets or on ferns. Water geraniums with beer to make sensational plants.

If you have too much water in a vase, don't move it; get your baster from the kitchen and draw out enough to lower the water level.

If water from your centerpiece has spilled onto your tablecloth, get out your hair dryer and blow your cloth dry in a few fast minutes.

If you place candles in your freezer overnight before using, they will drip less.

A little mint in a garden arrangement will add a delightful, subtle fragrance and absorb stale odors.

FOUR-STAR EVENTS

Helen R. Haddick   *Joan D. Siebenthaler*

GOLD RUSH SUPPER

Chilly Days Chili
Saucy Spinach Salad
*Sourdough Bread
Old-Fashioned Raisin Pie

C elebrating an event, almost any event, can bring bright sunshine into a winter-weary home. As an example, we are celebrating the discovery of gold in California, January 24, 1848, which started the great rush of pioneers westward. The discovery spawned a myriad of prospectors' camps and rough-and-tumble mining towns full of gamblers, saloon owners, and fancy women. It was a colorful and exciting era, so let's celebrate it.

Prospectors did not set a fancy table; in fact, they set no table at all. So a denim cloth or Indian blanket spread in front of a fireplace would work perfectly to serve this supper. Use bandana kerchiefs for napkins, and tin cups and tin pie plates for dishes.

A big kettle of steaming chili on the hearth, along with a basket of sourdough bread—what could be tastier or more appropriate? Sourdough was the prospector's staple fare. The Old-Fashioned Raisin Pie is included to remind you of the Spanish missions which dotted the California coast during the Gold Rush era. The menu is an easy one to prepare, ahead of time or that day. Emphasis here is on simplicity and fun.

A tin can or an enameled coffee pot filled with flowers or greens would make a great centerpiece for your cloth or blanket. A pierced coffee-can lantern also would be appropriate.

After supper, linger in front of the fire, and tell tall tales in the Mark Twain vein. And if anyone strums a guitar, revive some of the old mining town ballads.

All recipes except those starred are listed in the Index.

FOUR-STAR EVENTS

ST. VALENTINE'S DAY DINNER

Avocado with Crab
Dilled Cream of Green Soup
Roast Game Hens
Herbed Tomato Bake
Strawberries and Cream Pie

St. Valentine, the third-century martyred saint, probably had less to do with our February 14th celebrations than the pagan Roman festival of the Lupercalia, which coincided with the saint's day. Nevertheless, in his name we celebrate Valentine's Day, exchange lacy greeting cards, and offer expressions of love through hearts, flowers, and poetry. Here, then, is a feast for lovers.

A Valentine's Day dinner is an occasion to set the loveliest table you possibly can. A lace tablecloth, your family silver, Grandmother's antique china—all are appropriate. Add a touch of classic beauty with an arrangement of pink or red roses and baby's breath.

We have chosen a menu that includes a variety of colors—pink, red, green, and white—to add to the visual elegance of your table and complement the romantic mood. The dinner is prepared ahead of time. The Avocado with Crab and the soup are chilled, the Roast Game Hens and Herbed Tomatoes bake together unattended, and the pie waits in the refrigerator so that you can enjoy your leisurely evening at the table.

Background music is essential and now is a time to be sentimental about old favorites. Serve your finest bottle of wine with dinner and, perhaps, champagne as a finale to toast your Valentine.

FOUR-STAR EVENTS

EASTER EGG HUNT BRUNCH

Strawberry Soup
Ham Balls with Cumberland Sauce
Corn Custard
*Steamed Fresh Asparagus
Orange Date Bread
Maple-Nut Coffee Cake

Easter for children means the Easter Bunny, an Easter egg hunt, and be-ribboned Easter baskets of goodies. This Hunt Brunch is planned, there-fore, for the children, but doesn't a bit of the child remain in each of us? Give each child a basket and, weather permitting, hold the egg hunt out-of-doors. The Easter Bunny will have hidden colored hard-cooked eggs and foil-wrapped chocolates or cookies in not-too-obvious places among the trees and shrubbery. It is fun to include a golden egg and give a prize to the child who finds it.

To help turn your garden into an Easter wonderland and add to the excitement of the hunt, try tying balloons with trailing ribbons and spot them like colorful spring flowers through bushes, garden beds, and along fences or doorways. The children will be enchanted.

Daffodils, tulips, and flowering branches herald the Easter season. Bring them indoors to give your home a springtime mood. If Easter falls too early in the year for these blossoms, try forcing bulbs or branches as mentioned in the Potpourri Chapter.

Transfer the look of spring to your Easter table by using a blend of yellows, blues, and greens in your tablecloth and napkins. And an Easter egg tree makes an elegant centerpiece. If possible, schedule an egg decorating session before Easter and have the children decorate blown eggs. (Have the children initial and date the eggs. They can be carefully stored and brought out year after year to grace your table and be admired.) Hang the eggs on a flowering branch or a bare branch sprayed white, securely anchored in a low bowl or basket.

Carry out the Easter theme by using as many baskets, pottery bunnies or ducks, or flowery serving dishes as you can. The brunch menu has been designed to appeal especially to children, but they may be too excited to eat.

All recipes except those starred are listed in the Index.

FOUR-STAR EVENTS

CHRISTENING BRUNCH

Sherried Crab Soup
Crêpes à la Florentine
*Canadian Bacon Slices with Currant Glaze
*Fruit Bowl
Cranberry-Pear Sorbet

A christening is always a joyous event, and a lovely way to celebrate is with an elegant brunch following the baby's baptism. Most of the food can be prepared before you leave for the church. Last minute warming of the soup, crêpes, and bacon can be managed after you get home. Since this party may include several generations, remember the children in your planning. Have rolls and juices they will enjoy while the adults celebrate with stronger drinks before brunch.

A watermelon hollowed and shaped like a baby buggy to hold the fruit would make a spectacular centerpiece for your table. If you are not feeling that creative or you are the busy mother of the new baby, try an antique doll or teddy bear in a doll rocker. If flowers seem more appropriate, there is nothing lovelier than baby's breath with a few delicate rosebuds. Potpourri wrapped in netting and tied with pink or blue ribbons would be a nice touch at each place and would provide the guests take-home mementos as well. Chilled champagne should be on hand at the end of brunch to toast the baby, who may be sleeping soundly by now.

It would be fun to have on display baby books or pictures of grandparents, aunts, uncles, parents, or siblings attending. Predictions of family resemblances are inevitable.

All recipes except those starred are listed in the Index.

FOUR-STAR EVENTS

MEXICAN FIESTA

Spinach Dip with Green Chilies
Taco Dip
Cold Avocado Soup
Enchiladas
Green Pepper Sauté
Almond Flan

A fiesta can celebrate almost anything—All Souls' Day, Three Kings' Day, a birthday, a season. Take your pick or invent an occasion. Whatever you are celebrating, your fiesta must be gay, with bright colors, lights, and music. Luminaries (candles anchored in sand inside paper bags) lining your front walk will help establish a festive mood. Invite guests to bring along a musical instrument and create your own mariachi band during the cocktail hour. Have on hand some castanets. A few flamenco and carioca records might help get the band started. Warning: Your guests may get so carried away with the music, you will have a hard time luring them to the buffet table.

Here again, brilliant colors and lights are the mood-setters. Try a rebozo or bright strip of fabric for a table runner. For a centerpiece, use a piñata on a clay pot pedestal or hanging from an overhead chandelier; surround it with bright splashes of yellow, orange, or red zinnias or marigolds. Mexican tin candelabra are perfect for the table if you have them or you can scatter votive lights in hollowed-out lemon shells along your table. Terra cotta or painted pottery serving dishes are just right for this table. Add more color by wrapping individual silver place settings in bright paper napkins tied with contrasting color yarn.

Station the host or a trusted guest at the end of the buffet table to whir the cold avocado soup in a blender and pour into paper cups that match the napkins. The enchiladas are made ahead and can be frozen if desired. The flan is also made ahead and chilled. So except for reheating the Green Pepper Sauté and the enchiladas, you can stay out of the kitchen and enjoy the party. In this case, translate fiesta as "relaxed and easy."

FOUR-STAR EVENTS

LUNCH FOR THE BICYCLE BUNCH

White Wine Sangria
Cheese Shorties
Mediterranean Shrimp Salad
Oatmeal Muffins
Fresh Blueberry Pie

A bike treasure hunt in the cool of the morning, followed by lunch on a tree-shaded lawn, is a grand way to spend a summer day. Rally your bike-riding friends at your house about 10 a.m., and give them coffee or fruit juice, a pep talk, route map, and a list of "treasures" to bring back. (Suggestions: milk-weed pod, discarded beer can, smooth pebble, pine cone—whatever they might be likely to find en route.)

The planned menu is easy enough that host and hostess can go along on the bike hike, if they plan a shortcut toward the end in order to arrive home first.

Greet the tired returnees with a frosty pitcher of White Wine Sangria and a tray of Cheese Shorties. Then, after everyone has compared "treasures," serve your healthful, cool Shrimp Salad and Oatmeal Muffins. The muffins can be made ahead and frozen, the salad ingredients prepared the day before.

Picnic tables on the lawn covered with checked or patterned cloths, or sheets in cool colors, would be inviting for a leisurely lunch after a morning of activity. Roadside wildflowers such as Queen Anne's Lace, chicory, or goldenrod spilling from bicycle baskets would make easy and appropriate centerpieces.

Fresh blueberry pie, made ahead and chilled, tops off this "summertime and the livin' is easy" party.

292

FOUR-STAR EVENTS

MIDSUMMER'S NIGHT DINNER

Steak Tartare
Shrimp in Mustard Sauce
Summer Gazpacho
Grilled Lamb Chops
Brown Rice Salad
Snap Pea Stir-Fry
Pain (Extra)-Ordinaire
Cold Grand Marnier Soufflé

Soft summer evenings are meant for romantic dining with friends on a candlelit terrace. While Midsummer's Night is traditionally June 23rd, any mid-summer night can cast its spell if the mood is set. With the garden in full bloom, use as many blossoms, potted plants, and cut vines as possible. Torches around the terrace and white twinkle lights on background shrubs will add magic to the evening. Music is essential. If a strolling violinist is out of the question, pipe music from the house out onto the terrace.

Time cocktails and dinner so that your garden shows off to best advantage before dinner. Draw your guests into the garden before dusk by setting up your bar and an hors d'oeuvres table in a far corner. As dusk falls, begin serving dinner. Again, feature the opulence of summer with a buffet centerpiece of flowers or vegetables. (Refer to the Potpourri Chapter for suggestions on using eggplants, asparagus, or cabbage as containers.) Small round tables for four are best for this occasion.

To match dinner partners, pin a name on the back of each arriving guest, using names of famous lovers, e.g., Dante and Beatrice, Romeo and Juliet, Sampson and Delilah. Each guest must determine who he/she is by asking true or false questions of the other guests. Center each small table with a bud vase of flowers, and place flickering votive candles in stemmed glasses at each place.

Except for grilling the lamb chops and stir-frying the peas, all food preparation is done ahead and chilled or frozen, so that you, too, can enjoy the magic of this evening.

FOUR-STAR EVENTS

TAILGATE PICNIC

Savory Mushroom Tarts
Brandy-English Walnut Pâté
Carrot Soup
Pasta, Seafood & Basil Cream
*Crusty French Bread
Pumpkin-Apple Pie

Any autumn weekend near football bowls or stadia, you will find moveable feasts served from station wagon tailgates. The tailgate picnic is a uniquely American accompaniment to the "big game," and helps bring longtime rivalries to fever pitch.

Anything you have that heightens the rivalry and adds to the excitement of the game—team colors, mascots, pennants—should be used. Carry out colors in a tartan blanket spread as a tablecloth, in napkins, and serving dishes. Highly polished apples and nuts in a basket make a lovely centerpiece which can be dismantled for a mid-game treat.

Surprise, luxury, and plenty are the key ingredients of a moveable feast, according to Julia Child. Anything less is brown-bagging, an appropriate means of sustenance, but not what we have in mind for the "big game."

We have chosen a menu that is relatively portable without sacrificing the posh effect we are striving for. Counting on a crisp, cool day, we have chosen a hot soup to follow the appetizers and drinks, and then a cold entrée.

Containers are very important as they are decorative elements as well as serving and storage pieces. A wicker hamper for plates, silver, and food sets the tone. Covered terrines, pottery dishes, baskets, antique jars, school mugs for soup are all appropriate. Don't use paper or plastic—they are for brown-bagging!

Save the coffee and Pumpkin-Apple Pie to enjoy after the game. It will help bring the euphoric victors back to earth or dispel the gloom of defeat. And while you are enjoying dessert, the homebound traffic jam will have a chance to clear.

All recipes except those starred are listed in the Index.

FOUR-STAR EVENTS

YELLOW BUS PROGRESSIVE DINNER

An American Version of Sushi   Avocado Caviar Pie
Stuffed Cocktail Tomatoes   Brie en Croûte
Stuffed Mushrooms

* * * *

Artichoke-Chicken Casserole with Green Noodles
Lemon-Butter Carrots   Dilled Cheese Bread
Piquant Molded Beet Salad   Pea Pod Salad

* * * *

Mother's Shortcake with Strawberries or Peaches
Pecan Tarts
Mud Pies
"Cracker Jack" Popcorn

What could be more fun than having a yellow school bus carry you back through time—and three courses of delicious food—to your childhood? This is a progressive dinner for six couples to give, two at each bus stop. Hiring a waiter and cook's helper is recommended. It makes service for a large group much easier, and the cost of bus rental, waiter, and cook's helper, split six ways, isn't much. Bonus: Planning with your co-hosts can be as much fun as the party itself.

A yellow bus rented from your school district will move your guests smoothly from one house to the next and finally return them all to the starting point at a reasonable hour. At the same time, it is a nostaglic reminder of an earlier time.

Contemporary decorating, to go with the planned hors d'oeuvres, is in order at the first house. The music, colors, serving dishes, and centerpiece you choose should all be compatible with today's lifestyle. The sushi, caviar, and other appetizers that start the evening reflect sophisticated tastes.

If all six couples search through their memorabilia for mementos of their teen years, there should be enough posters, pennants, books, records, letter sweaters, and pompons to decorate a whole school, much less the second house for the main course. A menu on a blackboard and a tablecloth with napkins in school colors will help carry out the theme. Music of the '50s, '60s, or whatever decade fits your guest list is certainly in order.

Decorations at the third house are easy. Toys, balloons, party hats, strings of paper dolls, nursery rhymes—the possibilities are endless. Six couples at a planning session can come up with some really creative decorating ideas for all three of these themes. Let your imagination run wild.

The food planned for each house is not particularly easy, but preparation divided among six couples makes it light work. Plan the evening so that each couple is free to participate in most of the fun.

After the mud pies are devoured, give each guest a paper sack of "Cracker Jack" Popcorn and put them back on the school bus for the trip back to reality.

FOUR-STAR EVENTS

TREE TRIMMING SUPPER

Frosted Ham Roll   Hot Swiss Cheese Spread

Wassail Bowl

Pork Loin with Plum Sauce   Make-Ahead Potatoes

Sweet-Sour Beans   Cranberries in the Snow Salad

Christmas Cookies

Trimming the Christmas tree should be an occasion for fun and warm fellowship. By planning Pennsylvania Dutch-type decorations and supper to go with the trimming, we also are acknowledging the source of this treasured Christmas tradition. The Pennsylvania Dutch (Germans, really) credited Martin Luther with decorating the first fir tree and brought the custom to the colonies.

Put your family and a few close friends to work before supper stringing popcorn and cranberries to swag your tree as the Pennsylvania Dutch did. (Decorate the tree also with polished apples, nuts, and gingerbread cookies or with frosted cookies in the shapes of apples, birds, and tulips, as they did.) Meanwhile, serve your tree trimmers the Frosted Ham Roll and Hot Cheese Spread, and invite them to partake of the Wassail Bowl. (Actually, this is an old English tradition, not Pennsylvania Dutch, but it will promote "good will among men.") Vary the wassail recipe to suit the ages of children involved.

When it is time for supper, lead the group to a traditional table set with a red or green felt runner and place mats. Use votive candles at each place and a centerpiece of pine or holly sprigs in a stockade-type container made of candy canes or cinnamon sticks and tied with a red and green plaid ribbon.

The supper's entree, pork tenderloin, is typical fare for Germans, but we have compromised on the traditional seven sweets and seven sours by including the Sweet-Sour Beans. The Cranberries in the Snow Salad adds a festive holiday touch to the supper.

A small table tree, trimmed with extra cookies and apples to be eaten for dessert, would be a nice touch. Now, sit back, devour the cookies, and admire your Pennsylvania Dutch Christmas tree.

X | Potpourri

COCKTAIL PARTY GUIDE

	For 12	For 24	For 48
Liquor:			
Scotch	1 liter	1 liter	2 liters
Bourbon	1 liter	1 liter	1 liter
Vodka	1 liter	1 liter	2 liters
*Gin	1 liter	1 liter	2 liters
Blended Whiskey	1 liter	1 liter	1 liter
Light Rum	(optional)	1 liter	1 liter
Wines:			
White	2 liters	4 liters	6 liters
Red	1 liter	1 liter	2 liters
Mix:			
Perrier	1 six pack	1 six pack	2 six packs
Club soda	1 bottle	2 bottles	2 bottles
*Tonic	2 bottles	2 bottles	4 bottles
Ginger ale	1 bottle	1 bottle	2 bottles
Cola (regular and diet)	2 bottles	2 bottles	4 bottles
Ice	12 pounds	24 pounds	50 pounds

(Bottles specified are 28-oz. size.)

Note: One liter equals 33.8 fluid ounce or 1000 milliliters. A standard bottle of liquor contains 750 milliliters (ml.). Liquor for parties may be bought in the larger, one liter size.

*Amounts should be doubled for warm weather parties.

CHARTING YOUR COURSE

Betty J. Jones

SHOPPING AND COOKING FOR 12

Meat

Beef	5 pounds
Ham	5 pounds
Hamburgers	4 pounds
Meat Loaf	3 pounds
Pork	5 pounds
Weiners	3 pounds

Salads

Fruit	2½ quarts
Potato	1½ quarts
Vegetable	2½ quarts
Salad Dressing	1 pint

Bread

Sliced Bread	1½ loaves
Rolls	2 dozen
Buns	2 dozen

Vegetables

Baked Beans	½ gallon
Cabbage for Slaw	2½ pounds
Lettuce	2 heads
Potatoes	4 pounds
Vegetables	3 cans (17 oz.)

Dessert

Cakes	1 cake (2-layer round or 9x13 sheet)
Ice Cream	½ gallon
Pies	2½ pies

Other

Coffee	½ pound
Cream	1 pint
Milk	2½ quarts
Sugar	1 cup
Olives	1 pint
Pickles	1 pint

CHARTING YOUR COURSE

RECIPE INGREDIENT EQUIVALENTS

3 slices dry bread	1 cup dry bread crumbs
1¼ slices soft bread	1 cup soft bread crumbs
1 stick butter (¼ lb.)	½ cup
2 stalks celery, chopped	1 cup
16 ounces (1 lb.) processed cheese	4 cups shredded cheese
1 square chocolate	1 ounce
8-10 egg whites	1 cup
12-14 egg yolks	1 cup
1 pound flour	4½ cups, sifted
9 graham crackers, crushed	1 cup crumbs
1 lemon	2½-3 tablespoonfuls juice
8 ounces elbow macaroni	4½ cups cooked macaroni
1 pound fresh mushrooms	1 (6 oz.) can
8 ounces uncooked egg noodles	4 cups cooked noodles
1 medium-sized onion, chopped	½ cup
1 orange	6-7 tablespoonfuls juice
1 cup precooked rice	3 cups cooked rice
1 cup uncooked rice	3½-4 cups cooked rice
8 ounces uncooked spaghetti	5 cups cooked spaghetti
1 pound brown sugar	2¼ cups, firmly packed
1 pound powdered sugar	3⅓ cups

CHARTING YOUR COURSE

SUBSTITUTIONS

In Place of:	You May Use:
1 cup sugar	⅔ cup honey plus ½ teaspoon soda
1½ cups corn syrup	1 cup sugar plus ½ cup water
1 cup brown sugar	½ cup granulated sugar plus ½ cup molasses plus ¼ teaspoon baking soda
1 square unsweetened chocolate	3 tablespoons cocoa plus 1 tablespoon butter
1 square sweetened chocolate	1 square unsweetened chocolate plus 1 tablespoon sugar
1 cup whole milk	½ cup evaporated milk plus ½ cup water or 1 cup dry milk plus 2 tablespoons butter or 1 cup water plus 4 tablespoons powdered milk
1 cup skim milk	4 tablespoons dry non-fat milk solids plus water to make 1 cup
1 cup buttermilk	1 tablespoon vinegar or lemon juice plus whole milk to make 1 cup (let stand 5 minutes)
1 cup sour cream	1 cup yogurt or 1 cup evaporated milk plus 1 tablespoon vinegar or 1 cup cottage cheese blended with 2 tablespoons milk and 1 tablespoon lemon juice
1 cup butter or margarine	⅞ cup oil or lard, or ¼ cup rendered chicken fat
1 teaspoon baking powder	1 teaspoon cream of tartar plus scant teaspoon baking soda
1 cup cake flour	⅞ cup all-purpose flour
1 teaspoon cornstarch or 1½ teaspoons arrowroot	2 tablespoons flour
White wine	Apple cider or juice
½ cup tartar sauce	6 tablespoons mayonnaise and 2 tablespoons pickle relish
1 teaspoon dry mustard	2½ teaspoons prepared mustard
1 teaspoon lemon juice	1 teaspoon vinegar
1 teaspoon marjoram	1 teaspoon oregano
Fresh parsley	Fresh celery leaves

THE ADDED TOUCH

Nancy S. Barber

Items from your garden or grocery add color, flavor, and texture to food. Ranging from a sprig of parsley to an edible centerpiece, these added touches can turn any meal into a visual delight.

Food	Garnish	Procedure
Citrus fruits (oranges, lemons, limes, etc.)	Rose	Peel fruit in continuous ¼-inch strip; coil tightly, skin side out. Secure with toothpick.
	Bow	Cut radius from edge to center in thin slice. Twist in opposite directions.
Grapes	Frosted grapes	Dip small bunches into unbeaten egg white. Roll in granulated sugar and dry thoroughly.
Cherries (Maraschino or Queen Anne)	Poinsettia	Cut cherries into daisy-like shapes. Use wedges of green cherries for leaves. Use to top desserts or freeze in ice cubes.
Beets, turnips, or yams	Rose	Cut 6-8 thin diagonal slices. Wind several narrow slices tightly around pencil. Remove pencil and overlap remaining slices around coil. Secure with toothpicks.
Turnips	Gardenia	Cut 6 thin slices from large end and 6 from middle; place in ice water to curl. Skewer large slices in circular pattern; skewer smaller slices on top, forming second layer.

THE ADDED TOUCH *(continued)*

Food	Garnish	Procedure
Turnips *(continued)*	Peony	Stem end down, cut series of thin vertical slices around outside of peeled turnip to within ⅓ inch of bottom. Make a second series of slices, just inside and overlapping the first. Repeat layers to center of turnip. Place in ice water to bloom. Dry and lightly brush top of each petal with a little water-diluted food coloring.
	Tulip	Follow directions for turnip peony. As you finish each layer of slices, remove every second petal, alternating positions with each row. Scoop out center and place in ice water.
Radish	Miniature Rose	Peel as you would an apple with continuous long thin strip. Place in salt water (1 tablespoon to 1 quart water) for 5 minutes. Wrap in loose coil to form rosette. Skewer.
	Pompon	Stem end down, cut series of thin parallel vertical slices to within ¼ inch of bottom. Holding tightly, cut again in crisscross pattern. Place in ice water.
	Begonia	Cut series of horizontal wedges around bottom; cut second series of wedges just above and overlapping the first. Repeat layers to top of radish. Cut ⅛-inch thick disks from second radish and fit between wedges of first radish.
Broccoli and Cauliflower	Florets	Skewer small florets and slices from thick stems.

303

THE ADDED TOUCH *(continued)*

Food	Garnish	Procedure
Cucumber	Leaves	Cut thin lengthwise strips of peeling. Shape and notch to resemble leaves.
Gherkins	Tassels	Split the gherkin lengthwise almost through to broad end. Continue making as many horizontal slices as possible. Press with your thumb to fan out.
Onion	Chrysanthemum	With stem end down, cut series of parallel vertical slices through peeled onion to within ½ inch of bottom. Holding tightly, cut again in crisscross pattern. Place in hot water to open. Water may be tinted with food coloring.
Bay Leaves	Leaves	Tuck under fruit or vegetable flowers for finishing touch.
Ham, turkey, beef, or cold cuts	Cones	Roll or fold thin slices of meat and fill with pickle, olive, or small pickled corn. Secure with toothpick.

Edible Centerpieces

Fresh fruits, vegetables, and even scooped-out loaves of bread make interesting containers for many foods. Try hollowing out the center of eggplants, watermelon or cantaloupe, fresh pineapple, cabbage heads, gourds or pumpkins, onions, oranges, lemons, and grapefruit.

Make an asparagus stockade by placing upright stalks of fresh green asparagus around a can or jar and tying with a bright piece of yarn.

Use your imagination and creativity to create your own edible centerpieces.

THE ADDED TOUCH
Added Color

Red
Apples
Beets
Cherries
Cherry Tomatoes
Cranberries
Peppers, Red Bell or Chili
Radishes
Raspberries
Strawberries
Tokay Grapes
Watermelon

Orange
Banana Squash
Cantaloupe
Carrots
Kumquats
Peppers, Orange or Chili
Pumpkins
Yams

Yellow
Cheese
Crookneck Squash
Eggs, hard-cooked, sliced
Lemons
Pickled Corn
Pineapple
Turnips, tinted

Green
Artichokes
Asparagus
Broccoli
Chives
Cucumbers
Endive
Green Beans
Honey Dew Melon
Kiwi Fruit
Limes
Olives
Parsley
Pea Pods, Sugar Snap Peas
Peppers, Green Bell or Chili
Thompson Seedless Grapes
Zucchini

White
Bleached Endive
Cauliflower
Eggs, hard-cooked
Mushrooms
Onions
Parsnips
Scallions
Turnips
White Radishes

Purple & Blue
Blueberries
Concord Grapes
Eggplant
Purple Cabbage
Ripe Olives

QUICKSILVER RECIPES

WATERCRESS SOUP *Glenda Shrader*

Place 1 bunch of watercress, stems removed, and 2 cans of cream of mushroom soup in blender and blend. Add 2 soup cans full of cold milk and mix well. Heat and serve—with a dash of Tabasco sauce if desired. This soup may also be served cold. Yield: 6 servings.

NEW ENGLAND CLAM CHOWDER *Mrs. Paul T. Welch (Mary)*

Heat in double boiler: a 10¾-ounce can of cream of potato soup; a 10¾-ounce can of New England clam chowder; a 6½-ounce can of minced clams, drained; 5 ounces of milk or half-and-half; and 5 ounces of chicken bouillon or homemade chicken stock. Add a pat of butter to each serving. These are pantry items and, although preparation is fast and easy, your guests will think you worked for hours. Yield: 4 servings.

BEER BISCUITS *Elizabeth Donovan*

Mix together 4 cups of Bisquick, 2 tablespoons of sugar, and 1 can of beer. Spoon into ungreased muffin tins (tins should be about ¾ full) and bake at 350 degrees for 20 minutes or until brown. Yield: 2 dozen.

QUICK AND EASY BISCUITS *Mrs. William Curran Rogers, Sr.*

Combine 1¾ cups of self-rising flour and 1 cup of whipping cream. Mix with fork until all the flour is absorbed. Knead on floured bread board and roll out dough to ½-inch thickness. Cut out biscuits of desired size and bake at 375 degrees until lightly browned. Yield: 12-15 delicious, flaky biscuits.

CHOCOLATE CHIP ROLLS *Louise French*

Prepare a 15-ounce package of frozen white dinner rolls according to package instructions. When dough is partially risen, add ½ cup of chocolate chips, milk chocolate or semi-sweet. Bake according to package directions and serve warm with butter.

PRALINE CRACKERS *Marylizabeth Grefe*

Spread 27 whole graham crackers (broken in half) in a single layer in a jelly roll pan. Heat 2 sticks of margarine and 1 cup of brown sugar to boiling point, and continue boiling for 2 minutes, stirring constantly. Add 1 cup of chopped nuts and pour the mixture over the crackers, covering them as completely as possible. Bake at 350 degrees for 10 minutes. Separate crackers while still warm and cool on wire rack. Yield: 4 dozen.

QUICKSILVER RECIPES

ROASTED ORIENTAL CHICKEN
Betty Sue Wydman

Combine ½ cup of Italian dressing and ½ cup of soy sauce, and marinate a whole chicken (3 to 3½ pounds) for 1-3 hours, turning once or twice. Remove from marinade and bake at 350 degrees for 1-1½ hours. Baste once or twice with marinade. For a delicious salty gravy, heat marinade and thicken, if desired, with cornstarch mixed with cold water. Yield: 4 servings.

EASY, EASY CHICKEN
Mrs. Fred B. Davis

Place a fryer, cut up, in pan or pyrex dish. Season to taste with Jane's Krazy Mixed-Up Salt and lemon pepper (1 or 2 tablespoonfuls). Cover and bake at 350 degrees for 30-40 minutes, remove cover and bake another 15 minutes. This is also delicious cold, and makes a good picnic dish. Yield: 3-4 servings.

TIPSY CHICKEN
Mrs. Donald Peacock

Combine ⅔ cup of salad or cooking oil, ⅔ cup of bourbon, and ⅔ cup of soy sauce and marinate a whole chicken overnight or for several hours, turning occasionally. Bake in marinade at 325 degrees until chicken is tender, about 1 hour, basting a few times. Broth may be made into gravy or served as is over rice. If preferred, chicken may be cut into pieces. Yield: 4-6 servings.

ROSY MEATBALL SAUCE
Jocelyn Feeman

Mix together and heat an 8-ounce can of tomato sauce and a 16-ounce can of whole cranberry sauce. Add favorite meatballs. (Make meatballs days ahead; bake on a broiling pan to catch the drippings; freeze individually and bag.) This is a very different type of meatball sauce with a reddish color and zippy flavor. Yield: 12 servings.

MICROWAVE BAKED APPLE CHUNKS
Lorraine J. Armentrout

Slice 1 small, firm, ripe apple (peel, if desired) into microwave-safe custard cup. Pour small amount of maple syrup (about 2 teaspoonfuls) over apple and dot with butter (about 1 teaspoonful). Microwave for 2 minutes or until apple is soft and tender, stirring once. Serve warm. Good accompaniment for pork. Yield: 1 serving.

MICROWAVE CORN PUDDING
Lou Mason

Beat 2 eggs in a 1-quart casserole, add two 16-ounce cans of creamed corn, salt and pepper to taste, and mix. Cover with waxed paper. Microwave on high setting for 5 minutes. Stir well. Continue cooking on high until just set, 4-8 minutes more. Let stand a few minutes before serving. Yield: 6-8 servings.

QUICKSILVER RECIPES

GREEN BEANS WELL-DRESSED
Constance Klarer

Cook fresh or frozen green beans until tender-crisp, drain, and toss well with Marzetti's Slaw Dressing. Other dressings may be used, but a creamy dressing with a distinctive flavor produces the best result.

CARAMEL-CHOCOLATE SAUCE
Elsie Mason

Combine in double boiler an 8-ounce jar of chocolate sauce, a 14-ounce can of sweetened condensed milk, and 1 stick of margarine or butter. Heat over simmering water until thickened, stirring frequently. This sauce becomes very thick when cool. Yield: 2½ cups.

LIME SHERBET MERINGUES
Constance Klarer

Make or purchase the number of meringues (about 4 inches across) needed, allowing 1 per serving. Fill each meringue with a scoop of lime sherbet and spoon canned black raspberries over the sherbet.

GIFTS WITH A GLOW

Laura S. Fanning   *Susan J. Siebenthaler*

A gift from your kitchen can say many things—from "thanks for inviting us," to "sorry you are sick." Here are suggestions for those occasions when a gift of food might be just the right touch. (See Index for recipe page numbers.)

For Your Hostess

Invited to a friend's house for dinner? It is always nice to take a small gift of food. This is especially true when you go to a dinner party during the Christmas season. Here are some ideas for hostess gifts:

> Quick Fresh Cucumber Pickles
> Bleu Cheese Dressing
> Celery Seed Dressing

Pack the pickles in an old-fashioned canning jar. Pour the salad dressings into small bottles with a cork. To give them a festive look during the holiday season, cover the jar with a round piece of Christmas material, tie with a ribbon, and add a sprig of holly or other greens.

When the Cook Can't Cook

When a friend comes home from the hospital or when a special person you know has a baby, a ready-to-heat casserole can help out a hectic household or a brand new daddy. All that is needed to complete the meal is a salad or some fruit. Here are three casserole recipes that are especially good to take to someone:

> Artichoke-Chicken Casserole
> Asparagus and Chicken Mornay
> Crab-Shrimp Casserole

For a new mother, deliver the casserole in a paper bag decorated by your children with crayons or markers. For a sick friend, wrap the casserole in aluminum foil and accent it with a bow and a small package of herb tea, or silk or straw flowers.

To Say "Thank You" or "Congratulations"

A neighbor helps you out of a tight spot. A good friend gets a promotion. How often have you wanted to say "thank you" or "congratulations" with a little more meaning? Try these recipe ideas for an added touch:

> Marinated Mushrooms
> Spicy Pecans
> Millie's Sugared Nuts

Dress up the nuts by putting them in a measuring cup or china coffee cup and tying a bow to the handle. Or thread bright ribbons through a cherry tomato basket to make a colorful container for the nuts. Try putting the mushrooms in two wine glasses and you might be asked to stay and help celebrate that promotion or award.

GIFTS WITH A GLOW

For the Children

Do you know a child who has just broken a bone and needs to be reminded that life is really O.K.? Or do you want to remember the children of your hostess when you go to visit? Here are some recipe suggestions that can be counted on to please a child:

> Chocolate Pecan Cake Cookies
> Butterscotch Chewies
> Peanut Butter Temptations

Give those cookies extra appeal by piling them into ice-cream cones. Then wrap the entire edible bouquet with plastic wrap and a bow. Or place the cookies in a decorated shoe or cigar box. The children will enjoy the cookies and can use the container for all sorts of collectibles.

Shut-ins and Senior Citizens

It is thoughtful to take something special when visiting shut-ins or senior citizens, especially those who live in a retirement complex where all meals are provided. Check first to make sure there are no dietary restrictions. Why not arrange to take a party to them—a coffee in the morning or an afternoon tea? Call and offer to bring all the fixings for your party. Then arrive with pretty matching napkins, plates, even hot cups. Serve one of these recipes with tea or coffee. Then leave the leftovers so your senior or shut-in can share them with friends. Here are a few ideas:

> Carolina Tea Bread
> Chocolate Pumpkin Nut Bread
> Oatmeal Muffins
> Overnight Coffee Cake

If you place the bread or coffee cake on a cutting board and then wrap the entire package with plastic wrap, it will be handy for serving. Put the muffins in a shiny tin bucket or a planter. After the muffins are gone, the container can hold a plant and brighten your shut-in's room.

Leaving Home and Liking It

Do you have a friend going on a special trip to an exotic place? Do you know a family driving to Grandma and Grandpa's house, two states away? Send them off in style by cooking up a travel kit. Include games for the children and little jars of snacks as well as one of these recipes:

> Dilled Cheese Bread
> Spiced Fruit Bread
> Carol's Caramels
> "Cracker Jack" Popcorn

Pack your travel kit in a disposable fruit basket lined with colorful paper napkins. Another idea is to use a straw hat or sand pail. Then, after all the goodies are gone, the container can come in handy to help entertain the children.

GIFTS WITH A GLOW

New Neighbors

A new family in the neighborhood? Make them feel welcome by taking them a casserole or cake. It will give them a needed break and a new spurt of energy for unpacking. Here are three recipes that can brighten a new neighbor's day:
        Cabbage Casserole
        Apple Nut Coffee Cake
        Strawberry Butter
Assemble the casserole in an aluminum pan and fit the pan inside a box decorated like a house. Take the Strawberry Butter in a disposable cheese crock or jar. The containers will look nice for serving, but then can be thrown away.

The Big Game

You are invited to watch the Super Bowl, or the Derby, or the hockey finals. You are not asked to bring anything, but it might be nice to have something to nibble on while watching that championship game. Here are some appetizer ideas that are easy and good:
        Chicken Cashew Ball
        Winnie's Vidalia Onions
        Glop
If you arrange the Chicken-Cashew Ball on a cutting board, it will be ready for serving. The Glop can be poured into a glass canning jar and decorated with a miniature ball, a small horn, or pennant. You will have all the fixings for cheering on the home team.

Birthdays

How often do you find yourself pondering what to give someone who doesn't need a thing? When that happens, remember that a gift of food is always appropriate, and your birthday honoree undoubtedly will appreciate the time and thought you put into your gift. Here are some suggestions:
        Ohio Buckeyes
        Steamed Cranberry Pudding
        Maple-Glazed Nuts
        Grandmother's Chili Sauce
Make the buckeyes or the nuts look more festive by putting them in a large shell or in wine glasses decorated with silk flowers and a ribbon. Try putting the chili sauce in a special jar or bottle and tying a balloon to the bottle with a ribbon. Or tie a kitchen gadget—a cookie cutter, pizza cutter, wire whisk, or garlic press—to the neck of the bottle

SILVER BELLS AND COCKLE SHELLS

by Mary S. Martin

An easy, inexpensive centerpiece can be made by arranging ivy, pachysandra, and your favorite blossoms in a bowl. The greens look lovely by themselves and last for weeks in water. Changing colors and kinds of blossoms for different effects is quick and easy.

To prevent drooping heads when arranging tulips, stab a straight pin into each stem at an upward angle just below the bloom (this lets out the air bubble), or wrap each stem in damp newspaper and place in refrigerator overnight. Do not cover bloom.

When arranging gladioli, do not cut the stems; break them, and dip in hot water. Use warm water in the container. Bottom blossoms will last much longer.

Would you like to keep your paper white narcissus from growing too tall and flopping over? Start bulbs in pebbles and place in sunlight. Let bulbs grow to a height of six inches. Remove bulbs—roots and all—from pebbles, being careful not to damage roots. Replant in a small amount of potting soil and top with pebbles. Buds will appear on short, strong stems.

SILVER BELLS AND COCKLE SHELLS *(cont.)*

If your Reiger begonias get a fungus that blotches their leaves, spray them with an aerosol can of undiluted Lysol room deodorant.

The expanded styrofoam "peanuts" used in shipping cartons make excellent crocking for large hanging baskets. They are light and provide good drainage.

Beech, forsythia, peony, and crab apple leaves can be prepared by pounding stems and placing in glycerine (or anti-freeze) and water—one part glycerine to two parts water. Remove when leaves become the right color. Minimum time is 10 days. Green food coloring may be added to help preserve color.

To make a holiday arrangement of poinsettias, buy single bloom plants, water well, and remove from pot. Place earth and roots in a plastic bag and secure base with a twistem; put the poinsettias in a bowl with a few sprigs of holly, boxwood, or other greens. They will last many weeks.

Branches of flowering trees and shrubs can be forced into bloom the latter part of February. The easiest to force are apple, pear, flowering cherry, flowering quince, forsythia, and pussy willow. Split or pound stems and place in a bucket of warm water. Put in a sunny room. The closer to the normal blooming time of the plants, the sooner the flowers will appear.

If you would like peonies in July, cut unfurled buds which show color the end of May. Roll buds in newspaper and keep in vegetable drawer of refrigerator for two months. Arrange with baby's breath for your party in July.

The small green plastic cartons in which cherry tomatoes are packaged make reusable holders for almost any bowl or wide-mouth container. Cut a piece of floral foam to fit the carton snugly. Stems can be poked through holes of carton when it is placed upside down.

Flowers and Their Preferred Conditioning

"Conditioning" or "hardening-off" of flowers simply means the treatment given flowers before arranging. This usually consists of putting them in cold water overnight, but some flowers have special needs. The following chart may be helpful:

Cold Water	Cold Water Plus Sugar	Cold Water Plus Salt	Cold Water Plus Dash of Alcohol
Asters	Chrysanthemums	Carnations	Lilacs
Bleeding Heart	Delphiniums	Daffodils	Tulips
Lilies	Larkspur	Violets	
Nasturtiums	Petunias		
Pansies	Roses		
Queen Anne's Lace	Sweet Peas		
Zinnias			

SILVER BELLS AND COCKLE SHELLS *(cont.)*

Some General Guidelines:

Milky Stem Plants—Stem should be charred in flame or dipped in boiling water (protect blossoms and foliage), and then placed in cold water. (Peonies, lilies of the valley, geraniums, snapdragons, and poppies respond to this treatment.)

Woody Stem Plants—Stem should be cut slantwise and split so that water is drawn upward to keep flowers alive.

Greens, Vines, Foliage—Submerge in water for at least one hour.

Additional Suggestions:

Pyracantha (Firethorn) can be used in arrangements if leaves are removed and stems split and conditioned overnight in warm water. Spray berries with clear plastic or hair spray.

Evergreens should be washed in warm soapy water, rinsed in cold water, and stems split and conditioned in warm water.

Holly (red-berried Ilex) can be conditioned by splitting the stem and placing in brown sugar water (one cup brown sugar to one quart water).

Water in arrangements, especially in foliage, stays fresh longer with the addition of a few pieces of charcoal or a tablespoon of Clorox.

INDEX

A

U

V

W

Y

Z

NOTES

NOTES

Mud Pies & Silver Spoons

To order additional copies of this cookbook, complete the attached coupon and mail to the Dayton Philharmonic Women's Association, P.O. Box 632, Dayton, Ohio 45401.

All copies will be sent to same address, unless otherwise specified. If you wish one or more books sent as gifts, furnish separate list of names and addresses of recipients. Include $2.50 for postage/handling for each book. If you wish to enclose your own gift card, please write name of recipient on outside of envelope, enclose with order, and we will include it with your gift.

All proceeds from the sale of MUD PIES & SILVER SPOONS will benefit the Dayton Philharmonic Orchestra.

DAYTON PHILHARMONIC WOMEN'S ASSOCIATION
P.O. Box 632   Dayton, Ohio, 45401

Charge to my _____ Mastercard _____ Visa

Account # _____ Interbank # (MC) _____

Expiration Date _____

Signature _____
Required if using Credit Card

Make checks payable to DAYTON PHILHARMONIC WOMEN'S ASSOCIATION

Name _____

Address _____

City, State, Zip _____

Please send _____ copies of
MUD PIES & SILVER SPOONS at $13.50 each $ _____
Add postage/handling $2.50 first copy $ _____
Plus postage/handling
additional copies (same address) $ 1.00 each $ _____
Ohio residents add tax $ .81 each $ _____
Please gift wrap $ 1.00 each $ _____
CHECK OR CREDIT CARD   TOTAL $ _____

Prices subject to change.

Mud Pies
& SilverSpoons

To order additional copies of this cookbook, complete the attached coupon and mail to the Dayton Philharmonic Women's Association, P.O. Box 632, Dayton, Ohio 45401.

All copies will be sent to same address, unless otherwise specified. If you wish one or more books sent as gifts, furnish separate list of names and addresses of recipients. Include $2.50 for postage/handling for each book. If you wish to enclose your own gift card, please write name of recipient on outside of envelope, enclose with order, and we will include it with your gift.

All proceeds from the sale of MUD PIES & SILVER SPOONS will benefit the Dayton Philharmonic Orchestra.

DAYTON PHILHARMONIC WOMEN'S ASSOCIATION
P.O. Box 632   Dayton, Ohio, 45401

Charge to my _____ Mastercard _____ Visa

Account # _____ Interbank # (MC) _____

Expiration Date _____

Signature _____ Required if using Credit Card

Make checks payable to DAYTON PHILHARMONIC WOMEN'S ASSOCIATION

Name _____

Address _____

City, State, Zip _____

Please send _____ copies of
MUD PIES & SILVER SPOONS at $13.50 each $ _____
Add postage/handling $2.50 first copy $ _____
Plus postage/handling
additional copies (same address) $ 1.00 each $ _____
Ohio residents add tax $ .81 each $ _____
Please gift wrap $ 1.00 each $ _____
CHECK OR CREDIT CARD   TOTAL $ _____

Prices subject to change.

Mud Pies & SilverSpoons

To order additional copies of this cookbook, complete the attached coupon and mail to the Dayton Philharmonic Women's Association, P.O. Box 632, Dayton, Ohio 45401.

All copies will be sent to same address, unless otherwise specified. If you wish one or more books sent as gifts, furnish separate list of names and addresses of recipients. Include $2.50 for postage/handling for each book. If you wish to enclose your own gift card, please write name of recipient on outside of envelope, enclose with order, and we will include it with your gift.

All proceeds from the sale of MUD PIES & SILVER SPOONS will benefit the Dayton Philharmonic Orchestra.

DAYTON PHILHARMONIC WOMEN'S ASSOCIATION
P.O. Box 632   Dayton, Ohio, 45401

Charge to my _____ Mastercard _____ Visa

Account # _____

Expiration Date _____ Interbank # (MC) _____

Signature _____
Required if using Credit Card

Make checks payable to DAYTON PHILHARMONIC WOMEN'S ASSOCIATION

Name _____

Address _____

City, State, Zip _____

Please send _____ copies of
MUD PIES & SILVER SPOONS at $11.95 each $ _____
Add postage/handling $ 2.50 each $ _____
Plus postage/handling
additional copies (same address) $ 1.00 each $ _____
Ohio Residents add tax $ .72 each $ _____
Please gift wrap $ 1.00 each $ _____
CHECK OR CREDIT CARD   TOTAL $ _____

Prices subject to change.